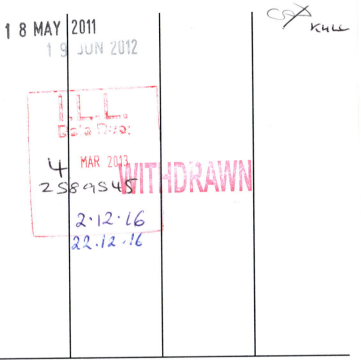
Books should be returned or renewed by the last date above. Renew by phone **08458 247 200** or online *www.kent.gov.uk/libs*

823.912

KATHERINE MANSFIELD
AND LITERARY IMPRESSIONISM

Julia van Gunsteren

Amsterdam - Atlanta, GA 1990

ISBN: 90-5183-199-4 (CIP)

©Editions Rodopi B.V., Amsterdam - Atlanta, GA 1990
Printed in The Netherlands

Acknowledgements

The search for Manfield's place in English literary history and the role of Impressionism in her aesthetics and fiction was an invigorating and rewarding enquiry, one that brought me into contact with many colleagues, students and friends all over the world, who contributed in various ways.

It is impossible to acknowledge everyone who assisted my labours, but a few people deserve special expression of gratitude.

Professor dr. Elrud Ibsch, always helped shape and criticise my thinking and writing, at whatever inconvenient moment. I am deeply indebted to my far away adviser, the Mansfield scholar and one of the editors of her letters, professor Vincent O'Sullivan in New Zealand, for supervising and invigorating this study.

I am pleased to acknowledge the helpful assistance of an other, far away scholar, professor Ulrich Weisstein, who, from Graz and Bloomington, checked the methodology and the scope of this study, and professor August Fry, who helped shape the English and paragraphing.

I am gratefully acknowledging the support of Dr. Keith Walker, my English brother-in law, who assisted in checking the English of the manuscript, dr. Dick Schram and dr. Marius Buning, who always stimulated my studies and writing.

My oldest debt is to Mrs Henriette Schalm-Timmermans, who first introduced me to Katherine Mansfield, many years ago.

JB vG-V

The Hague,
Koninginnegracht 67

To Frans, Fleur, Sofie, Michiel
and my brother H.

KATHERINE MANSFIELD AND LITERARY IMPRESSIONISM

CONTENTS

Acknowledgements

PREFACE

The total body of Mansfield's work is small and uneven in quality.* But even those with only a cursory knowledge of 20th century English literature would agree that Katherine Mansfield, 'the little colonial from New Zealand', must have been an intriguing woman-writer. (See the list of biographies). Mansfield was an excellent and talented writer of short stories; so much so that, after her death, Virginia Woolf confessed in her diary that she was 'the only writer I have been jealous of'.[1]

Interpretations of her work are various, often with a biographical bias. If a serious critic is willing to plough through 'Mansfieldiana' and forget the biographical interpretations and the myth built up around her life[2], he or she will be still confronted with differing views. Thus: 'Mansfield is the first and most important innovator of the English short story in the 20th century'[3], 'she has influenced Virginia Woolf in her Modernist impulses'[4], 'she was and remained a Symbolist'[5], 'she is a feminist and a Modernist'[6], 'she is an Imagist'[7], and finally, 'she is unique and cannot be classified into any literary period'.[8]

In some German, French and English literary histories Mansfield is grouped among the Impressionists in literature. Vincent O'Sullivan, one of the editors of her letters, speaking in 1988 at the Mansfield Conference at Wellington University, New Zealand, also argued that 'if we have to place her, it should be in Impressionism'. But, the reader and literary critic may wonder, 'What is an Impressionist in literature, or, if you prefer, 'a Literary Impressionist'?

This study attempts to answer this question. It will be argued that, *if* we have to place Mansfield, it will be in Literary Impressionism.

Literary Impressionism, one of the variants of Impressionism in the arts, has not yet been adequately described in literary history. However, as an incipient movement to Modernism it appears to play a significant role, particularly in the reaction against traditional Realism, Naturalism and the narrow confines of Symbolism.

Many writers at the beginning of this century experimented and searched for new forms and methods to describe the world around them. The Literary Impressionists, like the Impressionists in painting, focused on perception. They attempted to formulate reality by breaking it into momentary fragments, selected intuitively and subjectively. They relied on sensory (ap)perceptions, used clusters of images and rendered their emotions in a 'slice of life' picture of some everyday, ordinary experience. Their solipsistic visions of apparently directly perceived moments ('d'un moment de la durée') were presented in an atmospheric 'Stimmung', which surrounds events, characters and the narrator. This fragmentary, momentary, evocative

7

reality *is* or *becomes* reality for the Literary Impressionist.

Mansfield experimented in the form of the short story. She wrote satirical 'travelogues', sketches, dialogues, monologues, in which she could render her memories and personal visions in a picture of everyday life. She included many chains of images in her poetic prose, in which she recorded suggestive atmospheric impressions. Her short stories need to be read carefully. Mansfield's narrative methods are a good deal more complex than has generally been assumed, especially by those critics who focused on thematic or symbolist issues alone. Her perception of the surrounding world, the stress on form, structure, empathy and atmosphere (in Mansfieldian terms 'the prose writer's weather') in a writer's subjective vision with an expressive narrator (See Chapter 4.1) attempt to create a fictional illusion. There is the emotive correlative between images, narrator and character, in an apparently objective stance. She often renders a moment of sudden awareness in an epiphany (See Chapter 3), whereby one of her major themes, the disparity between illusion and reality, is revealed. All these characteristics are congruent with the basic concepts of Literary Impressionism.

Katherine Mansfield (1888-1923) wrote her best work between 1914 and 1922. At the age of eighteen she began publishing her short, fragmentary sketches. She was fascinated by Anton Tsjechov's short stories. Mansfield, being unclassifiable in the English social system, the 'underdog' of classy Bloomsbury, had to find her own way in literary circles. She was detached from the mainstream, and able to cross barriers.

The term Impressionism is not used by her. Only scant references to some Impressionist painters may be found in her writings.

Now, 70 years after her death, Mansfield may be related to Literary Impressionism, and her short stories may be read, interpreted and translated in a Literary Impressionist manner. It is argued that no reading of Mansfield's work can be complete if the significance of an Impressionist perception is not dealt with as both a methodological and a thematic component of these works.

* Mansfield's work has been translated into 24 languages. Penguin sells around 10.000 copies a year of the *Collected Short Stories*.

Chapter 1.   INTRODUCTION

This study is the result of an exploration of two concerns that became closely related. The first was a general interest in Mansfield's short stories. The second was a desire to assess Mansfield's role in the development of the 'modern' impulse in English literature. This involvement was found to be in need of a more precise definition. I found that definition in Literary Impressionism.

Reading the criticism of Mansfield's short stories I noted the many different critical attitudes - worldwide - and the rather vague nomenclature which the critics used to describe her style and technique. Some critics focused mainly on her early writing, searched her early notebooks, her unpublished annotations and letters, and decided that Mansfield was a Symbolist.[1] Others, after the flurry of criticism of Modernism in the seventies, grouped her rather loosely and vaguely under Modernism, even associating her with feminism. These critics never explicitly stated the reason why they did so and never defined the relationship.[2]

I was astonished to discover that in many works on the history of English literature the term 'Impressionism' is not mentioned at all[3], implying that, despite the impact of Impressionism in painting and music, the movement had had no influence whatever on English literature. This view, all too common among literary scholars, seemed in need of revision.

When describing two related art forms, as Impressionism in painting and in literature, there is a tendency to equate Literary Impressionism with a kind of pictorialism. Some critics will focus on literary style only.[4] I shall not adopt the stylistic approach, nor equate the two art forms, but attempt to trace Mansfield's aesthetic intentions and the basic aesthetic of Literary Impressionism. Despite a number of inherent problems, which will be discussed in this chapter, a plausible aesthetic and general construct of Literary Impressionism seems possible. The best method to achieve an understanding of the evident relationship between Mansfield and Literary Impressionism appears to be first to undertake a survey of the aesthetics and techniques in Impressionist painting (Chapter 2.1), as the movement had its roots in the visual arts, followed by a chronological survey of the use of the term *Literary Impressionism* in literary criticism to date (Chapter 2.2). Finally, I shall present the most significant and fundamental aspects of the aesthetics of *Literary Impressionism*. In the second part of this study I shall offer an account of Mansfield's Literary Impressionist aesthetics, based on an examination of her

9

journals, letters and reviews. In the last part I shall analyse her Literary Impressionist techniques on a structural level and with reference to the narrative methods (Chapter 4.1), themes (Chapter 4.2), structure (Chapter 4.3), characterisation (Chapter 4.4) and imagery (Chapter 4.5) throughout the entire body of her published work. I hope to demonstrate that the many dominant characteristics, selected and coordinated for discussion represent essential aspects of Mansfield's style and technique; that they, now grouped together for the first time, form a meaningful pattern, and that Literary Impressionism is the one term which best describes them.

But first some general questions of methodology require discussion. As regards the aim of this study, I shall first endeavour to define the problems inherent in the study of a collection of literary works which need to be placed within a literary period from the beginning compared by critics with a parallel movement in painting.

My conviction was that, when a literary critic attempts to describe a parallel movement in the different arts, 'it is literature that must always be at the heart of what a comparatist does'.[5] Of course, when comparing, we must ask ourselves: What are the types of linkage which make up the subject matter of the area known as 'literature and art' and what are the most urgent *desiderata* in the parallels? Ulrich Weisstein has listed some types useful in deciding on a direction for further investigation. I shall restrict myself to mentioning only the three types which are relevant to the discussion. Type no. 4 is 'literary works emulating pictorial styles', type no. 5 'literary works using artistic techniques' and type no. 8 'literary works sharing a theme, or themes, with works of art'.[6] I shall combine some aspects of these three types into a new, different, and more structured method of investigation, based on a discussion of literary techniques related to the basic aesthetics of Literary Impressionism and Impressionism in painting.

A difficulty in attempting to describe Literary Impressionism is the lack of agreement among critics as to the different exemplars of the movement. There is some consensus as to the aims and techniques comprising the phenomenon, but much difference of opinion as to who is to be included among its ranks and who is not.[7] Some of this disagreement may be accounted for by the fact that, unlike the painters, the Literary Impressionists did not form a movement, at least not in the formal sense of officially constituting a group or of issuing manifestos. Another fact is that critics rarely discuss the same aspects of art when they speak of a movement. Some regard a movement as basically historical, others merely as an autonomous artistic category; some in terms of sociological developments, and others as the expression of philosophical principles. Besides, many writers, and Katherine Mansfield among them, experimented with a variety of modes and rarely wrote their works with complete fidelity to one school. We must recognise, therefore, that a definition of a literary mode describes tendencies rather than absolutes, and provides only indicators for distinguishing a literary period.

Literary Impressionism is not the only impulse discernible in Mansfield's short stories. Her work touches on a range of literary movements, but Literary Impressionism is far more than an occasional tendency. It is a fundamental aesthetic impulse. The other movements other than Literary Impressionism that play a discernible role in her development are Naturalism, Realism, Symbolism and Modernism. At the end of this chapter these movements will be discussed in relationship with Mansfield's work.

Let us first discuss the analogies between the two arts. We must, above all, as Mario Praz has observed, always bear in mind that we 'are entitled to speak of correspondences only where there are comparable expressive intentions and comparable poetics, accompanied by related technical media'.[8] On the aesthetic level, then the question arises: 'How extensively are a writer's 'expressive intentions' recorded in a writer's aesthetics?' And on a more general personal level, the question to be addressed is: 'Were the Literary Impressionists consciously attempting to recreate the goals of the painters? Do we have recorded statements that the Literary Impressionists were imitating the painters?'

Though a collective tendency among a group of writers inevitably suggests that Impressionism was a cultural or social phenomenon, there is no documentary evidence to support such a thesis. Some art critics - one of them René Huyghe - attempt to establish common ties between the painters and the writers. In his introduction to a centenary exhibition catalogue of Impressionist painting, Huyghe describes the painters' relationship to the Impressionist era and argues that the features of this era link the painters and writers. They shared a vision of a new universe that included 'rational sensualism, instinct and intuition, intellectual relativism, anti- materialism, consciousness of immediate sensory data and 'la durée'.[9] We must, therefore, answer the question: 'Did Mansfield consciously intend to write Impressionist short stories or did she consciously imitate the Impressionist painters?' There is little evidence that the French Impressionist painters had any direct impact on Mansfield, although she often made trips to Paris, and some minor references to Renoir and Manet may be found in her letters. She can hardly have been unaware of the phenomenon, though, for Impressionism had in these years become a widely accepted term. Mansfield, however, never commented on Impressionism as such. She was probably aware of the movement, but not consciously struck by an affinity. When Mansfield visited the exhibition where she saw Van Gogh's *Sunflowers* (this is the only reference of influence we have) she did not start writing in the manner which Van Gogh or the other Impressionist painters had advocated. Only ten years later did she realise that this painting, these sunflowers 'brimming with sun, (...) had lived with (her) (...) and had given her a kind of freedom - or rather, a shaking free' as she noted in a letter to her painter-friend Dorothy Brett.[10] Mansfield did not consciously analyse Van Gogh's aesthetics and set to work. Obviously writing is a different medium, which has its own techniques and aesthetic principles. But no art and no artist exists in a vacuum. Models of reality, epistemologies, ethical principles and techniques that define one artistic and aesthetic movement may find their way into another discipline, and may find themselves translated, or 'transliterated' into another medium. Writers, painters and philosophers - in Mansfield's case Virginia Woolf, D.H. Lawrence, Bertrand Russell and her painter-friends Richard Murry and Dorothy Brett, to name but a few - do of course tend to exchange ideas on techniques and aesthetics.[11] This means that the germ of one movement, in this case mainly initiated by certain painters and the aesthetic lines of its development, can be carried over, and in the process a new art and new narrative techniques can be created in order to express a new vision of the world. It is evident, when investigating Mansfield's aesthetics and short stories, that she found and employed a new style, new narrative techniques, different themes, structures and characterisation that had a great deal more in common with the concerns and aesthetic ideas of Impressionist painters than with those of any group of writers.

Returning to the discussion of comparable aesthetics when describing a literary period style, we must assume - as Mario Praz has again suggested - that 'the description is based on the assumption that each epoch has its own peculiar handwritings, which, if one could interpret them, would reveal a character, even physical appearance, as from the fragment of a fossil palaeontologists can reconstruct the entire animal'.[12] Such a description, or reconstruction based on a mere fragment, selected from the entire corpus of an author, may remain wishful thinking. However, an investigation of an author's aesthetics as recorded in all the available letters, journals and reviews, and an examination of the author's complete works, does appear to provide a sound basis for a plausible reconstruction.

In studying the interrelationships between the various arts, the problem of selection must be addressed. Which features should be involved in the comparison? Ulrich Weisstein quoted J.D. Merriman saying that 'a feature possible to one art but definitionally impossible to others can only show non-relationships'.[13] On the level of analogies, when discussing two related art forms, there is a tendency to discuss only shared features. In the entire critical history of the literary phenomenon, the important misunderstanding has persisted that

Literary Impressionism may be equated with a kind of pictorialism.[14] I shall not adopt this approach, which leads to the painters only, but refer to the basic aesthetics of the phenomenon. As previously stated, writing is not painting. In any comparison we must first attempt to 'transcribe' the basic aesthetic assumptions of Impressionism in general, related as they are to Impressionism in painting, and as 'transliterated' by the literary artists.

In this discussion of the interrelationship between the two arts on the aesthetic level we must decide what is a relationship and what is not? To be more specific, how can an author transcribe or 'transliterate' an aesthetic technique or principle from painting? In order to discuss the problem of 'transliteration', let us examine two recent articles describing Mansfield's Literary Impressionism. In both articles Ulrich Weisstein studies Mansfield's Literary Impressionism in a single short story "Her First Ball". In the first article 'Verbal Paintings, Fugal Poems, Literary Collages and the Metamorphic Comparatist'[15], he immediately links Mansfield's style with Claude Monet's Impressionist aesthetics and argues that it is 'a style whose champions - Claude Monet at the helm - stoutly maintained that things existed only insofar as they were seen'.[16] Apart from the link with 'sensationism', Weisstein draws parallels between 'the philosophy of Impressionism' in general and Mansfield's selection of setting and theme. Here the occasion is a ball, where a young girl is enjoying herself, even when she meets the old, bald man, who warns her that she too will soon be old and fat. Weisstein very aptly describes the Impressionist atmosphere, in particular its sensationist aspect, but does not hint at the narrative and thematic consequences of a sensationist's restricted point of view and its parallax (See Chapter 4.1) with the old man's perspective. He does not refer to the story's structural design, in which the main character, as so often in Mansfield's stories, may experience (but does not: why not?) a sudden 'moment of awareness', or flash of perception, which is often described as another characteristic of Literary Impressionism. Equally there is no investigation of the evocative patterns of Mansfield's images. If Weisstein had studied some other, or - preferably - all of Mansfield's stories, he might have realised that 'sensationism' is not the only Impressionist aspect of "Her First Ball". In his more recent article Weisstein presents a more elaborate analysis of the same Mansfieldian text.[17] Again it is the painter Monet who is selected from among the Impressionist painters to prove Weisstein's point. Weisstein states that Mansfield's "Her First Ball" is 'a deliberate attempt on the part of the author to tackle Impressionism on her own, decidedly, literary terms, a *tour de force*, if you will, which (...) goes to the very heart - I am tempted to say the esthetic, if not philosophic, root, of the matter, by recreating Impressionism in another, namely verbal medium'.[18]

Weisstein stresses the temporal aspect of literature and contrasts it with the atemporality of painting. Monet and his colleagues are introduced to prove his point. Weisstein argues that Monet in his desire to evade the deprivation caused by the atemporal aspect of his art, resorted to a 'trick' when he depicted the same object - a haystack or a facade of a cathedral - at various times of the day or seasons of the year and so created a series which, viewed consecutively, conveyed the beholder an intimation of time passing. Again Weisstein immediately links this supposed Impressionist aesthetic principle with a discussion of theme and setting in Mansfield's story "Her First Ball" and refers to Mach's philosophy of 'sensationism', which he uses as his 'methodological compass and theoretical anchor'.[19]

Returning to the question of comparable poetics, on the aesthetic level, we must examine the question of Monet's supposed aesthetic principle which is here at stake. We must ask ourselves: 'Why indeed did Monet paint his series of many haystacks or cathedrals?' Reconsidering this particularly painterly device or 'trick', as Weisstein calls it, it is evident, as the painter himself and many later art critics have all argued, that Monet wished to paint series of different haystacks or cathedrals, because he had discovered, that the effect of light (one of Monet's technical concerns) could constantly change the appearance of any object and each canvas could be devoted to one specific effect. To quote J. Rewald, a reference which Weisstein also quotes :

He (Monet) thus strove to attain what he called 'instantaneity' and insisted on the importance of stopping work on a canvas when the effect changed and continuing work on the next one, so as to get a true impression of a certain aspect of nature and not a composite picture.[20]

This sensivity to an altering attitude towards one's environment, when studying the shifts of light, colours and forms that winter and summer bring to the same motif, is now seen as one of the basic Impressionist characteristics. Monet constantly qualifies his view of an object by slightly shifting his angle in time and space to represent the truths of flux and relativity. In other words, Monet represented the Impressionist's epistemological view of reality as subjective and relative. Therefore he juxtaposed and contrasted his multiple pictures of the same object to convey the Impressionist vision of pervasive ambiguity. For Monet it is a matter of perception and of rendering the sensory nature of life itself. 'Transliterated' into literature, this means that an Impressionist writer, as Mansfield often suggested in her reviews (See Chapter 3), wishes to convey to the reader the basic impressions that a single human consciousness could receive in a given

14

place during a restricted duration of time. The qualification of the
'reality' of these impressions is that they are necessarily filtered
through the intermediate minds of a narrator and a character. They
are personal and subjective. The impressions may be rendered with
meticulous fidelity, or they may not; they may be momentarily
changed and even distorted because of restricted data or faulty
perception. Impressionist fiction thus rests on a philosophic basis, well
described by Paul Ilie:

> The assumption is (...) that the immediate is in an incessant state of
> rapid flux, with an infinite number of sensory phenomena
> occurring in as many moments in the time continuum (...)
> Impressionism, consequently, is the technique by which one
> moment of reality is comprehended after the sensation has been
> modulated by consciousness and arrested in time.[21]

Here is another, slightly different, formulation of the basic aesthetic
principle of Impressionism:

> It establishes reality entirely in the stream of sensations.
> Fundamentally, impressionism is a statement of the subjectivity of
> reality and the variety of human response to (...) experience.
> Memory, imagination and emotion guide the mind in its ordering
> of individual consciousness and become the basis for artistic
> representation of experience.[22]

In literature, therefore, we are forced to the uncomfortable realisation
that, as Bender explains, 'the impression of the perceiving mind is
quite distinct from the phenomenon stimulating the impression, and
although impressions may be the only source of human knowledge, the
perceiving intelligence in recognising the stimulus apprehends it in
terms formulated by the mind itself'.[23] The result is a persistent
unreliability of narrative stance. This is why the crucial device of
Literary Impressionism is the method of narration. It is the central
concern of Impressionist literature, a basic concept aptly stated by
Ford: '(we) saw that life did not narrate, but made impressions on our
brains. We, in turn, if we wished to produce on you an effect of life,
must not narrate, but render'.[24] The Impressionist writer discredits the
authority of a single point of view.
     Returning to Monet's 'trick' of painting series of multiple haystacks
or cathedrals, which Weisstein relates to Mansfield's Impressionist
'fashion', it may be argued that Monet's aesthetic principle in painting
multiple views of haystacks and cathedrals, may be related merely to
the aesthetic principle of subjective perception, i.e., 'transliterated'
into literature, to a restricted, relative point of view. Mach's

15

'sensationism' is not the only basic aesthetic principle.[25] If Mansfield wished to present the theme in Weisstein's phrase of 'an intimation of time passing' - which, in his discussion of motion, movement and space, he links with Monet's creation of a series of paintings - Mansfield had different literary tricks to resort to. And this, in fact, she often did. When treating the theme which in this study is termed 'Life and Death' or 'The Flight of Time'[26] she often structured her text and its evocative images into a sudden 'glimpse' or a sudden moment of awareness, in which the character achieves a new realisation i.e. an epiphany. This aesthetic principle is not dealt with in Weisstein's discussion, although Mansfield clearly defined and illustrated the concept of a 'glimpse' (the Mansfieldian term for an epiphany) in her aesthetics.[27]

Finally, returning to the main issue of this introduction, the question of how a comparatist may best illustrate the evident relationship between Mansfield's short stories and Impressionism in painting, it is important in periodisation to reject any large-scale syntheses in comparing two related art forms. 'The study of periodization may best be limited in its object and must always rigorously refer to the possible different features, which are relevant to a discussion of a literary text'.[28]

I have opted therefore for a 'transliteration' of the most characteristic and relevant literary features, to be investigated when studying Mansfield's work. I have grouped them into narrative methods, themes, structure, characterisation and images. In the main part of this study, the analyses (Chapter 4) of Mansfield's work, all these features will be discussed separately. The interrelationship with painting will be discussed fleetingly, and only when it is relevant to the general analysis. Once again, it is literature that must be at the heart of what a comparatist does, and it is literary devices that must be investigated. As Weisstein has suggested, 'we must sharpen our precision tools'.[29] In periodisation we must refer to literary techniques and integrate these findings into a larger whole.

In this study I will start from the assumption that Impressionism in the arts was begun with the painters in the 'movement' represented in the various works by Monet, Renoir, Pisarro, Sisley, Degas, Cézanne, Morisot and Van Gogh 'grouped' together and described as Impressionist by Gombrich, Rewald[30], Hartt, Honour & Fleming[31], a label which may be used as a conterminous, symbiotic parallel. A brief introductory postulation like the following is theoretical and, of course, no single work will be consistent with this model in all respects.

In painting, Impressionism was a reaction against the orthodox realism that had culminated in the mechanical, sterile work of the academicians, and in fiction it was a reaction against the fact-mongering of the Naturalists.[32] Although the terminology of the movement in painting was controversial from the first, a spectrum of ideas and methods united the various painters, without the formalised rules of a 'school' of art. The fundamental concept was an attempt to paint what was actually seen, what the sensory impressions produced on the individual painter at a given time and place. The variety of concerns involved in the concept of 'Impressionism' is suggested by the works and comments of the French painters themselves. Cézanne in particular[33] indicated the sensory nature of Impressionism when he declared: 'I have not tried to reproduce Nature: I have represented it (...) Art should not imitate nature, but should express the sensations aroused by nature'.[34] On another occasion he wrote: 'we must render the image of what we see, forgetting everything that existed before us'.[35] Visual emphasis is the most striking feature of Impressionist painting. Of particular interest is the obscuration of vision, a systematic limitation or change in the sensory reception of the essentials of a scene. This obscuration is generally the result of natural phenomena, such as distance, darkness or smoke.

Another striking dimension of Impressionist painting that links it to literature in the same mode is a concern with the transience of reality. Human perceptions of the most stable of objects are ineluctably fleeting. Monet will present his numerous paintings of haystacks from the same perspective at different times and under differing light conditions. Colours, emphasis and the essence of reality change. The fundamental ideology of Impressionism is clear: reality is a matter of perception. It is ever-changing, elusive, inscrutable and unstable.

From the very start, one of the fundamental ideas of Impressionism was regarded as a structural principle: 'a picture should be a unified impression (...) (it) should be the staged and reproduced effect of a single section of the world of color upon the eye'.[36] Garland's view is close to that of Cecelia Waern, that the sensory effect of reality, not reality itself, is the subject of such a mode of art, and that the Impressionist aesthetic, although not a formal philosophy, 'indicates a radical change in attitude toward the physical universe. It stands for an advance in the perceptive power of the human eye'[37], an aesthetic principle which may be related to Mach's contention that the only reality worth referring to is that of the surface, the place where objective (physical) elements meet with their subjective (psychological) counterparts.

In writing, too, there was a change of mode. The authors Joseph Conrad and Ford Madox Ford played a role in the development of Literary Impressionism. It was Ford who observed that 'you must render, never report ':

We saw that life did not narrate, but made impressions on our brains. We in turn, if we wished to produce on you an effect of life, must not narrate, but render (...) You must never, that is to say, write: 'He saw a man aim a gat at him'; you must put it; 'He saw a steel ring directed at him'.[38]

Ford's remark implies a form of literature in which direct sensory experience is rendered without expository intrusion. The existence of a gat (a gun) in Ford's passage is not asserted; the reader must interpret the sensory data for himself. This method lies at the heart of Literary Impressionism.

The narrative methods may present the reception of a sensory experience, or the subjective interpretation of a sensation, or two or more modes in narrative counterpoint. The purpose of Literary Impressionism is to render the sensory nature of life itself, especially to make the reader 'see' the narrative described.[39] It is not polemical, often not even 'thematic', in the sense that it points clearly to any predetermined idea. As Mansfield's comments often suggest, she wished to convey the basic impressions of life that a character could receive in a particular place, during a limited period of time. These impressions may be subject to distortions from restricted data or incoherent interpretation. In a subjective sense the impressions may be rendered accurately, or they may not. The reader is forced to exercise a permanent scepticism about the reliability of narrative assertions. Literary Impressionism implies a basic assumption, well described by Paul Ilie:

Ultimate reality, however, belongs to the realm of human consciousness, whose instruments for monitoring those phenomena are the sensory faculties, through the medium of sensation.[40]

Implicit in an art form based on a confluence of sensation with interpretation, is the necessity to distinguish between reality as perceived by the character (or narrator) and reality itself. The two may be in harmony, but often there is discord caused either by external factors that distort sensory signals or by distorting factors within the interpreter. The logic of Literary Impressionism suggests that the correspondence between perception of the factors and interpretation of the signals is never certain and that reality is always inscrutable. Literary Impressionism involves a constant awareness that any description of reality depends upon the clarity with which it is perceived, apperceived or understood. A fictive mode that presents such an assumption must render its reality in an aesthetically compatible form, in a manner which suggests a restriction of perception and knowledge in shifting, uncertain points of view.

Impressionist fiction that renders life must be evocative and dramatic, must limit exposition and narratorial intrusion and must present the sensory life of characters. It will focus on episodes of isolated activity, rather than on lengthy coordinated events. Characters will be presented in dialogue rather than in lengthy descriptions. The emphasis will be placed on their minds.[41] The central concern is the manner of presentation, a basic concept aptly stated by Ford in his advice to render rather than narrate, to show rather than tell.

A narrative method (See Chapter 4.1) that is consistent with the idea and themes of Literary Impressionism is a method with a narrator who pretends to be the character, or a character who serves as a narrator, or a number of different characters who see reality in different terms. Another method is the complex device of uncertain or unreliable narration, in which the narrator attempts to discover the truth about his own experience. The narrator is as restricted in his interpretive power as any of the characters. There is a persistent unreliability of narrative stance. Narrative assertions are limited to sensory experience, or to reflective moments and fantasies. As a result, the reader receives fragmented and potentially unreliable information which is often distorted and ambiguous. A significant method is the device of 'parallax' (See Chapter 4.1) the method of presenting an event or scene as perceived by multiple characters or narrators.[42]

Authors of literary texts based on these concepts necessarily experience difficulties in the generation of themes. (See Chapter 4.2) Empirical sensation does not organise itself around consistent ideas. In both central premise and narrative methods, Literary Impressionism suggests that 'reality is ephemeral, evanescent, constantly shifting its meaning and hence continually defying precise definition'.[43]

Structure (See Chapter 4.3) in Literary Impressionism also derives from the various implications of its narrative methods. A Literary Impressionist wishes to create a coherent narrative based on fragmentary episodes. Episodic structure may be presented in narrative parallax or in a juxtaposition of scenes from a variety of points of view, presented in any order, not necessarily chronological.

Characters (See Chapter 4.4) in Literary Impressionist works have, therefore, to interpret the world around them for themselves and have to distinguish between the 'real' and their own perception of it.[44] What is true and what is illusion? This theme, a major one in Literary Impressionism, concerns itself with a character's ability to understand the world around him. A character's ability to 'see' is synonymous with his ability to interpret his own experience coherently. Comprehension becomes apprehension or understanding. Literary Impressionist characters exist in a state of flux; they seldom fully comprehend themselves or the world around them. There is no generalisation that explains life to them. They may be uncertain,

19

deluded, but they may also be capable of a percipient state in which they achieve a new insight into their world. What is known about the characters emerges from what they say or do, and from what other characters say about them. This represents a severe limitation for the narrator, in comparison with various omniscient modes of narration. Characters in Literary Impressionist works have a tendency to seem shallow. Only the surface of characters is presented in their thoughts and action, without the depth of any philosophical or psychological analysis.

Impressionist narrative methods also have an impact on the use of figurative devices. (See Chapter 4.5) Since in Impressionism reality is largely sensory, the images that may formulate a sensation form a basic unit of narration. In Literary Impressionism, a character's experience is not presented as an organised association of thought or action, but rather in a series of images which may suggest a subjective coherence. One of the early critics of Literary Impressionism argued:

> Seeking an impression for an ever changing and transitory appearance the impressionist's images naturally tend to be particular and personal rather than general and universal. They do not profess to reveal about the objects or situations described any deep and hidden truth which will be valid for all time. The aim is merely to convey the immediate impression evoked by a certain set of circumstances, the interplay of which would most probably occur only on that one and unique occasion.[45]

This implies that a Literary Impressionist would not tend to use symbols, for symbols require an abstract and consistent frame of reference and an extensional meaning for the literal vehicle is usually provided. The use of a dominant symbol is not consistent with the philosophy of Impressionism. Symbolisation is rare and potentially inconsistent with the assumptions of Impressionism. The clusters of images used in Literary Impressionism often relate to its source in the consciousness of a character. Sensory images serve as correlatives of empirical data. They tend to be suggestive rather than definitive. They relate only to fleeting sensations, without organisation or interpretation.

Literary Impressionism, in its total aesthetic, derives its coherence from the assumption that human life consists of the involvement of an individual character in a reality which is apprehensible only in terms of sensations. The result is a text that renders and resembles the sensory nature of human experience. It is no less dramatic or meaningful than life itself.

As previously stated, Literary Impressionism is not the only impulse discernible in Mansfield's work. Because in this study I argue against the concentration on 'Symbolism' prevalent in Mansfieldian criticism, I shall first discuss her relationship with the Symbolist movement. A complicating aspect in the discussion remains the poetical textual organisation of the two movements, which has often misled critics into assimilating the attempts of Literary Impressionists with those of the Symbolists. Ruth Moser, too, in her monumental work on French Impressionism[46] draws no sharp distinction between Symbolism and Literary Impressionism. The search for 'symbols' in some of Mansfield's major short stories has also produced an excessive output of studies, finally leading to a dead end.[47] This study argues that Symbolism, with its possible initial attractiveness for Katherine Mansfield, was consciously rejected at a fairly early stage. My position is that Mansfield quite early fought to rid herself of narrow Symbolist tendencies, of the postulate of a correspondence between the Symbolist world of appearances and a 'higher' outside world of Absolute Beauty and Truth.

Despite the blurred line dividing the two -isms, it has become an acknowledged fact that there are two different aesthetics underlying Impressionism and Symbolism respectively. The Symbolist seeks to escape from reality to an ideal 'Absolute'. He focuses on a solipsistically encapsulated world. As M. Décaudin tells us: 'symbolism is turned toward the absolute, the dream and the ideal'.[48] Impressionism holds to the real, stabilises the ephemeral. The Symbolist is spiritualistic and idealistic in outlook. The Impressionist, having no faith at all in transcendental values, lives 'earth to earth', both enjoying and rather passively undergoing instantaneous fragmentary impressions.[49]

Mansfield's more mature fiction does not present a rounded off, finished Symbolist entity. On the contrary, it becomes progressively more Impressionistic in its momentary, fragmentary, episodic structure.[50] In June/July, 1919 Mansfield recorded her rejection of 'dishonest' Symbolist poetry, which she believed was 'decomposing'. She is quite clear in her intentions:

Nowadays one of the chief reasons for one's dissatisfaction with modern poetry is one can't be sure that it really does belong to the man who writes it. It is so tiring, isn't it, never to leave the Masked Ball - never - never (...)
(...) Why these young men should lean and lean over the decomposing vapours of poor Jules Laforgue is inexplicable (...).
I do believe that the time is come for a 'new word' but I imagine the new word will not be spoken easily. People have never explored the lovely medium of prose. It is a hidden country still - I feel that so profoundly.[51]

Symbolist influences were shaken off. Instead, her lifelong admiration for Tsjechov must be remembered. Tsjechov's Impressionist vision and techniques[52] clearly influenced Mansfield's Literary Impressionism.

> I have re-read *The Steppe*. What can one say? It is simply one of *the* great stories of the world - a kind of Iliad or Odyssey. I think I will learn this story by heart. One says of things: they are immortal. One feels about this story not that it *becomes* immortal - it always was. It has no beginning or end. (Tsjechov) just touched one point with his pen (...) and then another point: enclosed something which had, as it were, been there for ever.[53]
> (Italics KM)

Literary Impressionism offered a more fluid, easier means of development for Mansfield, who had a natural, intuitive eye for a fragmentary, sensory presentation of an obliquely individualised everyday reality. In Literary Impressionism and in Mansfield's stories things often 'seem' to be.[54] The famous 'pear tree' in "Bliss" is best interpreted in the light of its associations within the story itself[55] and cannot be endowed with any Symbolist significance, as Bertha '*seems* to see (...) the lovely pear tree (...) as a symbol of her own life'.[56] No absolute 'Truth', as forming the basis for Symbolist poetry, is evident in "Bliss".

The other movement that needs to be discussed is Naturalism. Of the stories with some Naturalistic elements, perhaps the most significant are the early "The Woman at the Store", "Ole Underwood" and "Millie", the 'brutal stories' with a New Zealand setting, in which a pathological state of mind is examined. Social setting and natural environment are presented as causal; characters are victims, moved by external and internalised forces. In Naturalism deflation beneath the crushing forces would be overwhelming, resulting in a defeated, defenceless character. In this sense "The Woman at the Store" and "Ole Underwood" may contain some elements of Naturalism, but the bulk of the mature stories certainly do not. Mansfield's stories are brief, episodic and fragmentary. Naturalism tends towards epic scope in length and focus, and employs an omniscient narrator, who analyses the themes of the narrative in long, expository passages. Mansfield's fiction usually adopts a detached narrative stance which projects the restricted interpretations of the characters in a 'slice of life' portrait. A Naturalistic narrator builds with straightforward sincerity towards elevation and broad social significance. Mansfield's short stories tend ironically towards reduction, specificity and individual human concerns.[57] Naturalism forces its characters into the common lot, Mansfield's Literary Impressionism, with its focus on unique sensory evocations and a subjective, personal, often expressive interpretation of experience, tends towards isolation and individuality. If in these stories Naturalism, in the form of genetic, environmental determinism[58] plays a role in the portrayal of the characters from the lower classes, it is quite inadequate as a term to describe Mansfield's overall work. Atmospheric and epistemological processes are more important to Mansfield than deterministic forces. Nature is generally described in compensatory and Impressionist terms. Free will plays a more important role than either chance, coincidence or fate. As Yuan She Yen has argued:

> The reason that the characters in these stories suffer lies in a combination of factors, both in themselves and in the environment in which they find themselves. Katherine Mansfield does not believe that social environment is the source of all evils. An individual should be responsible for himself at least to a certain extent; if he fails, there must be something wrong in his personality. Thus Bertha Young is guilty of hedonism and mental immaturity, Mr. Hammond of bossiness, the little governess of carnal temptation.[59]

Moreover, Mansfield's use of thematic and compositional irony in all of her major short stories is at odds with Naturalism, which most often drives on towards the 'tragic' inevitability with steadfast seriousness. The dominant and unifying element in Mansfield's work is not inexorable destiny, but the ironic and problematic disparity between truth and illusion in everyday life.[60] At the heart of Mansfield's work there is always an ironic disparity[61], often presented in some apprehensional distortion or misinterpretation that gives the narrative an ironic twist beyond the bare structure of events. The most frequent source of such irony is some false estimate of self or reality.[62] Mansfield's Literary Impressionist method often makes ironic what in Naturalism might be tragic.

Another -ism that needs to be discussed, because Mansfield together with most 20th century writers reacted against the influences of this movement, is Realism. Both Realism and Literary Impressionism may employ 'objective' narrative methods, but in Realism there is more access to information derived from sources beyond sensory data. A Realistic narrator is likely to know the names of the characters, the setting and time of events. A Literary Impressionist narrator often does not, or supplies this information only indirectly and casually. Fictional biographical background is much more important in Realism than in Literary Impressionism. Realistic works often provide such information directly. Differences in the roles the characters play may offer some lines of demarcation. This aspect is not obvious in simple 'slice of life' Realism, which may resemble Impressionism, but may be more apparent in Realistic works that focus on discussions of ethical matters and culminate in a moral crisis in the life of the main character. Although some of Mansfield's short stories touch indirectly on various ethical matters[63], very few of them have a moral crisis as a climactic moment. Most of her stories have as a central scene some key juncture, some 'sudden moment of awareness' in the perception of a character, in which something is realised, perceived in a new manner, or not perceived when it should have been.[64] Climactic scenes may function in Realism, because the character understands reality well enough to ponder a complex choice of alternatives. The irreducible norm of Realism is that reality is recognisable and known, it can be mastered and may be defined and recorded in the narrative. This assumption is not present in Impressionism. Characters struggle to perceive reality. Their grasp of circumstances is often inchoate and blurred. Realism often concentrates on determining what to do about reality. Impressionism focuses on attempting to apprehend it in a fragment of experience.[65]

Some overt structural distinctions may also help place Mansfield within Impressionism. In Realism there is no injunction for brevity. Since reality is known, it may be presented as a continuum of experience; it is comprehensible and reasonably stable. On the other hand, in Impressionism 'reality' is in rapid flux, always changing, evanescent; to portray Impressionistic 'reality' therefore, episodes must be brief, capturing fleeting and more or less intense moments of experience, in which characters and the world are perceived but not arrested. They are touched for an instant but not known. In this regard, Mansfield's stories are Impressionistic. They tend towards accumulations, aggregates of episodes, rather than towards any continuous action. A story rarely proceeds from beginning to end with no lapses in chronology, or breaks between scenes. There are no expository links to explain what has happened between episodes. Scenes begin and end abruptly, are often mixed with sensory descriptions of the environment (or fantasies or dreams) and suddenly conclude in the midst of dialogue or action. Mansfield does not attempt to circumscribe reality or give it full definition.

Mansfield's work shares with the norms of Realism a rejection of many of the tendencies of Romanticism and transcendental Symbolism, symbolisation, metaphysics, pantheism and a general inclination to represent people and events as emblematic of some significance beyond themselves. Mansfield portrays ordinary people, who speak ordinary language sometimes tinged with dialect and describes situations drawn from within a common range. But, unlike the Realists, Mansfield depicts the process of perceiving reality in an

24

unstable changing world. What is compelling about the mental lives of her major figures[66] is that they are of the most ordinary, everyday sort and it is the ordinary mental distortion of the characters' perception that carries the most force. Mansfield's Impressionism is notable as an epistemological record of sensory experience, to be accompagnied by reflection, internalisation, fantasies and dreams. It is the ordinary, everyday-life aspect of this problem that gives the sense of being real.

No discussion of Impressionism would be complete without some reference to Expressionism. Outside of Germany, Expressionism has been poorly understood and little investigated. In Anglo-Saxon literature its influence has been restricted to drama[67], and perhaps in poetry, where a few practitioners of Vorticism may be related to Expressionism. The Expressionists sought to grasp the essence of things, rather than portray outside appearance. The close link and continuous contact between the plastic arts and literature is a characteristic feature of the movement, which manifested itself predominantly in Germany at the beginning of the 20th century, as a reaction against prevailing Impressionism, but also against Realism and academism. The Expressionists strove to transcend the passive registration of Impressionism and moved towards a more violent, hectic and energetic creativity in a dissolution of conventional forms, abstract use of colour, the primacy of powerful emotion, and above all, the turning away of mimesis. A major feature is its anti-mimetic aspect. The Expressionist refuses to imitate, repeat and reproduce that which already exists.

As Expressionism has mainly been investigated in Germany, and in general by German critics, we might expect some criticism from this region in relation to Katherine Mansfield. However, none of the German critics who have analysed Mansfield's short stories refer to Expressionist influences. They all, directly[68] or indirectly[69], refer to Literary Impressionism. It is evident that Mansfield was far removed from the anti-mimetic aesthetics of expressionism, from its symbolical themes ('Man' in its criticism of modern contemporary life and his inner disintegration), its 'types' as characters, experimental structures, its autonomous and visionary images, dynamism and vitalism and above all in its radical intensity of feeling which is poured out into its works of art.

The extent to which Modernism can be perceived as having influenced Mansfield's work depends on the definition of the term. It is nowadays agreed that Literary Impressionism anticipated the most striking qualities of Modernism.[70] One of the latest critics on the concept of Literary Impressionism, Stowell, writes: 'Literary Impressionism discovered modernism'[71] and: 'James's multiple impressions of consciousness led them to the architectonic prose of

25

modernism'.[72]

The two movements may be described as having common roots in a set of shared assumptions in which there is a primacy of perception, with a fragmentation of perceived reality, no chronology, and no clear beginnings or endings. They share the realisation that time is both successive and durational, that Bergson's individualised flow of duration merges with the moments of chronometric time, and that memory cannot be relied upon.[73]The Modernist believes that actual historical events are best presented indirectly, as the subject-object relationship may be recorded through the reactions of one or more characters, in a 'stream of consciousness'[74], when responding to time through events. There is also a common acceptance of chance in a world which is complex and unknowable. Thus a character has to come to terms with reality through selection and induction.[75] Characters learn to adapt to a changing environment. They perceive and know through inductively perceived impressions, while they are also aware of the subjective limitations of knowledge. For they no longer believe in Truth, but only in various truths which are a matter of interpretation, always differing, and fleetingly experienced in a momentary coalescence of fragmentary impressions.

Both the Literary Impressionist and the Modernist distrust language.[76] Characters frequently fail to communicate meaningfully through words. There are silences during which something might have been said, but wasn't. Something might have been said *if* something had been said. There are soundless reflections and privileged moments, seconds and minutes of silent waiting, but also signs and impressions that communicate more than words ever could.

Literary Impressionism discovered a new way of seeing and knowing, a vision which was continued in Modernism. There are traces of common characteristics, elective affinities and philosophical agreements, but there are also differences, and reactions in Modernism against the 'supersensual multiverse' of Literary Impressionism. The Modernist goes some steps further. He comes to distrust any intuitive feeling of the heart. His own critical mind is the most reliable basis for any argument. The Modernist expects to gain from intellectual hypothesis[77], not from subjective impressions. Not unlike the Impressionist, he doubts and offers no definitive evaluations but fragmentary, hypothetical conjectures.[78] He will, however, question man's relationship with his social and material environment.

The relativistic aspects of Mansfield's Literary Impressionism surely play a part in the development of what came to be known as Modernism, in its sense of an indifferent, undefinable universe and the lack of individual significance.

If, however, Modernism consists of themes involving a great interest in intellectual conjectures, or a non-acceptance of values of the contemporary scene, for which the Modernist needed the scope of a novel, then Mansfield cannot be described as a Modernist. Modernism was too intellectual to be convinced by any subjective feeling of the heart. If Modernism is described as a literary period that takes the individual critical mind to be the most reliable argumentative source for a (Modernist) view of the world, with many hypothetical implications and abstractions of experimental philosophical thoughts, borrowing mythical narrative structures to help generate its themes of solitariness and solipsism, then Modernism played no role in Mansfield's fiction.

Modernism is a literary phenomenon only recently developed in literary criticism, and the concept of Literary Impressionism still needs to find its niche among competing yet compatible literary movements. Many contemporary literary critics still identify Literary Impressionism with some aspects of Modernism, when defining Modernism as a broad historical phenomenon. A great deal of comparative literary research remains to be done.

Finally, when comparing and contrasting Realism, Naturalism, Impressionism and Modernism, the main criterion to be employed is the extent to which reality is regarded as recognisable and describable. In Realism, reality is thought to be definable. The first step is to observe phenomena, which are then subjected to a scientific analysis in terms of cause and effect, after which separate phenomena are combined and generalised. In Naturalism, social and biological factors are viewed as determinants of individual behaviour. The Naturalist believes that moral choices can be made, if based on an optimistic belief in science and progress.

Both Impressionism and Modernism, on the other hand, reject the assumption that broader conclusions can be drawn from observation and analysis of details. No ethical implication is available to support scientific certainty, for the limited experience of the Impressionist and the Modernist allows of no epistemological or ethical generalisation. In Modernism it is believed that reality is made up of conjectural deduction. Causality is regarded as a mental exercise. Time, space and language are viewed as intellectual constructs. In Impressionism, however, it is not believed that the concept of reality can be extended into hypothetical arguments. The Impressionist approaches 'existing' reality from his own subjective, personal experience.

Viewed in their totality, Mansfield's short stories exceed the limits of Realism, Naturalism and Symbolism and do not concur with Modernistic argumentative or conjectural impulses. By concluding that Mansfield was a Literary Impressionist first and foremost, this study may not have come up with sensational news. But I hope that, besides showing why and how Mansfield was a Literary Impressionist, the method may be employed in studying other possible Literary

Impressionists and may contribute to the introduction of Literary Impressionism as a more precise and meaningful term in the analysis of 20th century English prose.

Interpreted within a Literary Impressionist concept, the Mansfield canon reveals a multifarious contribution rather different from that so far acknowledged. Mansfield appears a less complex writer than has generally been suggested in modern scholarship.

Chapter 2.1   IMPRESSIONISM IN PAINTING

In order to grasp the aesthetics of Impressionist painting more clearly, let us first survey some historical data and views which were common among Impressionist painters.

The modern usage of the term *Impressionism* is derived from an exhibition organised by the *Société Anonyme des Artistes, Peintres, Sculpteurs et Graveurs* in the Paris studio of the photographer Nadar in 1874. The exhibition contained 165 pieces by thirty artists, among them Cézanne, Degas, Monet, Pisarro and Renoir. Their works had been rejected by the conservative judges at the official 'Salon' in Paris. One of the paintings shown was Claude Monet's *Impression, Sunrise* (1872), a work sometimes credited with giving the name to the whole movement, but the word 'Impressionist' was also used in a review of the exhibition, and it was quickly adopted as a term of derision as applied to Monet's bold complexes of colour and brushstrokes. Originally intended as a label of derision, the designation was taken on willingly by the group and the currency of the word *Impressionism* to describe this new mode was assured with the formation of an artistic journal entitled *The Impressionist* in 1877. Brunétière, borrowing the term from painting in 1883, was one of the first critics to apply it to literature.

In artistic circles there was from the first a good deal of confusion surrounding the word. Emile Zola, for example, persisted in referring to the painters and their works as Naturalistic. Renoir refused to be grouped among them because the term implied a 'school' of painting and Degas failed to understand how it could be applied to his own work. There was no consensus: the term was conceived in disharmony, nurtured in derision and never applied with precision. Moreover, by 1886 the first wave of enthusiasm about the new aesthetic and its techniques was over and at the eighth exhibition the term was formally renounced by the painters of the original 1874 exhibition.

The terminology used by the critics was controversial from the beginning. We may, first of all, certainly discount the more loose or merely lyrical usage in which *Impressionism* means anything 'fanciful', 'disorderly' or 'illogical'. Having done so, however, it is possible to penetrate to a fairly solid core of new ideas and methods, which gave the group cohesion even without the formalised rules of a 'school' of French painters. It is evident now that the early Impressionist painters tried to strip themselves of many intellectual preconceptions; they wanted to forget that the sky is blue, the grass green and shadows black. They attempted, therefore, to paint what the eye actually saw, in order to render their immediate, naive sensory impressions, as experienced by an individual painter at a given time and place.[1] Their concern for direct, immediate impressions required an intense interest in the fluctuations of light and colour, with the effect of a more accurate 'realism' in the rendering of nature as it is perceived by a particular individual.[2]

This position had had its intellectual antecedents. Comte, the originator of Positivism, had also distrusted 'a priori' assumptions, and stressed the importance of empirical data. There was the exploration of a mere scientific basis for the modifying influence of juxtaposed colours in *The Principle of Harmony and Contrast of Colour and their Application to the Arts* by the French chemist Eugène Chevreul in 1839. Moreover, a good deal of work, relevant to Impressionistic ideas, had been done by British empirical philosophers, perhaps best represented by Hume's *A Treatise of Human Nature* (1739-40).[3] The Impressionist movement in painting was not, however, an essentially philosophical one. The painters seemed more interested in artistic effect than in intellectual coherence.[4]

In Camille Pisarro's instructions to his fellow painters we can read about the practice of their new aesthetics:

Look for the kind of nature that suits your temperament. The motif should be observed more for shape and colour than for drawing. There is no need to tighten the form which can be obtained without that. Precise drawing is dry and hampers the impression of the whole; it destroys all sensations. Do not define too closely the outline of things; it is the brush stroke of the right value and colour which should produce the drawing. In a mass, the greatest difficulty is not to give the contour the detail, but to paint what is within. Paint the essential character of things, try to convey it by any means whatsoever, without bothering about technique. When painting, make a choice of subject, see what is lying at the right and at the left, then work on everything simultaneously. Don't work bit by bit, but paint everything at once by placing tones everywhere, with brushstrokes and try to put down your perceptions immediately. The eye should not be fixed on one point, but should take in everything, while observing the reflections which the colours produce on their surroundings. Work at the same time upon sky, water, branches, ground, keeping everything going on an equal basis and unceasingly rework until you have got it. Cover the canvas at the first go, then rework it until you can see nothing more to add. Observe the aerial perspective well, from the foreground to the horizon, the reflections of sky, of foliage. Don't be afraid of putting colour, refine the work little by little. Don't proceed according to rules and principles, but paint what you observe and feel. Paint generously and unhesitatingly for it is best not to lose the first impression. Don't be timid in front of nature:

one must be bold, at the risk of being deceived and making mistakes. One must have only one master-nature; she is the only one always to be consulted.[5]

In Pisarro's *The Defense* we are informed of the role of suggestion and the restriction of expository background information and the use of synechdoche. The practice of Cézanne, Matisse, Van Gogh and other so-called post-Impressionists was even more revolutionary. Cézanne cherished 'the innocence of the idea' in the perception of reality. He wished to achieve greater purity and a more scientific accuracy of colour. His final aim was not a more sensitive reproduction of surfaces but a 'realisation' of inner meanings or essences. In other words, art should not imitate nature but should express the sensations aroused by nature. His direct image was a means to an end. His impressions were visionary as well as visual and his paintings, in some measure, mirrors of his reality.[6] He freely distorted appearances, not only by blurring, but also by breaking up contours, in order to clarify or emphasise the underlying reality. Although he himself retained recognizable forms from the objective world, his followers increasingly sacrificed representation to 'expression' until finally they landed in pure abstraction.

The Impressionists wanted to dissolve firm outlines in shimmering light. But how were these achievements to be preserved without leading to a loss of clarity and order? How could the 'messiness' of early Impressionist paintings be structured into absolutely sensory impressions of nature? The painters wanted an oblique sense of order and repose horizontally and vertically without the painter imposing firm lines on nature. The brush strokes were to be arranged so as to fall in with the main lines of the design and so to strengthen the feeling of natural harmony by creating an impression of poise and tranquillity. Their efforts were directed at achieving a sense of depth without sacrificing the brightness of their colours and at achieving a strong design without sacrificing the sense of depth. In all their struggles and gropings there was one thing they were prepared to sacrifice if need be: the conventional 'correctness of outline'. They were not out to distort nature, but they did not mind very much if it became distorted in some minor detail if this helped them obtain the desired overall effect.

As Cézanne had suggested, visual and individual emphasis is the most striking feature of Impressionist painting and this may be influenced by the obscuring of vision, by a systematic limitation on a sensory reception of the essentials in a scene. Such obscurity was generally presented by means of introducing into the painting natural phenomena such as trees, fog, snow, darkness or distance, or by breaking perspective by the use of buildings, a crowd, flags or smoke.

31

Monet paints his *Impression, Setting Sun* in dominant red tones, but his *Sailboats at Argentueil* in more delicate pastels. Pisarro portrays a river on a misty and fog-laden morning as in *The Isle of Lacroix, Rouen* and Monet paints a railway depot, hardly visible through the heavy smoke pouring from the locomotives.

Another important aesthetic feature, also related to the act of perception, is the painter's preoccupation with the transience of reality. More correctly, the painters realised that there was an ineluctable flux in human perception when perceiving even the most stable of objects. Monet produces different paintings of haystacks, from the same perspective but at different times and in differing light conditions. He paints *Rouen Cathedral* in full and in veiled sunlight. Only the light effects have changed and yet the nature of the reality portrayed is quite different. The fundamental Impressionist aesthetic is evident: reality is a matter of perception. It is unstable, elusive and subjective, because everchanging and inscrutable.

To summarise the most essential Impressionist techniques in painting and some aesthetic principles, it may be said to consist of a number of ideas and techniques[7] which may be described as follows:

Firstly, the rendering of a direct, momentary and fleeting impression, as perceived by the artist's eye. Monet's interest in capturing the direct personal visual sensation is seen to good advantage in his *Sailboats at Argenteuil* (1874). T. Duret emphasising Monet's predilection for portraying water in all its evanescence indicated that Monet's originality lay in his rendering of 'les aspects fugitifs que les accidents de l'atmosphère donnent (au passage)'.[8] An interest in seizing instantaneous visual effects runs throughout the work of the leading Impressionists.

The desire of the Impressionist to express the moment of change and chance seems to imply the domination of 'l'instant fugitif' over the solid qualities of life in general and of the external world in particular. William Harms has characterised the Impressionist vision as being one which apprehends human experience in terms of 'phenomenological mutability'.[9] Monet often attempted to capture these fleeting impressions of the world in his out of doors work:

> Everything painted directly and on the spot has a strength that can never be attained in the studio; three brush strokes from nature are worth more than two days' studio work at the easel.[10]

A picture of Monet in pursuit of 'l'instant fugitif' is provided by Guy de Maupassant, who followed Monet in his search for out of door impressions:

> He was no longer in truth a painter, but a hunter. He went out,

followed by a child who carried his canvases, five or six canvases representing the same subject at different hours of the day and with different effects. He took them up and put them aside in turn, according to the changes in the sky. And the painter, facing his subject, lay in wait for the sunshine or for the cloud that passed, and disdainful of error or propriety, painted them rapidly on his canvas. I have seen him thus seize a glittering play of light on the white cliff and fix it with a flow of yellow tones which rendered in a strangely surprising way the effect of that unseizable and blinding brilliance. Another time he took the rain beating on the sea in his hands and dashed it on the canvas.[11]

The Impressionist emphasis upon the 'moment of perception' thus implies the prevalence of a relation to things. Its property is to be non-committal as well as changeable.[12] This complex is expressed clearly in a painting such as Manet's *Concert at the Tuileries* (1862) in which the quick sweep of the brushwork lends a sense of transience to the gaiety of the scene. Monet wished to eternalise 'the moment'[13] although it changed so rapidly, for example in *Rouen Cathedral-in full Sunlight* (1894). The painting is not only a representation of the Gothic cathedral in Rouen but presents the atmosphere of the moment. This momentary atmosphere suggests a living fluid. The form of the cathedral can only be inferred from the differing intensities of light reflected from the surfaces, which seem to be in dissolution.

Secondly, the painters emphasised the importance of seizing the effects of light and the different colours, when painting out of doors. Monet's *Impression, Sunrise* (1872) combines a lyric touch with the immediacy of an open air impression. The actual light of day became the vital principle for the Impressionist painters. Their visual experience of the world inevitably depended upon light and its power to change the whole atmosphere.

A third principle was to move around a subject and painting consecutively from several different angles. Monet, Sisley and Pisarro, to name but a few, insisted upon recording only one particular impression at one particular moment of the day and in one particular prevailing light.[14] Like most Impressionist techniques and ideas[15], this was not wholly original. The idea of painting the same subject in different weather, from different angles and at different times of the year had been anticipated by Valenciennes - the founder of 19th century historic landscape painting - who also painted one subject from nearly identical viewpoints at different hours of the day. Another influence may have been other 19th century landscape painters who used delicate colours and employed a technique of circling around a subject. Here is Duret on Monet:

Claude Monet has succeeded in setting down the fleeting impressions which his predecessors had neglected or considered impossible to render with the brush. The thousand nuances that the water of the sea and rivers takes on, and the checkered reflections of foliage in the rays of a burning sun have been seized by him in all their truth. No longer painting merely the immobile and permanent aspects of the landscape, but also the fleeting appearances which the accidents of the atmosphere present to him, Monet transmits a singularly lively and striking sensation of the observed scene. His canvases really do communicate impressions. One might say that his snow scenes make you cold and that his brightly lighted canvases give off warmth and sunshine.[16]

Monet seems to have been following Delacroix's comments on the subject of the part that the mind plays in the mental perception of the world:

Even when we look at nature, our imagination constructs a picture. We do not see the blades of grass in a landscape, minute blemishes in the skin of a charming face (...) the mind itself has a special task to perform without our knowledge; it does not take into account all that the eye offers, but connects the impressions it receives with others that have gone before.[17]

This passage in turn calls to mind the reflections of the chemist Chevreul, whose writings so impressed Seurat. In his *de L'Abstraction* Chevreul wrote:

When it is a question of representing the view of a landscape or a group of figures participating in some action, whether public or private (...) the painter to be truthful can represent only a moment in a landscape in which light and shadow vary continually, he is obliged to choose *this moment* from among others; henceforth this moment should be considered a *veritable abstraction of the moments making up the duration* (...).[18]

Illustrative of this idea in painting is Degas' *Woman with Chrysanthemums* (1865?). This seems at first sight not to be a posed picture; it gives the impression that the woman might almost have sat down at the table by chance. Yet everything in the scene is very carefully arranged, even down to the carelessly placed gloves and the crystal water pitcher. In fact, the lady, the bouquet and the table all contribute to the total 'impression', and it would be difficult to say which is the most important element in this audacious composition. Many of the Impressionists convey something of the impermanence

34

and insubstantiality of the visible world through their depiction of water (an effect that Monet rendered in his *Garden at Giverny*). But something of the same effect, too, is generally conveyed in the Impressionist portrayal of human figures. For example, in Berthe Morisot's *Young Woman in Party Dress* (1879) everything about the woman's appearance suggests the passing moment, the powdered face, the expectant look, the luminescent skin and the revealing dress. When this painting was shown at the Salon des Impressionistes in 1880 (Vth Exhibition) an art critic remarked: 'There are five or six lunatics there, one of them a woman'. The woman herself (Morisot) confessed that her ambition was merely 'to see something as it passes, oh, something, the least of things'.[19]

A fourth characteristic was the use of broken, empathetic and evocative brushwork, which requires to be viewed from a distance. Arnold Hauser has noted that 'nothing is more typical of an Impressionist painting than that it must be looked at from a certain distance and that it describes things with the omissions inevitable in them when seen from a distance'.[20] Minute details are excluded and elaborate finishing touches eschewed. In Manet's *Bar at the Folies Bergères*, for example, many of the figures painted are suggested rather than defined. Special mention should also be made here of Van Gogh, with his idiosyncratic brush strokes. When Van Gogh abandons dark earth colours and flings himself into the conquest of primary colours, of the broad brush strokes and the short touches of his fellow-Impressionists, the particularly wavy strokes he uses (after 1899) give his shapes an intense inward life. Van Gogh reinforces the essentials, in the colour of yellow, and every tint and hue is highlighted in order to convey his personal impression of the world around him. Van Gogh has produced in his paintings the basic motivation of a simple, sincere human feeling penetrating into his impressions of what he saw to be the truth behind any external appearance. He used the individual brush stroke not only to break up the colour, but also to convey his own excitement or depressions.[21] In *The Church at Auvers* he exteriorises his reaction to the world. Both space and the object of the impression suddenly start to shake and move. Van Gogh cared little for what he called 'stereoscopic' reality, i.e. a photographically exact representation of nature. He would exaggerate and even change the appearance of things, if it suited his purpose to do so.

A fifth feature was the juxtaposition of colours for artistic effect. The Impressionist painters realised 'that the so-called local colour was actually a pure convention and that every object presents to the eye a scheme of colour derived from its surroundings and from atmospheric conditions'.[22] Monet and Pisarro showed in their work a great interest in the effect of light and shadow. In a winter landscape the shadows on the snow could be blue in the sunlight instead of the traditional black.

A final important characteristic was the presentation of scenes in a hazy atmosphere, in order to create an atmospheric perspective. The boundaries in Impressionist paintings are blurred, not sharply demarcated and contours are seldom drawn.[23] Something of this quality of indistinctness may be found in Monet's *Impression, Sunrise* (1872), the painting which the art critic Leroy had ridiculed in his attack on the Impressionist painters. Monet wanted to convey above all 'instantaneity', and 'the envelopment of the same light spread over everywhere'.[24] Monet's *The Gare St. Lazare in Paris* (1877), which struck the critics as sheer impudence, may serve as an example. Here is a truly, 'blurred' impression of a scene from everyday life. Monet's fascination with the effect of light streaming through the glass roof onto the concealing clouds of steam surrounding the shapes of engines and carriages emerging from the confusion, creates an unusual atmospheric perspective of a public station. Other examples are Renoir's *A Dance at the Moulin de la Galette* (1876) and Pisarro's *The Boulevard des Italiens, Morning, Sunlight*. (1897).

Before finally describing the break-up of the Impressionist movement in painting, consideration should be given to the kind of subjects the Impressionists dealt with in their paintings. There can be no doubt that the Impressionists, for the most part, made a conscious break with the powerful Paris 'Salon', which favoured dramatic, religious and historical scenes. The Impressionist's principle of painting from the life opted for a different kind of subject, more everyday and less dramatic: buildings, panoramas, still lives, ordinary people, and people in their own circle - dancers, singers, musicians, barmaids, cafe-waiters or fellow-painters at work - or people at leisure, enjoying themselves at concerts or in rowing-boats. By selecting mundane subjects they broke with artistic tradition. They were disengaged, and little inclined (apart from Van Gogh and Pisarro) to deal with issues of great social concern. Their paintings had no 'message'.

With their ambition to capture merely the accurate momentary impression, the painters of the Impressionist movement broke with most of their predecessors for whom 'subject' was of primary importance. As early as 1882, profound differences of opinion were felt among most of the original Impressionist painters and by 1883 the idea of organising another communal Impressionist exhibition was abandoned in favour of separate exhibitions by Monet, Renoir, Pisarro and Sisley. By this time several of the old-timers among the Impressionists had begun to question the value of the aesthetic course that they had chosen. Renoir had already become disenchanted with the Impressionists and had moved into the direction of a more classical technique and Pisarro was beginning similar experiments. Degas was beginning to paint in a style that increasingly diverged from that of his Impressionist colleagues, and Gauguin, Cézanne and Van Gogh had modified and eventually rejected Impressionist principles.

The Impressionist painters continued to paint into the first years of the 20th century but by the early 1880's they had ceased to show their paintings as a group. Their position as 'the antennae' of the art world was taken over by other artists, who had profited from the lessons of Impressionism but modified or even rejected its aesthetic principles. The term *Impressionist*, however, soon came to be applied to analogous techniques in the other arts: in music, sculpture, architecture and literature.

Chapter 2.2   A CHRONOLOGICAL SURVEY OF
THE USE OF THE TERM LITERARY IMPRESSIONISM

The first recorded use of the term *literary impressionism* is found in Brunétière's article on Daudet, written in 1879, in which he describes Literary Impressionism as a stylistic development of Naturalism, incorporating the main principles of Impressionism in painting.[1] He defines the new style as 'une transposition systématique des moyens d'expression d'un art, qui est l'art de peintre, dans la domaine d'un autre art, qui est l'art d'écrire.'(p. 87). Daudet's 'painterly-poetic' style was strongly rejected by Brunétière. It was Desprez who, in his volume *l'Evolution Naturaliste* (1884) presented the Goncourt brothers as Literary Impressionists. Since they had consciously transposed the Impressionist techniques of the painters into language many stylistic characteristics were summarised : the painterly imperfect, broken sentences, lack of logical syntax, accumulation of adjectives and a great number of synonyms.[2] In 1896 also Gilbert, in *Le Roman en France Pendant le XIXe Siecle*, vaguely introduced the concept of Literary Impressionism.

Summarising the discussion in France so far, enough evidence can be found that the concept of Literary Impressionism at the end of the 19th century was applied to the description of a stylistic phenomenon. Brunétière and Desprez define Literary Impressionism as a formal style with grammatical characteristics and include Flaubert, Zola and Balzac in their analyses.[3] In 1899 Petit de Juleville, and M. Spronk, however, were the first critics to treat Literary Impressionism as a new, modern vision of reality. Juleville emphasised the subjectivity of experience and Spronk stressed the presence of 'an intensified sensitivity'.[4] Meanwhile, in Germany at the turn of the century, the term was also being used by German scholars studying French literature.[5] As a result of Herman Bahr's *Die Überwindung des Naturalismus*, German literary critics recognised a post-naturalistic modern impulse in Germany after 1890 and began to employ the term Impressionism. In 1890, however, C. Grottewitz, in an analysis of contemporary literature, still applied it as a term of abuse. He concluded that literature had changed from 'Naturalismus zum Impressionismus, Obskurantismus usw.'.[6] In 1891 the term was used by M.G. Conrad, as signifying a literary style, closely connected with photography.[7] Some years later, in 1902, the historian Karl Lamprecht presented an analysis of Impressionism as an art form, influenced by science and Positivism. In a later study Lamprecht distinguished a division within Impressionism between a psychological Literary Impressionism registering inner events, found in e.g. Hofmannsthal,

George, Bierbaum, and a physiological type, representing outward characteristics, found in e.g. Liliencron.[8] The same distinction is to be found in Ernst Lemke's study.[9]

Another important literary critic, Hermann Bahr, writing in 1904, discussed Impressionism and contrasted it with Naturalism. He viewed Impressionism in painting as a progressive art form, firmly based in modern times. Bahr draws parallels with Ernst Mach's philosophical views, as presented in *Die Analyse der Empfindungen* (1886):

> 'Die Technik des Impressionismus bringt eine Anschauung der Welt mit oder setzt sie vielleicht sogar voraus, die in den letzten hundert Jahren allmählich erst möglich geworden ist (...) Ich meine nicht, (...) es sei notwendig, erst einen Kurs bei Heraklit, Kant und Mach durchzumachen. Aber es sei bei mir entschieden, dass der Impressionismus auf uns nicht nur durch seine Technik, sondern noch vielmehr als Ausdruck jener Anschauung wirkt'.[10]

Mach believed that sense experience lies at the root of scientific knowledge. He rejected the traditional subject-object differentiation. For Mach there was no 'Ding an sich', only perceptions or sensations of reality, which always pertain to a subject who perceives. For Mach 'the world consists only of sensations'.[11] Herman Bahr foretold that Mach's philosophy of sensationism would be called 'die Philosophie des Impressionismus'.[12] In 1909 the parallel between Mach's philosophy of sensations and Impressionism was drawn when E. Friedell described Mach as the 'klassischen Philosophen des Impressionismus'.[13]

In 1907 the first general and comprehensive study of Impressionism, including Literary Impressionism, was published by Richard Hamann in *Der Impressionismus in Leben und Kunst*.[14] Hamann described Impressionism as the ultimate stylistic development, as an 'Ende der Entwicklung, das Altern eines in ununterbrochener Kontinuität wachsenden Kulturorganismus' (p. 197). Hamann was the first critic to apply a moralistic and cyclical-mystical concept of history to Impressionism, as 'Impressionismus als Äusserung (...) eines Zeitgeistes', when designating the concept 'Dichtung aller Perversionen einer dekadenten Zeit' (p. 149). In literature it is especially the tendency towards a 'Stimmungskunst' (art of mood + atmosphere) and a loss of form (p. 64) that are described, together with 'Klang, Akzent, Neuheit und Gedrängtheit, Sinnlichkeit und Lebendigkeit, Schwulst der Vorstellungen und der Gefühle' (p. 81). Unfortunately, Hamann's moralistic views influenced many successors in Germany, like Max Picard[15], who in 1916, described Impressionism as a form of 'decadent' existence, rather than a stylistic phenomenon.

Up to 1940, the discussion on Impressionism in Germany followed two main tracks: the conservative-nationalistic, ideological path and the approach which saw Literary Impressionism as a stylistic phenomenon. The latter is usually incorporated into the former. It is not only literature of the last century that is analysed.[16] Oskar Walzel blamed Impressionism for not being politically involved.[17] Negative French influences were described e.g., by Erich Köhler, who claimed the Goncourt brothers as the founders of Impressionism[18] in *Die Impressionistische Syntax der Goncourt*.[19] The studies by Wenzel and Hans Hoppe[20] and W. Melang[21] presented Literary Impressionism as a genuine French concept.

Walter Melang was the first to disconnect Impressionism in painting from Literary Impressionism.

Contrary to Brunétière, he concluded that Impressionistic tendencies were to be found as early as in Flaubert. According to Melang it was mere coincidence that Impressionism in painting took the lead. Melang's argument is important since he acknowledged that the Impressionists were objective in their presentation: 'Die Umwelt wird so objektiv als möglich und unbeeinflusst vom empirischen Wissen und von dem Bestreben, irgend etwas Persönlich-Subjektives auszudrücken, von den Sinnesorganen des Einzelnen, der das Sinneserlebnis wiedergebt, aufgefasst'. This argument was introduced by Wenzel in 1928. Hans Hoppe[22] analysed two contrasting phenomena, Impressionism and Expressionism, as co-existing styles, based on the subjectivistic principle. Between 1918 and 1940, a different group of French writers was introduced as Literary Impressionists.[23] Verlaine and the Goncourt brothers were generally accepted; Proust was still problematic; but when Zola and La Fontaine were mentioned the problems of the historical demarcation of Literary Impressionism were again evident. Meanwhile, in analysing these very different authors, the traditional argument was again adduced: that Literary Impressionism may be considered merely a possibile stylistic classification of literature, which may be introduced unconditionally as it is not linked with any periodical demarcation. But it was also argued that Literary Impressionism was the expression of a highly sensitive and nervous experience of life which manifested itself mainly at the end of the 19th century. Haman's and Walzel's influence was still noticeable in the strongly nationalistic studies[24] in which the affirmation of nationalistic ideology seemed to be more important than the analysis of a work of literature. Betz mentioned Liliencron, Dehmel, Dauthendey, Heinrich Mann, Schlaf, Wedekind, Rilke and Schnitzler as Literary Impressionists.

Three other studies are important, as they attempted to define Literary Impressionism mainly as a linguistic-stylistic phenomenon.[25] Loesch developed and described some characteristics of Impressionism in painting. He attempted to transpose into the Goncourts' works a subjective perception of reality, which was conveyed by e.g. a loose sentence-structure, substantivization, a preference for the nominal style and many strings of synonyms.[26] Large numbers of examples (4300) were carefully tested, but Loesch introduced a priori arguments. He described every possible grammatical form in any particular set of conditions, adding a special semantic ordering principle as a typically Impressionistic one. Kurt Brösel, in his *Veranschaulichung im Realismus, Impressionismus und Frühexpressionismus*, offered no criteria for a classification either.

In 1928 Luise Thon attempted to define Impressionism as a literary concept, on the basis of stylistic (syntactical and lexical) characteristics. Thon investigated a number of German authors of the 19th century: Schlaf, Holz, Liliencron, Dehmel and Dauthendey, but also von Altenberg, Hofmannsthal, Kerr, Th. Mann, Nietzsche, Rilke and Schnitzler. She defined Literary Impressionism as a concept identified with a particular period running from 1890-1910 and attempted 'das Gemeinsame zu erfassen, das allen diesen Dichtern eignet, und daraus einen Typus zu gewinnen, der die Eigenart einer ganzen Epoche umschreibt.' (p. 1) Thon distinguished four main characteristics. The first is 'Die Kunst des Treffens' (borrowed from O. Walzel), which describes the effort to express the complex presentation of an impression, with all its different nuances. The second is a passive outlook on life. The third is syntactical coordination and a loss of coherence, due to the influence of ordinary colloquial speech, and its inevitable syntactical consequences. The last characteristic is a vague presentation, or less resolution to give a concise one.[27] All these features may be evoked by a large number of grammatical indexes, mainly lexical ones, e.g. compositions, as 'möglichst vieles' is introduced in 'einem Komplex' (p. 137), adjectival and adverbial ones, short comparisons, in which 'Vergleichsgegenstand und verglichener Gegenstand (...) nicht mehr gleichwertig nebeneinander (stehen), sondern (...) ineinander (fliessen) (p. 29), and finally, adjectival participles, 'denen eigentlich ein präpositional angeschlossenes Substantiv beigestellt werden müsste' (p. 129). There are two problems inherent in Thon's approach to formally grammatical and lexical indexes. First, it was very difficult to define and describe a literary period concept using only formal and a-historical categories. Thon herself realised this, since she was careful to point out that these stylistic examples may also be found in other literary period concepts: 'Wenn hier Spracherscheinungen als typisch impressionistisch dargelegt worden sind, so soll das nicht ohne weiteres bedeuten, dass sie *nur* Sprachmittel der Eindruckskunst sind' (p. 2). The second problem was that Thon's bases for evidence appeared to be rather restricted and limited. They cannot be representative for a whole period concept and the results cannot be generalised.

Meanwhile the discussion on Literary Impressionism was also continued internationally, e.g. by Bally and Richter[28], and a good deal of attention was paid to Impressionism in the thirties. In 1932 Joseph Warren Beach described its basic outlines in his chapter on Modernism.[29] In 1935 Ford Madox Ford wrote an essay on 'The Impressionist Group', in which he included H. James as a writer who 'builds suggestions of happenings on suggestions of happenings' and who influenced Joseph Conrad. According to Ford Madox Ford, there was a time when a group of English novelists accepted without much protest the label *Impressionist*. Ford not only accepted the term, he also made it the core of his literary theory, which was based on Henry James's famous sentence: 'A novel is in its broadest definition a personal, a direct impression of life'.[30] In 1938 Herbert Müller, in an article evocatively entitled 'Impressionism in Fiction: Prism vs. Mirror' claimed that Impressionism was 'one of the key words in modern literature.'

In Buenos Aires, in *El Concepto Linguistico de Impressionismo*, the authors Amado Alonso and Raimundo Lida rejected the idea of constructing a restricted linguistic theory of Impressionism. In raising the issue they summarised a number of theories proposed by Bally, Wenzel, Lerch, Brunétière and Hatzfeld. Their analysis is most valuable in synthesising many ideas from various sources, but most of all for their fundamental conclusion that there is no such thing as an inherently Impressionistic language. They argued that the same linguistic constructions used in one stylistic context may also be employed in other contexts, in order to create different effects. What determines whether a style is Impressionistic, according to Alonso and Lida, is an aesthetic, as deduced from a 'voluntad de estilo' ('a will to style'), a linguistic philosophy which is conceptual, together with the use of a special pattern of words and structures, the handling of linguistic devices designed for a particular aesthetic purpose, which produces Impressionism.[31]

Consequently, it was realised that any attempt to define Literary Impressionism by positing an inherent linguistic configuration is a mistake. Alonso and Lida discredited the term 'impressionistic language'. They believed that it is impossible to verbalise an instantaneous sensorial impression, as a word or a sentence alone cannot express a pure and isolated perception without being altered to some degree by empirical knowledge or by memory.[32] Though it may be theoretically applicable as a criterion for formal logic, Alonso and Lida's criticism was not taken up in the international discussion after the fifties.

An increasing number of art studies then appeared in which art and literature were seen as parallel. Hatzfeld, writing about European and particularly French literature, claimed that 'art (...) [is] the key to a better and deeper understanding of literature'.[33] René Wellek, however, did not assert this view in 'The Parallelism between Literature and the Arts'. He warned against too simple analogues.[34]

During the fifties and sixties, Impressionism was not only considered to be stylistically classifiable for describing authors around 1900. Considering the parallels between art and literature and the influences of historical, social, political and philosophical views and events, it was presented as a valid literary concept, comparable to Romanticism, Symbolism and Naturalism. In Germany, stylistic research persisted, attempting to define a literary period (Cf. Walzel and Thon), but now with the help of some new categories, such as 'Verselbständigungstendenzen des Optischen'[35], 'Verundeutlichung' and 'Auflösung der gegenständlichen Ganzheitsvorstellung'.[36] In Germany, Literary Impressionism was described as an anti-movement or development from Naturalism. In Alker's study it was analysed as 'Nervenkunst'.[37] It was described as a 'Kunststil' and a 'Seelenhaltung' supporting Mach's philosophy of subjectivity and sensationism.[38]

Impressionism as a general socio-historical term lay dormant for some twenty years until, in 1951, Arnold Hauser's very influential chapter appeared in the final volume of his *The Social History of Art*.[39] According to Hauser, Impressionism was an outgrowth of and a reaction to Realism. It had its roots in a malaise afflicting the middle classes of Europe because of the consolidation of capitalism and the rapid pace of industrialisation and urbanisation in European society. Impressionism manifested itself in each of the arts in different ways, reflecting a heightened sensibility, a new irritability in modern man, and a perception of the world as in a state of constant flux and transition, presenting the impression of a continuum in which everything coalesces and in which there are no differences other than the various approaches and points of view of the beholders (p. 169). In painting, where Naturalism 'marked an increase in the elements of composition (...) an extension of the technical means', Impressionism involved 'a system of restriction or simplifications' (p. 171). The 'anecdote' or 'literary element' of the subject was eliminated, the motif reduced to landscape (...), portrait or still-life. What was reproduced was an immediate (subjective) visual experience, the discrete features of the subject matter being less important than the visual sensation produced by them. A new emphasis on colour and light dissolved outlines and smooth surfaces into a system of spots and dabs, seemingly casually arranged:

Impressionism is less illusionistic than naturalism; instead of the illusion, it gives elements of the subject, instead of a picture of the whole, the bricks of which experience is composed. Before impressionism, art reproduced objects by *signs*, now it represents

43

them through components, through parts of the material of which they are made up. (p. 171).

According to the social-art historian Hauser, various trends in literature exhibited different features of Impressionism: the Decadents and Symbolist poets expressed the transitoriness of life and a revolt against bourgeois values in a hedonistic sensualism and a metaphoric language that attempted to link the material and non-material worlds. Another type of Impressionism remained materialistic, as opposed to spiritualistic, and was committed to the world of the senses. It was characterised by a philosophy of 'unresisting absorption in the passing moment.' (p. 206) Poetry expressed 'fleeting, scarcely palpable sensations, indefinite, indefinable sensual stimuli, delicate colours and tired voices' (p. 205). Eventually all forms of literature were affected: 'The story is reduced to mere situations, the plot to lyrical scenes, the character drawing to the description of spiritual dispositions and trends. Everything becomes episodical, peripheral to a life without a center.' (p. 206) Impressionism lasted, according to Hauser, until the early 1920's, by which time the post-impressionistic movement in painting had infected all the arts. Cubism and Surrealism were the logical outcome of the fragmentation of reality, instigated by the Impressionists. The 'Zeitgeist', the growing anxiety over the complexity of life, of the lack of permanence and continuity, had by then been expressed in all the arts. In literature, beginning in the 1880's, reality was depicted in ever smaller segments, as though men were able to seize and apprehend ever smaller portions of their experience - isolated moments, sensations and subjective impressions. This fragmentation was begun by the Impressionists. Hauser classifies James as an intellectual Impressionist and Tsjechov as 'the purest representative' of Russian Impressionism. Since Hauser is a social art historian from the school of Max Weber and Karl Mannheim rather than a literary historian, he fell short of giving a workable definition of Literary Impressionism. He overstated Tsjechov's lack of 'all formal organization and integration' as he failed to note the indexes of an internal ordering principle in e.g. Tsjechov's imagery, which is highly selective and concentrated.[40] Hauser's socio-historical arguments seemed, however, convincing, since he always based them on historically verifiable political, economic and social references.

In 1961 Hugo Sommerhalder based his argument on the same concept[41] when describing modern German literature between 1880 and 1910, as being characterised by two basic Impressionistic impulses, i.e. 'die Impression pure und den Augenblick, in dem sich die Wahrheit offenbart'.[42] Sommerhalder analysed a number of works by Liliencron, Bierbaum, Rilke, Hofmannsthal, Schnitzler, Holz, Schlaf, Hauptmann and George. Another social-historical account on

Impressionism in Germany was presented by Hamann/Hermand in 1977.[43] This was heavily influenced by Hamann's 1907 analysis in *Der Impressionismus in Leben und Kunst*. In order to analyse the Impressionistic 'dekadenten Stimmungsklang', they proposed to analyse a series of stylistic characteristics, such as 'Formlosigkeit', 'Flüchtigheit', 'Pikanterie' and 'Nuancenkult', as well as moralistic norms, to prove their points. According to Hamann/Hermand, Impressionism remains a 'Kulturerscheinung' in almost all European countries 'vorausgesetzt, dass sich in ihnen eine ähnliche gesellschafliche und ökonomische Entwicklung vollzog'. (p. 10) Hauser and Hamann/Hermann were the first to place Impressionism within a wider context, i.e., within the framework of a general European literary historical pattern. In 1973 Manfred Diersch applied the general period concept of Impressionism to a discussion of philosophy and art around the turn of the century. He underpinned his argument with empirio-critical studies by Avenarius and, more especially, by Ernst Mach.[44] Diersch also leant on Bahr's discussion in 'Aesthetics of Modern Literature'. Although his descriptions of social, political and philosophical conditions seemed convincing, Diersch's concept of Impressionism has not been pursued in Germany.

Most significant for Anglo-American criticism has been the discussion of Impressionism in the USA over the last two decades.[45] The argument was instigated by Orm Overland's analysis of Stephen Crane in 1966.[46] Overland did not refer to a historical period concept as deduced from Impressionism in painting, but offered a loose definition of certain stylistic features of Impressionism. He stressed the distinction between Naturalism and Impressionism, especially in their underlying philosophies. Overland's discussion provided precise documentation on the elements of style, syntax, and structure and on the quality of Crane's imagery. A year later, Stanley Wertheim contradicted Overland and described Crane as a Naturalist, a discussion which was continued by R.O. Rogers, Kenneth E. Bidle and James Nagel, all writing on Crane.[47] Nagel departed from an aesthetic perspective. He did not define a literary historical concept, but used a text-immanent approach, based on discernible aesthetic matters and impulses, to conclude that Crane was an Impressionist.

The Symposium on Literary Impressionism in 1968 introduced some interesting new issues concerning the concept in general. Herbert Howard, a literary historian, linked Impressionism in painting and in literature and analysed its aspect of vitalism in George Moore, V. Woolf, Joyce, and even D.H. Lawrence.

The second speaker, Paul Ilie, discussed Spanish Impressionism and departed from Alonso and Lida's basic conclusion that, apart from an all-embracing aesthetic issue, we cannot speak of an inherently impressionistic language. Phrases in themselves may not be

Impressionistic but, as Ilie contended, there is no denying that the Literary Impressionists favoured certain idiomatic constructions. Ilie departs from the Alonso/Lida notion of the 'voluntad de estilo', the 'will to style', as 'it is style and form, rather than themes, which gives Literary Impressionism in Spain its special quality'. Spanish Impressionism in painting is closer to French Impressionist literature than to French Impressionist painting in its themes and forms (p. 48). Ilie discussed the aesthetic concept of the Impressionists Miro, Jimenez, Azorin and Ramon, revealing stylistic similarities and a similar philosophy underlying their techniques. Ilie rejected the 'pictorialism' point of departure of the former speaker. He resorted to the basic aesthetic of Impressionistic painting, as the model for applying philosophical principles to an artistic end:

> Impressionism designates a style, a method and a psychology, rather than a movement. Its prototype is the French school of painting, and it reveals similarities with the latter, in the treatment of sense perception (...), the psychology of forming impressions and the concept of time (...) [and] the preoccupation with color and light.(p. 53).

The most provocative speaker, Calvin Brown, speaking on musical Impressionism and its relationship to other art forms, proposed to drop the term Impressionism from the musical and literary vocabulary: 'We have nothing to lose but confusion'. (p. 59) He proposed to maintain the term 'impressionistic', as 'it is useful to describe certain literary techniques' and 'some short works which derive their effect primarily from these techniques.' (p. 59). He admitted that 'Impressionistic' works were 'more prevalent in 1890 than in 1200, (but) (...) Impressionism 'dominated the work of very few writers, it was not sufficiently conspicuous in literature or music as a whole to warrant our giving its name to a literary period'. Brown rejected the term as applied to the novel: 'The novel as a whole can never be an impressionistic work whether in its essential techniques or in its primary impact on a reader.' (p. 58). He continued: 'it has generally been recognized that Impressionism is essentially an art of fragments, sketches and small forms. The determined Impressionist who undertakes a large work must go outside his aesthetic theories in order to give it some coherence, and hence it follows that the work will not be a purely Impressionistic production, but that the artist's expressed intentions will probably not be carried out.'(p. 58) Since 'shorter works (...) can be composed in a single creative impulse, relatively pure Impressionism is perfectly possible.' Brown adduced some literary and musical works (by Verlaine, Maeterlinck, Liliencron, the Goncourts and Debussy). The last two speakers, Remy Saisselin and Michael

46

Benamou, both discussed the relationship between Impressionist painting and poetry in general, which was not very relevant to the subject of the symposium.

Maria Kronegger studied a wide variety of authors in France (Flaubert, Gide, Proust, Sartre, Robbe-Grillet, Claude Simon), Germany (Rilke) and in Japan (Osamu Dazai).[48] Kronegger started from two basic assumptions: firstly, that the concept of Literary Impressionism is basically a cultural one; and secondly that the concept may be described as 'a style with its own devices' (p. 13): 'Impressionist creations in various countries are different expressions of the same basic idea. The common denominator of these various literary and artistic expressions is the Impressionist style'. In her discussion she included themes, characters and structure. Kronegger mixed up chronology and departed from the aesthetic norms of the painters, which 'did not precede the writers'.[49] Paris is said to be the 'indisputable cradle of French Impressionism' (p. 32), by which the German Impressionists, George, Rilke, Hofmannsthal and Liliencron were influenced: 'Impressionism became a Parisian movement of cosmopolitan character.' (p. 32) Kronegger's historical framework alternated between two opinions. On the one hand, she wrote: 'We wish to establish the notion in Western Europe of 'Impressionist literature' within a given period' (p. 29) and, on the other hand, she concluded: 'that impressionism is not limited to a short period, its high point in 1875 and its end in 1885.' Kronegger pointed vaguely to many different philosophical influences on Impressionism, Kant, Mach, existentialism and phenomenology. The result is a considerable mental confusion, listing everything from Ernst Mach's influence on Impressionism to the much later existentialist Merleau-Ponty.

R.M. Werner, writing in Germany in 1979, presented in *Impressionismus als Literaturhistorischer Begriff*[50] an excellent survey of mainly German arguments on the issue. Werner's aim was to analyse L. Thon's 1928 study, using computer-aided analyses, and to find out whether a so-called 'purely stylistic and statistical analysis' may be representative of a literary period concept:

> 'Dabei soll herausgefunden werden, ob der Begriff in seinen wesentlichen Charakteristika auf den literarischen Texten basiert oder ob vielmehr die Analogie zum Sinngehalt des Begriffs in der Malerei konstitutiv ist, die in der Literatur zwar partiell belegt werden kann, aber nicht die übergreifenden Sinnzusammenhänge repräsentiert.'(p. 4).

Since Werner questioned any general literary research based on the parallellism between art and literature, which he describes as a subjective experience, his main question is 'in wiefern eine subjektiv empfundene Parallelität zwischen Kunst und Literatur zulässig generalisiert werden darf (p. 5).' In this major study Werner restricted himself mainly to an analysis of word categories, parataxis and word-complexity, and concluded that on this basis Arthur Schitzler was the least impressionistic of the authors mentioned by Thon. Werner also rejected any purely stylistic classification and questioned Thon's arguments: 'Die Thonschen Kriterien, die von dieser Untersuchung zunächst kritiklos aufgegriffen und operationalisiert worden sind, müssten für den Fall, dass man mit ihnen einen Zeitstil institutionalisieren will, zunächst kritisch überpruft und mit dem malerischen Ursprung des Impressionismusbegriffes verglichen werden.' (p. 250) Werner rejected any thematic derivation (p. 196) from painting into literature. As a kind of afterthought, he would opt for a different point of departure and a new term for the movement: the (re)introduction of the concept of 'Aesthetizismus' which was also applied by Peter Bürger to post-naturalistic German literature[51]; this had the advantage that: er eine eingeschränkte Perspektive der Autoren impliziert, ohne sie gleichzeitig als Subjektivisten oder Solipsisten zu brandmarken. Er zielt (...) auf einen autonomen, selbstzweckbestimmten Kunstbegriff.' (p. 197)

This is what Sarah F. Paulk did in *Aesthetics of Impressionism: Studies in Art and Literature*[52] in which she analysed painting, sculpture, poetry and the novel - in general terms, introducing a large amount of biographical information into her arguments. In the chapter on the novel she discusses H. James, J. Conrad, F.M. Ford and V. Woolf. Concluding with an assessment of common features between Impressionistic painting and the art of the novel, she writes: 'Each sought a suppression or disappearance of the artist from his work. All comment by the artist was purged. The painters produced non-narrative works, and the novelists eliminated plot. Both are concerned with the moment and the senses. Still the comparison goes deeper to the very core- the essence of each is the attempt to render perception. The whole of Impressionistic painting is bound up in its attempt to capture what the eye perceives; likewise the Impressionist novel attempts to capture the perceiving mind in action.' (p. 161)

Two other studies, *Henry James and Impressionism* by James Kirschke (1981) and *Stephen Crane and Literary Impressionism* by J. Nagel (1981), also viewed the two concepts, Impressionism in painting and in literature, as directly parallel and proceeded to an interpretation of two American authors, James and Crane.

Meanwhile, Hauser's chapter on Tsjechov and James seems to have inspired Peter Stowell's important analysis of H. James and A. Tsjechov.[53] Stowell, in a profound philosophical analysis, based on psychology and Gestalt-thinking, maintained that Literary Impressionism is not simply a stylistic phenomenon that tried to capture the blurred and ephemeral images of the Impressionist painters in their moments of literary pictorialism, but that 'it was a literary phenomenon of major proportions, as it rendered a furiously changing world, precariously perched for the flight of modernism into the 20th century. Literary Impressionism is the incipient moment of modernism. It cannot be neglected.' (p. 9) His study centred around the Impressionist's act of perception, the subject-object relationship, change and time and space. Unfortunately, he did not translate these philosophical ideas into literary critical or narrative terms.[54]

In conclusion, most German critics on Literary Impressionism seem to have agreed that there is a close connection between Naturalism and Impressionism. At the beginning of the century in particular, German scholars formulated a system of *Stilentwicklung* in which the development of Naturalism into Impressionism (and Expressionism) was depicted as a series of steps following one another in a thoroughly logical manner. The first, they said, was dominated by the outer world (Naturalism), the second by the meeting of the outer world and the inner Ego (Impressionism), and the third wholly by the inner ego (Expressionism).[55] Even in German literary histories, Literary Impressionism was not always accorded the same weight as Naturalism, Symbolism and Expressionism. This is not the place to decide to what extent the writers discussed in these works can be classified as Literary Impressionists. Besides, a possible stylistic comparison of English works with their French and German counterparts can only be valid if the specific structure of each language is taken into account.[56] Stylistic features in one language need not be expressive of the same quality in another language. Hallmarks of Literary Impressionism in Germany may well be common usage in English.[57]

In criticism dealing with French literature, Literary Impressionism has often been lumped together with Symbolism.[58] The Literary Impressionist kept a middle course between subjective Symbolism and objective Naturalism. He did not create an artificial world, although his impression might be highly 'subjective'. His world was that of the Naturalist - but 'vu à travers d'un tempérament'.[59]

Criticism in the Anglo-American world has remained scattered and elusive, although some major critical works have recently appeared. Literary Impressionism is considered not simply as a stylistic phenomenon presenting the blurred and ephemeral images of literary pictorialism[60], but also a stage in literary history that paved the way for Modernism in the 20th century. It cannot be neglected and must be included among the many categories that attempt to regulate our critical vocabulary, because it embodies a new aesthetic concept in the art of fiction.[61]

In the final analysis this chronological survey of the different concepts and descriptions of Literary Impressionism reveals three possible currents which may be important for future research. Firstly, the concept of Literary Impressionism may be based on a parallel with social, philosophical, artistic (e.g. painting and music), political and economic conditions, and described within a period concept. Secondly, it may be analysed formally as a stylistic classification, using grammatical and lexical indexes. Thirdly, fusing the two possibilities, it may be analysed, described, and codified as an aesthetic 'will to style'. Reference may be made to foregrounded indexes as to narrative methods, themes, structure, characterisation and images. These indexes may be analysed with the help of traditional and more recently developed literary historical and critical terms.

This study will attempt to describe Mansfield's Literary Impressionist aesthetic impulses and techniques, (No. 3), fusing the two possibilities. Literary Impressionism is not seen as a merely stylistic manipulation of a mode of expression (as in no. 2), but as a way of perceiving and presenting the surrounding world, which will set its unmistakable and aesthetic stamp on an author's work at a variety of levels.

SOME BASIC AESTHETICS
                   OF LITERARY IMPRESSIONISM

THE PERCEPTION OF REALITY

At the centre of Literary Impressionist aesthetics is the act of perceiving the outside world and the manner in which it is perceived. The Literary Impressionists not only reacted against the cumbersome paraphernalia of ordinary realistic investigation, they also objected to conventional Realism because it was mechanical, clumsy and superficial, creating a merely orderly catalogue of externals, but most of all because they thought it was unreal. Whereas traditional writers started from a definable subject, i.e. experience previously organised and interpreted by the observing mind, Literary Impressionists started from perception. For them the surrounding world is not well ordered but constitutes an indistinct and obscure picture made up of an irresistible flood of confused and ever changing sense impressions.[1] Through sensory experience they discover a new relationship with the everyday world. As André Gide puts it in *Les Nourritures Terrestres*: 'I see, I feel, I hear, I smell; therefore I am'.[2] This sensory experience is a synthetic, intuitive feeling of oneness with reality, which becomes a subjective experience.

For the Impressionist the perceived world is neither the sum of its objects, the solid reality of matter, the brute reality of an inhuman world divorced from the subject as in the Realist or Naturalist tradition, nor the symbol of a hidden reality, a representation of both the idea and the unseen, or the embodiment and revelation of the infinite, as in the Symbolist philosophy.[3] According to the Literary Impressionist, reality cannot be analysed, but can only be intuitively perceived; it is a synthesis of pure sensations, modulated by consciousness and changed into impressions. Human experience consists of fragments, therefore the Impressionist's experience *is* these fragments. Instead of describing life, the Literary Impressionist attempts to convey directly the actual sensation of living - he tries to suppress, or at least subordinate the habitual concepts that separate us from actuality.[4] The Literary Impressionist attempts to communicate the live, instantaneous, total sensory perception of reality around him before common sense has transformed it, or intellect has abstracted or relativised its 'meaning', in short, to give a full intense realisation of a mere apprehension of experience.

One of Joseph Conrad's aims in his writing was: 'to make you hear, to make you feel (...) before all, to make you *see*'.[5] He presented his intuitive perceptions of objects, people, events. He offered no logical analysis or indexes, but a vivid rendering of sensory impressions, with

51

a disregard of chronology but a lively concern for atmosphere. He wanted to render the immediate impression that life makes upon us. In his attempt to create order where there is none, the Literary Impressionist intuitively selects and interprets reality. He fuses form and meaning through the portrayal of the human condition, and compresses this into a concentrated momentary impression.[6] He sees the world subjectively, as it presents itself to the senses in varying perceptions and from varying points of view. The sensory apparatus of each Literary Impressionist differs.

As Emile Zola already anticipated, an artist should express his personality and his temperament in his depiction of reality.[7] In his attempt to be as 'realistic' and personal as possible, the Literary Impressionist presents the undeveloped consciousness and all its arbitrary associations. He will avoid analysis, and content himself with the apperception in the mere representation of a momentary impression. His aim is to present an immediate, pure recreation of the actual sensation of living as opposed to an orderly analysis or generalisation of experience, since he wants to present a subjective, intuitive experience, with great intimacy. This does not imply an utter rejection of logical analysis, or a denial of its validity, but judgement follows rather than initiates, and it does not dictate.

The aim is to create an atmosphere, in subtle evocation, with discontinuous, retrospective or unfinished actions, in streams of consciousness channeled by emotion, corresponding to the way in which we experience life. No analysis or inventory of set pictures or comments on the characters is given nor is there a chronological report with a definite beginning, middle and end. In its effect on the reader, it is highly suggestive. The subjective aspect of Literary Impressionism and its rhetoric was noted as early as 1894 when H. Garland ponted out: 'It must never be forgotten, that they (the Impressionist painters) are not delineating a scene; they are painting a personal impression of a scene, which is vastly different'.[8]

The Literary Impressionist believes that reality is illusory. An impression of the surrounding world is often determined by circumstances. Any mental condition at any given moment must be taken into consideration. These factors are beyond any power of influence. The Impressionist's only responsibility is to render a character's reactions to the external stimuli as truthfully as he can. Here we are back again with Naturalism and its view of man at the mercy of natural forces. The Literary Impressionist presents an illusory reality rather passively, but as truthfully as possible. This passive attitude is basic to the entire 'Weltanschauung'.[9] In the end, the Literary Impressionist technique, with its assumed and apparent objectivity, creates a fictional illusion: the suggestive illusion that the reader is participating in the events, scenes or actions described.[10]

The emphasis on the act of perception leads us to the perceiver, who regards the process of perceiving impressions as reality itself. At any given moment of time, one impression is as valid as any other. The Literary Impressionist sees everything anew, through fresh and 'innocent' eyes.[11] Impressionism does not simply record the impact of raw and unadulterated sensations on a (passive) receptor. If that were so, Literary Impressionism would be little more than a compendium of impressions. But Literary Impressionism is the process by which impressions are absorbed by a perceiver.[12]

Passivity is often considered to be a most fundamental element in Literary Impressionist fiction.[13] It has been argued, correctly, that characters are the passive receptors of sensory stimuli and that the 'reduction of the artistic representation to the mood of the moment is, at the same time, the expression of a fundamentally passive outlook on life, an acquiescence in the role of the spectator'.[14] But it is too much to claim, that all Impressionist characters are passive.[15] They may, in fact, have an active, restless consciousness. They may passively absorb a bewildering flood of an outside world moving in constant flux, but apperception continually intermingles with the sensory fragments, searching for relationships, patterns and meanings. Impressionist characters, including Mansfield's characters, often find a 'creative synthesis' in passive perception and final 'active conception'.[16] The rendering of events and objects is a combination of carefully selected, yet seemingly random details in a vision of fragmented reality in which all contours are blurred. But at the same time the perceiving characters often attempt to find some unifying configuration, some 'merging of subject and object' in Stowell's terminology, some 'centrifugal' (Müller) unification of the perceiver and the perceived in the Impressionist's sensory world.[17] The Impressionist's characters seem to be caught in the moment of transition between a passionate desire for a transcendental glimpse of the 'Truth' of human consciousness, and their realisation that there is no 'Truth', but only perceived fragments of highly ambiguous sensory stimuli. Between the irresolution of these two paradoxes, a major theme of Literary Impressionism, is the struggle for identity in a constantly shifting balance of perception and knowledge: the disparity between subjective and objective 'truth' and 'reality'. Characters will never be able to perceive enough during their fragmentary existence to obtain definitive 'knowledge', and their 'knowledge' can never be acquired without apperception. They must perceive carefully, then guess and intuit enough to believe that they know - not all, but just enough. A character in Impressionist fiction often balances between an attempt to perceive and know his fluid relationship to the ever-changing world. The Literary Impressionist attempts to have the reader partake of the very process and the entire experience of perception, he does so by concentrating on the atmosphere which surrounds the object or scene presented, and on the feeling and sensations which are aroused by this experience. It is only the direct experience that counts - everything beyond the actual sensations or impressions of the characters is eliminated: what cannot be sensed does not exist for the Impressionist.[18]

We have seen that the Literary Impressionist begins (like the Impressionist painter) with an empirical reality, rather than an abstract idea. His vision is a vision which is seen, felt and heard, rather than imagined. It is a vision in which everything stable and coherent is dissolved and assumes the characteristics of the unfinished, the fragmentary. An atomisation of the world of the mind and of matter, as well as relativism and subjectivism characterise the Impressionistic vision of the world.[19] Everything turns around sensory impressions: objects are converted into light and colour effects or barely tangible shapes. As the critic Jules Laforgue explained: 'The Impressionist sees and represents nature just as it is, that is, solely in coloured vibrations. Not design, nor light, nor perspective, nor chiaroscuro[20] - such childish classifications: in reality all of that is resolved in coloured vibrations (...) The object and the subject are then irretrievably moving, unseizable and unseizing'.[21]

With the Impressionists, the colour of an object is not something which belongs to the object but rather a product of the ways in which sunlight, shadow and reflected light play upon it. In traditional literature colour is a frequently used metaphor in the ordinary sense of vividness or piquancy; but in the context of an Impressionist literary creation, the meaning of such words as red, purple, yellow becomes an important issue, because colour is susceptible to change, and therefore alive. Colour, like touch, smell, hearing and taste, is a sensation which has been variously defined as a way in which a consciousness is affected by an object and as a property of the object itself. The critic Albères defines Impressionism in literature as 'a plunge into consciousness':

'Multiple, swirling around, made of luminous dust suspended in nothingness, Impressionist reality is not told, nor is it even described at all. Words and men's eager gestures, their hesitations and arabesques, scarcely indicate several lines on the surface of that nebula of reality that is Life (...) Bewildered by a new perspective, the reader is thus transported into a molten universe (...) Far from being an objective vision, impressionism is in effect a plunge into consciousness'.[22]

Consciousness for the Literary Impressionist is a play of reflections. It is shine and countershine, and reality is seen as a harmony of subjects and objects, merging together in terms of time and space within which the character moves.

In Literary Impressionism the act of perception is more important than either the perceived or the perceiver.[23] No longer is there the narrator and/or character on the one hand and the perceived on the other. There is no separation between subject and object. There is only seeing and retaining.[24] With many Literary Impressionists, the act of perceiving and the act of remembering are homologous and sense impressions become an impression in the reflecting consciousness, receding into the past and invoking other impressions. The Literary Impressionist[25] stresses the fragmentary discontinuity of remembered experience, reflecting the discontinuity of human perception itself.[26]

Critics such as Gustave Geffroy in 1894, Bally in 1936 and Albères in 1966 and 1970 have associated Literary Impressionism with phenomenology. Geffroy defines an Impressionist painting as a kind of painting that tends to represent the appearance and meaning of objects in space, and attempts to synthesise these aspects in the semblance of the moment.[27] As Kronegger writes:

With the Impressionists' perceptive experience, the reality of the novel changes; the traditional frozen forms of description (Balzac) set themselves into motion spatially. The protagonist sees reality from several angles of vision at once and the objects are released without losing sight of their earlier positions.[28]

In this indecisive universe where subjectivism mingles with objectivity, the novel is no longer a story but a confused colliding of sensations, impressions and experiences. It is not 'ready-made', shown in advance, shaped and packaged by a trained writer-narrator. It is proffered to the reader like some fluid, poetic, enigmatic substance, and instead of following the plot line we wander around as if in a daydream. The 'real' world exists only insofar as it is reflected in a character's consciousness.

The parallel with science also seems valid, as the art critic René Huyghe has observed:

Science divides matter into billions of atoms which make the universe an immense magma of swirling, infinitesimal particles where the haphazardness and the logic of associations create bodies, shapes and objects, like so many provisional phantasms. The Impressionist for his part practices a similar divisionism: no more contours, no more shapes, no more distinct objects; a powdery haze of coloured dots whose convergence and grouping generate an illusion of things.[29]

Impressionism means a new attitude towards reality in life. The Literary Impressionist wants to express what the eye actually sees. What it often sees is a vibration of light on an object in dissolution. As Jules Laforgue says: 'a natural eye (...) reaches a point where it can see reality in the living atmosphere of forms, decomposed, refracted by beings and things, in incessant vibration. Such is the first characteristic of the Impressionistic eye'.[30]

LIGHT AND ATMOSPHERE

The Literary Impressionist, like the Symbolist, is preoccupied with images of light.[1] For the Symbolist, light is the equivalent of the highest spiritual principle; it exists apart from matter; it opens up a world beyond space and matter. For the Literary Impressionist light loses all such sacrosanct connotations. The Literary Impressionists do not assimilate light to 'the True', to God, or to 'the Universal Soul', but to themselves[2] and the 'Stimmung' (mood + atmosphere) they want to express. The word 'Stimmung' or 'état d'âme' becomes all important. This fusion of the individual's consciousness with the world at large creates a unity between visual appearance and mental reality.

Hugo Sommerhalder explained: 'if we are in such a 'Stimmung' that inner and outer worlds coincide, then the conditions are fulfilled for the assimilation of the ego and the impressions from the outside world - and for the fusion of outer and inner space into one single space'.[3] The 'Stimmung' is the medium into which Impressionist literature condenses itself. What the reader perceives from the Literary Impressionist's work is light; often not the objects which reflect the light, but the colours, in an atmospheric 'Stimmung'.[4] Kronegger, in her analysis of the harmonies of light and colour, argued that 'the quality of light in Impressionist literature is a psychological as well as a narrative ambience; it envelopes both protagonists and scenes. This light never dramatizes action, but lends it calm'.[5]

The Literary Impressionist also blurs the contours and presents intensity and expressiveness through images of light. There is no solidity and rigidity to life, no neat outlines, or symmetry, as in its traditional presentation. The mysteriousness of Literary Impressionist fiction, when the shadows are deepened by the very brilliance of its illumination, is meant to convey the mysteriousness of all experience that is deeply felt. A world and an atmosphere are created, in which everything seems to have lost its natural identity. The reflexion of light on this reality creates an impression of remoteness and distance. Since the definition of character is inseparable from a novel's plot, character cannot thrive in a plot without a form. Literary

Impressionism breaks down characterisation. Figures are presented who have no shape to speak of, who defy simple summary or categorisation. The most solid characters seem at times to melt away into an Impressionistic atmosphere.[6] Even when given sharp perceptions, the main characters in Mansfield's short stories remain enclosed in a sort of envelope. (See Chapter 4.4) There is more stress on connotation than on denotation. Images of haze, darkness, damp air, water, darkness, and obstruction dominate the scene[7] and convey the impression of a distant vision through unity of colour, under specific light.[8] Through unity of colour, tint and tone, blurred outlines and vagueness of meaning, the Literary Impressionist attempts to achieve a harmonious internal reality. The motives of characters are also rendered as though they lay far, even unattainably removed, also from the reader, in half-dissolving shapes transformed by atmosphere, moods and memories. The light which plays over these shapes does not bring them nearer to us, but removes them from us in dissolving contours. Space, time and the light in it have become a surrounding atmosphere, which can only be grasped intuitively and in a synthesis.

CHANGE

Change has also become one of the basic motifs of the Literary Impressionists. As the painters watch nature and people change, in the process of perception they themselves are changing. The Literary Impressionist attempts to express that mutual and reciprocal change by means of changing patterns of narrative methods, techniques and images. He emphasises the internal changes of characters and the external changes of the world around him: 'subject and object are then irretrievably in motion, inapprehensible and unapprehending'. In these flashes of identity lies the nature of the Impressionist's art, and 'any attempt to codify such flashes is but an academic pastime', writes Laforgue.[1] Change also brings 'flashes of identity' between subject and object'. By these 'glimpses', the artist enables the reader to share these flashes of insight with the character. In this process the Literary Impressionist seems to stand one step removed from the painter. In his attempt he presents the expression of an impression, in which the characters or perceivers become the Impressionist painter, seeing nature, objects and people through immediate, fresh, intuitive and prismatic eyes.[2] Characters may make errors of perception, when seeing fragments of nature and forms which decompose before their eyes. They may hear words and phrases that make little sense to them. They cannot grasp the relationships around them.

In Literary Impressionism everything is in flux and characters may not be able to see the outlines and contours of the fleetingness of time.

The natural, intuitive innocent eye of the Literary Impressionist immerses itself in his character's perspective.[3] Demarcation lines do not exist for Impressionist painters, nor for the Literary Impressionist. The apprehension of the undemarcated whole, of present, past and future must be captured in the total synthesis - through intuitive and inductive means, and therefore from a perspective that affords a view of 'the whole'. The Literary Impressionist steers his characters through a vast maze of seemingly meaningless and disconnected details. He has the character's mind register snatches of sight, sound, smell, hearing and touch. The 'trivial' sensory touches flow together through the character's mood and his sensory associations direct his mind. However, as soon as these images coalesce, they dissolve just as quickly into the flux of space, time and human consciousness, and dissolution of images brings the possibility of new combinations that may be added to the fabrication of new nuances in new impressions.

Impressionist characters often look into the distance and see 'someone' or 'something' that for the moment, through the blur of undemarcated lines and the haze of distance[4], is their reality. But an image or gesture, which might be identified through months or years of perceptual experience, may change the whole atmosphere. Details that are vague, even in their concreteness, may evoke the one crucial arresting feature. Only the impression made on the perceiver is presented - neither facial features nor expressions are described by the Literary Impressionist, but masses of seemingly arbitrary details support the fleeting image of an impression. What is perceived in the distance will change through space, time and light, giving reality a multiplicity of nuances to be absorbed by both the senses and the mind.

SPACE AND TIME

The physicist and philosopher Ernst Mach diagnosed the widespread cultural phenomenon of Impressionism in *Die Analyse der Empfindungen* (1885) in which he calls 'space' and 'time' sensations comparable to colours and sounds. The unity of space and colour sensation is for Mach and the Impressionists an interplay of the individual's consciousness and the surrounding world.

The Literary Impressionist believes that we cannot know reality independently of consciousness, that we cannot know consciousness independently of reality, and that reality is a synthesis of sense impressions, because Literary Impressionism suggests an 'emotional reality'. Space is defined as the relationship which pieces of matter, in our experience, have with one another. Time creates the relationship between different occasions, linked with the experience of the individual's consciousness. With Mach, and with the Literary Impressionist, the antithesis between the ego and the world, between sensation and the object vanishes. All that exists is in contact with everything else. The German critic Hermann Bahr calls Mach's view 'the philosophy of Impressionism':

> All distinctions are here eliminated, the physical and the psychological coincide, and sensations are one and the same, the ego dissolves and everything is an eternal flux which in some places seems to stop, in others to flow swifter, everything is merely a movement of colours, sounds, temperatures, pressures, spaces and times, which on this side of the ego appears as moods, feelings, and desires (...) before long Mach's world view will probably be called simply 'philosophy of impressionism'.[1]

Time seems to be abolished. Characters, gestures, objects and words seem to be the elements of the same atmosphere. Only characters are presented as rather static figures, in a moving atmosphere perceived at a certain distance. The self of these characters is not simply split, as with the Romantics, with the Literary Impressionist the character is atomised in the same way as light has dissolved the solidity of matter.

THE ACT OF BECOMING IN A FRAGMENTARY MOMENT IN TIME

When adapting a character's heightened consciousness to a new illusory fictional reality, the Literary Impressionist attempts to fuse the inner ego with the outer world. This relationship underlies the entire vision and aesthetic of Literary Impressionism and must be recognised as its nucleus.[1]

There no longer seems to be a separation between subject (e.g. the perceiving character, narrator) and object (e.g. the perceived object, other characters, setting, scenery). Reality is the synthesis of perceiver and perceived - each exists and each creates meaning for the other. The new aesthetic is based upon integrated juxtaposition. The perceiving character superimposes on a perceived object actual physical qualities, based upon his own subjective and intuitive memory, mood, and the perspective the object takes on. He then reflects on the physical properties of the surrounding environment. All is perceived through the senses of one or more selected narrators and characters. The object and its reflections - the entire *mise-en-scene* - simultaneously infuse the perceiver's own set of physical and psychological characteristics. This process continues ad infinitum,

59

turning, spinning, reacting, blending - all in moments of durational and phenomenological time. In this centrifugal process all outlines become hazy, 'all distinctions are eliminated, the physical and the psychological merge and sensations are one and the same, the ego dissolves and everything is an eternal flux which in some places seems to stop, in others to flow faster. Everything is a movement of colours, sounds, spaces and times, which on this side of the ego appear as moods, feelings and desires'.[2]

The Impressionist painters had been struggling to capture 'the moment' on their spatial canvas[3], in order to seize the instant in time and isolate it, transposing space into time through the vibrancy of colour juxtapositions, the movement of objects in the surrounding world and the outlines of their frames.[4] The language of Literary Impressionism is suffused with 'instants', 'moments', 'seconds' and 'minutes', creating harmonies of immediacy.

The Impressionist's fragments of the present are submerged into the relentless flow of enduring time. If the instants are lost and never meaningfully connected to other fragmented moments, the sense of tragedy brought on by irremediable loss is implicit. However, this tragedy may be mitigated through a superimposed vision of cyclical time. Impressionist characters are often unable to hold onto the moments of beauty in their lives either in the past or in the present (as they fade into the past), but if the disparate elements of momentary time coalesce in an 'epiphany' brought about through keen observation and awareness, and if the moment of 'coming together' can be carried over into the future, then the tragedy of loss may be compensated for or obviated.[5] These new conceptions formed the basic structure of 'the impressionistically architectonic fiction that has come to dominate modern literature'.[6] Stowell claims 'Gestalt'-thinking to be at the heart of all Impressionist art.[7] He argues that the 'Literary Impressionists were synthesisers, who did not attack the concept of chronologically absolute time, but instead found that their sympathies lay more with fusing objective and subjective time, moment with duration, space and time'.[8]

The Literary Impressionist also depended on simultaneity when cross-cutting scenes, or when fusing the fragmentation of image clusters and the sensory blending of past (flashbacks) and present (dreams, phantasies). These elements formed the basis for their 'glimpses', the 'moments of being', the 'priviliged moments' or 'epiphanies'. New impressions were created when redirecting the inherently temporal process by giving characters a respite from the flux of continually changing moments. Many Literary Impressionist characters do not realise that it is only through a geometric redefinition of their relationship with their kaleidoscopic environment that they may begin to reshape their own identity. Therefore the epiphanies often take place in moments of heightened awareness, when the character reacts to an object, an action or another character in such a way that he/she achieves a new synthetic experience, a new perception. This kind of moment has been given many different names in literary criticism and it is not strictly the property of Impressionism, but these epiphanies (priviliged moments, moments of being, visionary instants, impressions, 'instantanés' or 'moments bienheureux') do form a crucial basis for the Impressionistic vision.

These moments are not always transcendental, as they must be for the Romantics.[9] An epiphany may not 'mean' anything beyond what it is, but it may result in a new way of seeing, a change in direction for the character. Time may also be 'frozen', in what seems to be an eternal moment, 'a hope for reprieve from the continually multiplying prism of relations'.[10] Eventually the epiphany seems to detach itself from the background of normal awareness, and the 'ephemerally crystalline'[11] returns to the flux and flow of durational time. An instant that emerges from 'la durée' seems to hypostatise time, but the moment itself has its own duration, after which it returns to the flow of fleeting time. It is like the 'frozen' image on the television screen, in which time is suspended. What is experienced in this privileged moment may also be lost, forgotten or even blurred, but these moments may lead to new actions or, indeed, to a fresh or expanded consciousness, or a changed perception, as none of these moments have inherently positive or negative qualities. They offer only an instant of synthesis or apparent stability in an entire life of change. Such a discrete moment is one of many, it is not *the* moment of truth, as it is subjectively conceived. Some critics of Literary Impressionism state that the basic aesthetic of Literary Impressionism grew out of these moments, as these moments were those rare instances of composed impressions.

The many images in Literary Impressionistic texts, though created in the linear progression of language, create a certain stasis in the reader's perception. Stowell now draws the comparison with the cinema and argues that 'impressionistic time had the feel of presentness, even if narrated in the past'. Images and their kinetic fragmentation offered both a seamless persistence of vision and a simultaneous immediacy of controlled juxtaposition. The Impressionist painters' aesthetic vision grew out of their seizing a moment of light and movement: the transfer of the mood, atmosphere and feeling of that moment onto the canvas with a sense of immediacy and simultaneity. The Literary Impressionists saw their aims in basically the same terms but had to deal with a more complex temporal structure. In the 'glimpses' hypostatised time is detached from the flux and flow of durational time, a mysterious stasis which endows the arbitrary trivial with significance. As already noted, time for the

Literary Impressionist is a subjectively experienced sense of objective events and it is the Literary Impressionist's aim to present the transitory, the immediate and fresh perception. Each brush stroke for an Impressionist painter asks for reappraisal in terms of its relation to some other brush stroke. The more strokes, the more possibilities of new meanings. The Literary Impressionist piles on detail in concrete terms. Therefore, the accumulative technique is a major characteristic of Literary Impressionism and vague blurrings, random perceptions and concatenation, coordination, contraction and repetition prevail. In the dissolution of plot, the broken cycle of causality, the Literary Impressionist tends to reverse the order of cause and effect, because it is the effect that counts. There is the unknowable ambiguity of reality. The relativism of space and time and the perceptual subjectivity of characters has brought about a movement away from directness and clarity of description. The Literary Impressionist shifts away from a narrator's 'objective' description of a concrete material reality to the sensory rendering of a character's momentary, subjective impressions, sensations, and the mood and atmosphere surrounding a perceived reality in which objects and events lose their cleanly delineated shapes and forms. The Literary Impressionist does not want to separate subject and object. Both are one in the impression and life is seen as a sequence of impressions. There are no clear beginnings or sharp endings.

The feeling and tone of the Literary Impressionist's 'canvas' is enhanced by fleeting impressions and images; vague pictures are glimpsed hurriedly; details are arbitrarily selected, sometimes to the point of triviality. There are splashes of different colours and shades, blurred movements and nuances of mood, perceptions and consciousness. There is a sense of insufficiency, vagueness, of 'a something' in the inner world and 'a somebody' in the outer world, in order to catch that famous diffuseness of Impressionist painting, in which only particles of human gestures and ambiguous human attitudes are perceived. The angle of vision is oblique, the object of perception is often in movement or half hidden behind a smoke screen. As Stowell writes: 'Perception as a process of becoming, inevitably leads to the arbitrary and inconclusive ambiguity that characterises Literary Impressionism'.[12]

To sum up, it is argued that Literary Impressionism did not emerge full-blown from the work of the French Impressionist painters, since the Literary Impressionists stepped back from the painters. They rendered human consciousness and acts of perception in prose. Literary Impressionism is indeed something more than a series of separate fleeting impressions. As Calvin Brown suggested, 'Literary Impressionism's aim is to catch and reproduce the shifting, fleeting, intangible impressions by which the outside world impinges on our senses, - or as some more philosophically minded critics like to put it, 'to break down the distinction between the subject and the object.' In his pursuit, the Impressionist abandons causality, formal logic, or any attempt or desire to fit his impressions into predetermined forms. The image of a unified and knowable universe seemed to the Literary Impressionists a complete impossibility. There was no rigid ideology for the Literary Impressionists. They formed a disparate breed, an important and influential set of shared literary assumptions in the fifty years surrounding the turn of the century (1870-1920).[13]

The Literary Impressionists expressed their artistic responses in highly individualistic and experimental forms, as they faced the issues of a fragmented, accidental and accelerating world - and they realised how ill-prepared they were to absorb and adapt to such a world.[14] But Stowell believes: 'they lived in a prismatically impressionistic world, they must recreate that world of individualized sensory perception, epistemological indetermination, and surfaces (...). Retaining empiricism, they rejected the thinly veiled moral didacticism of the Realist's aesthetic omniscience. Subjective and limited sensory perception became the empirical truth for the Impressionist'.[15]

From this flux emerges the Literary Impressionist's primary tenet: the rendering of apperception, with a shift to rendered atmosphere. It was in their approach to time and space that the Impressionists made their greatest contribution. All the components of Literary Impressionism - the shift from description of objects to the rendering of atmosphere and mood, the importance of a perceiving consciousness - are, of course, inextricably woven into the Impressionist tapestry. Yet 'the dominant thread is the paradoxical union of Bergson's durée and phenomenological time and space'.[16] The Impressionist intuitively felt that Bergson's subjective current of human time neglected the privileged moments of spatialised presentness. Phenomenological time stresses the 'moment' of events, which, because they are imperceptibly framed and spatially perceived, take on the Literary Impressionist's hallmark of temporally extended frozen moments of spatialised time that dissolve and return to the flow of durational time.

The Literary Impressionist appropriated certain primary tenets, which formed the backbone of their writing and which may now be formulated as follows.[17] To the Literary Impressionist the surrounding world is not a unified and knowable universe, but constitutes an indistinct picture, made up of an irresistible flood of confused, ever-changing sense impressions, in a fragmented, relativistic, accidental and accelerating world. This world is incapable of analysis and can only be grasped intuitively. The Literary Impressionist will therefore avoid analysis and content himself with the rendering of impressions[18], recreating and suggesting them as they appeared to him at a given moment. At the centre of the Literary Impressionist aesthetic is the act of (ap)perceiving the outside world, and the manner in which it is perceived. Through sensory experience the Literary Impressionist opens up a new relationship with the perception of this world, which is a synthetic, intuitive feeling of oneness with this reality. It becomes a subjective experience, as reality is a synthesis of sensations, modulated by consciousness and changed into impressions. His experience consists of an epistemological indeterminacy, of individualised sensory fragmentary perceptions. He regards this process of perceiving impressions as reality itself. It consists of fragments.[19] The first image of a scene may be a vague, indistinct, blurred impression of a whole, but it is this impression that the narrator will attempt to convey. It is left to the reader to create a coherent and meaningful picture.

In his attempt to create order, the Literary Impressionist intuitively selects and interprets reality. The subjective and limited sensory perception becomes the empirical truth for the Literary Impressionist. In this indecisive universe, where subjectivism mingles with objectivity, the Literary Impressionist creates his characters.[20] His narrative is no longer a 'story' with a plot, but a confused colliding of fragmentary sensations and experiences. His primary tenet, the rendering of this (ap)perception, is presented like a fluid, poetic and enigmatic substance. It is within the view of Man's subjective, but also solipsistic definition of freedom, based upon limited knowledge and active choice, that the Literary Impressionists discovered their aesthetic goal: the fusion of form and meaning in a 'slice of life' portrayal in ordinary circumstances, compressed into a concentrated momentary impression.

The Literary Impressionist emphasises the internal changes in characters and the external changes in the world around them, in which subject and object are irretrievably in motion. The characters, in their new perception, may experience a 'glimpse' into the fragments of their existence in a temporal stretch of time. The disparate elements of objective and subjective time are fused in a moment of 'coming together', in an epiphany. This moment may be carried over into a new synthetic experience, a new perception; it may be lost, forgotten or blurred; or it may return to the flux and flow of durational time.

In his subjective immersion, the Literary Impressionist concentrates directly on the surrounding atmosphere and the feelings and sensations aroused by it. He attempts to make the reader even more involved in his subjective experience by concentrating on a character's mood or 'Stimmung', in subtle, suggestive evocation. No analysis or inventory of pictures, and no comments on characters are given, nor is there a chronological report with a definite beginning, middle or end. In his attempt to be as 'realistic' as possible, the Literary Impressionist presents the consciousness of his characters as it functions from moment to moment by rendering its undeveloped impressions and associations. It is only the direct experience that counts. What cannot be sensed does not exist for the Impressionist. The Literary Impressionist attempts to make the reader apprehend life at the instant when it is being experienced, in order to communicate the live, instantaneous, total sensory perception of reality around him, before intellect has transformed it.

The Impressionist character seems to be caught in the moment of transition between a passionate desire for a transcendental glimpse into the 'truth' of human consciousness, and the realisation that there is no 'truth': there are only perceived fragments of highly ambiguous sensory stimuli. Between the irresolution of these two paradoxes the Literary Impressionist presents one of his major themes: the struggle for identity in a constantly shifting balance of perception and knowledge - the disparity between subjective and objective 'truth', between illusion and reality.

The Impressionist's technique springs from the belief that reality is illusory, phantasmagoric. His sole responsibility is to render his impressions as truthfully as he can, although an impression of the surrounding world will often be determined by circumstances. This 'passive', expectant attitude is basic to his entire 'Weltanschauung'. Images of light may evoke new moods, create a new 'Stimmung', which is the medium through which the Literary Impressionist condenses experience. A world and an atmosphere are created in which everything seems to have lost its natural identity in an erosion of blurred contours. There is more stress on connotation than on denotation in a surrounding atmosphere, in which space, time and light can only be grasped intuitively, in a synthesis, but spatially in a moment of time. Characters, gestures, objects, colours and words all seem to be elements in the same atmosphere.

Part II

Chapter 3 MANSFIELD'S LITERARY IMPRESSIONISM
IN HER SCRAPBOOKS, JOURNALS,
LETTERS AND REVIEWS

In order to evaluate Mansfield's aesthetic and critical stance we
must concentrate predominantly on her technical and practical remarks
on writing, more evident in her letters and journals, than in her
reviews. These views - which will be discussed here in order of
importance - were expressed when writing about her art and her
intentions for new short stories. They were also formalised in the
reviews which she wrote for *The Athenaeum* in 1919/1920, collected
in *Novels and Novelists* (1930).

This chapter aims to examine Mansfield's aesthetic principles. The
prior assumption is that she was a writer with a coherent, solipsistic,
intuitive aesthetic vision. A focus on her aesthetic may shed a new
light on her work as it may offer an explanation of her purposes on
writing.

When reviewing her aesthetic issues one has to be alert to certain
pitfalls. Firstly, the details of Katherine Mansfield's life are often
painful. When reading her letters and journals, one has to be alert to
the fact that many utterances were coloured by her illness, her
personal stresses and conflicts.[1] When examining source material, the
reader has constantly to consider the circumstances in which they were
made. Secondly, the reader has to be aware that Mansfield, the
'polymorphous poseuse'[2], presented many different faces or masks to
her audience and her readers. The *letters* especially still fascinate the
modern reader, for the many different 'personae' that the author
created. Her letters show her deadly serious, warm and friendly,
cynical and sarcastic, absurd and loving, morbid, though human in
conforming to the recipient's wishes and expectations. However, when
we read her comments on the literary history of her time - in her
own metalanguage, often full of images - we are struck by her
original and sensitive perception of her literary environment. Thirdly,
one has to be alert to utterances made primarily to protect herself
from Murry's sentimental manner of reviewing. Fourthly, one has to
beware of a number of casual, jejune utterances, which are merely
thrown off in her letters, journals or scrapbooks and are never
repeated. When reading Mansfield's secondary resources, we should
also be aware of the fact that there is not a great deal of evidence that
she had in mind publication in the form chosen by John M. Murry. In
fact, on the flyleaf of the 1915-Diary (now in the Alexander Turnbill
Library, Wellington, New Zealand), we find: 'I shall be obliged if the

contents of this book are regarded as my private property'.[3]

When concentrating on Mansfield's aesthetics the main Literary Impressionist impulses will be examined in consequential and logical order. A number of concepts will be discussed and illustrated in quotations, arranged under a number of major Mansfieldian ideas, such as the relationship between 'Life and Art', 'Art and History', 'Defeat of the Personal', 'Intuition', 'Emotion', 'Empathy', 'Epiphany', 'Atmosphere', 'Oblique', 'Structure' and 'Fragments'. I will attempt to present these aesthetic views in an analytical manner, without synthethising them too much into large-scale concepts.

LIFE AND ART

Mansfield felt that a writer should be free to express his personality and his temperament. She stressed the importance of an author's personal experience and was reluctant to analyse experience intellectually. When she wrote to J.M. Murry in 1920, she expressed her distaste of intellectualism:

Not being an intellectual, I always seem to have to learn things at the risk of my life.[4]

In another letter she noted 'that dreadful glaze of 'intellectuality' which is like a curse upon so many English writers'.[5] She often reproached Murry for his intellectual approach to criticism, for:

this intellectual reasoning is never *the whole truth*. It's not *the artist's truth* - not *creative*. If man were an intellect it would do, but man *isn't*.[6] (Italics KM)

'That dreadful glaze of intellectuality' is no substitute for 'the freshness and warmth and suppleness' and the 'warm emotional tone'[7] which characterise the true voice of feeling. Mansfield wrote that, not only in literature but also in life, mere intellectuality is a bane and not a blessing:

It is this life of the *head*, this formative intellectual life at the expense of all the rest of us which has got us into this state. How can it get us out of it? I see no hope of escape except by learning to live in our emotional and instinctive being as well and to balance all three.[8] (Italics KM)

According to Mansfield, an ideal author is someone, whose 'head' and 'heart' go hand in hand, whose affectivity is controlled by

67

rationality. In a review she wrote:

> You must feel before you can think; you must think before you can express yourself. It is not enough to feel and write; or to think and write. True expression is the outcome of them both, yet a third thing, and separate.[9]

Mansfield did not trust the mind. Her distaste for an intellectual approach was recorded in a review:

> The only form of government is government by *the heart* alone, and for the heart alone. There is a dreadful black monster, a kind of wild bull, looking over the fence at the innocent undefended picnic and plotting and planning how he may come in and upset and trample all. It is the mind. Beware of it. Have nothing to do with it. Shun it as you would your mortal enemy.[10] (Italics KM)

In a perfect work of art, thought and feeling should be harmoniously blended. Mansfield's aim was to present an immediate, pure recreation of the actual sensation of living, as opposed to an orderly analysis or a generalisation of experience. She transformed her earlier principle 'all art is self-development'[11] into a more general 'life-art' relationship, which became one of the fundamental Literary Impressionist aesthetics in her work. She focused on the delicate balance between her subjective, intuitive concept of reality and her actual experience. Her understanding of the 'life-art' relationship that 'life and work are two things indivisible' formed one of the basic principles for her writing:

> Life and work are two things indivisible. It's only by being true to life that I can be true to art.[12]

Artists will have to accept Life - and give themselves up to it unreservedly:

> It seems to me that the *secret* of life is to *accept* life. Question it as much as you like after, but first accept it.
> (...) It's only by risking, losing yourself, giving yourself up to Life', that you can ever find out the answer.[13] (Italics KM)

In 1920 she wrote:

> I don't believe a writer can ever do anything worth doing until he has - in the profoundest sense of the word - accepted life. Then he can face the problem and begin to question, but not before.[14]

and in 1921:

Chekhov said over and over again (...) that he had no problem (...) And when you come to think of it, what was Chaucer's problem or Shakespeare's? (...) The artist takes a long look at life. He says softly, 'So this is what life is, is it?' and he proceeds to express that. All the rest he leaves.[15]

Mansfield wanted 'life in literature' and she judged other fiction according to the extent to which 'life' was present or not. 'Good work has life in it' she wrote in 1920. When reviewing George Moore's *Esther Waters*, written in the Naturalist mode, Mansfield argued:

And yet we would say without hesitation that *Esther Waters* is not a great novel, and never could be a great novel, because it has not, from first to last, the faintest stirring of the breath of life.[16]

Once Mansfield had reached a more self-conscious awareness of the 'Life-Art' relationship, she began to express her views more forcefully and was prepared to state that 'Good work takes upon itself a life - bad work has death in it'.[17] According to her, Art and Life are inseparable. They minister unto each other. The artist, however ingenious, cannot create anything *ex nihilo*, or make an experiment *in vacuo*. He has to store impressions from the outside world, whittle them into necessary shapes and then incorporate them in his stories. 'I have looked at this tree so long', she wrote in a letter to Richard Murry, referring to 'a tree called a datura' (...), 'that it is transplanted to some part of my brain - for a further transplanting into a story one day'.[18] She ascribes her difficulty in writing to the dearth of sense impressions:

The reason why you find it so hard to write is because you are learning nothing. I mean of the things that count - like the sight of this tree with its purple cones against the blue.[19]

She wrote almost to the same effect in a letter to her cousin, the Countess Russell:

If I had been well I should have rushed off to darkest Africa or the Indus or the Ganges or wherever it is one rushes at those times, to try for a change of heart (...) to gain new impressions. For it seems to me we live on new impressions - really new ones.[20]

But how should the writer convey his 'Life-Art' relationship in his work? Mansfield decided that the writer must be rooted in his time :

The question of the Artist and his Time is, I am sure, the Question of Questions. The artist who denies his Time, who turns away from it even so much as the fraction of a hair is false. First, he must be free; that is, he must be controlled by none other than his deepest self, his truest self. And then he must accept Life, he must submit, give himself so utterly to Life that no personal qua personal self remains.[21]

The artist must commit himself to life in order to create his own vision. To Richard Murry she wrote:

I think I understand exactly what you mean by 'visionary consciousness.' It fits the writer equally well. It's mysterious and it's difficult to get into words. There is this world, and there is the world that the artist creates in this world, which is nevertheless this world, and subject to his laws, his 'vision'.[22]

Mansfield's longing to be a 'real, a living writer'[23] and express the feeling of 'reality', of history and actuality, is often commented on by critics when focusing on the relationship with Virginia Woolf. In various other reviews she also commented on this aspect of 'being real'. According to Mansfield, writers should not remain detached from the outside world and only observe it without any sense of feeling:

I'm doing Virginia for this week's novel. I don't like it, (...) My private opinion is that it is a lie in the soul. The war never has been: that is what its message is (...) but the novel can't just leave the war out. There *must* have been a change of heart. It is really fearful to see the 'settling down' of human beings. I feel in the *profoundest* sense that nothing can ever be the same - that, as artists, we are traitors if we feel otherwise: we have to take into account and find new expressions, new moulds for our thoughts and feelings. (Italics KM)

In the same letter she wrote:

There is a trifling scene in Virginia's book where a charming creature in a light fantastic attitude plays the flute; it positively frightens me - to realize this *utter coldness* and indifference (...).

Inwardly I despise them all for a set of *cowards*.[24]
(Italics KM)

On 13 November 1919 she continued:

I am reviewing Virginia to send tomorrow. Its devilish hard. Talk
about intellectual snobbery - her book *reeks* of it. (But I can't say
so).[25] (Italics KM)

On 16 November 1919 she commented on the effects of World War
I in general:

What is this about the novel? (...) the more I read the more I feel
all these novels will not do. It's not in the least a question of
material or style or plot. I can only think in terms like 'a change of
heart'. I can't imagine how after the war these men can pick up the
old threads as though it had never been. Speaking to *you* I'd say we
have died and live again. How can that be the same life? It doesn't
mean that life is the less precious or that 'the common things of
light and day' are gone. They are not gone, they are intensified,
they are illumined. Now we know ourselves for what we are. In a
way it's a tragic knowledge: it's as though, even while we live
again, we face death. But *through life*: that's the point. We see
death in life as we see death in a flower that is fresh unfolded. Our
hymn is to the flower's beauty: we would make that beauty
immortal because we know.[26] (Italics KM)

In a letter to Dorothy Brett in 1922 she revealed her 'Art-History'
concept again. Interested in politics, as she now is, she wrote:

I hang on the newspapers. I feel I dare not miss a speech. One
begins to feel, (...) that it's one's duty to what remains of
civilization to care for those things and that writers who do not are
traitors.[27]

When formulating her 'Art-History' concept Mansfield often
stressed the particular significance of the artist's immersion in history.
A writer is responsible to history, she wrote. He should not deny his
time and leave history and its consequences to humankind out of his
writing.[28] One should include the acknowledgement of one's past and
one's mortality. For Mansfield, to deny one's Time is to deny Life
itself. Almost a year later she argued once again in favour of this
view, which had been close to her heart for a long time. She wrote:

I cannot conceive how writers who have lived through our times

71

can *drop* these last ten years and revert to why Edward didn't understand Vi's reluctance to be seduced or (see Bennett) why a dinner of twelve covers needs remodelling.[29] (Italics KM)

Authors cannot ignore their time, according to Mansfield, except at their peril. The pre-war and post-war world, for example, are not the same, even though one is the continuation of the other. Authors, who fail to take this notion into account, are rejected out of hand by Mansfield. This happened to Virginia Woolf when she published *Night and Day*, because Woolf did not accept the notion that a new world had emerged out of World War I. In her review, Mansfield wrote that it is a novel 'in the tradition of the English novel, which 'makes us feel old and chill.' To Mansfield writers of fiction should be responding to actual history. Besides, writers should not be influenced by simplistic and false views of war, as propagated by the popular press, but emphasise on a transformation of a subjective, consciousness:

Art is not an attempt of the artist to reconcile existence with his vision; it is an attempt to create his own world *in* this world. (...) We single out - we bring into the light - we put up higher.[30] (Italics KM)

Mansfield could not abide 'simple' views on war and writers who presented them, were 'written off' disdainfully.[31]
As many critics have realised[32], the central theme of many of Mansfield's short stories is the disparity between reality and illusion or appearances. Frequently, a character's impression of the surrounding world is determined by a subjective perception and an arbitrary selection of circumstances. In 1922 she wrote in one of her scrapbooks:

Denn jeder sieht und stellt die Sachen anders, eben nach seiner Weise.[33]

Any mental condition at any given time must be taken into consideration. In her scrapbook she hints at the dichotomy: 'What is life really? What is real and not real? Oh God!'[34] and in 1922 she conveys the (Literary Impressionist) solipsistic choice merely to suggest, without directly stating or telling directly, that reality is illusory:

Why must thinking and existing be ever on two different planes? Why will the attempt of Hegel to transfer subjective processes into objective world-processes not work out? It's the special art and object of thinking to attain existence by quite other methods than that of existence itself. That is to say, reality cannot become the ideal, the dream; and it is not the business of the artist to grind an axe, to try to impose his vision of life upon the existing world. Art is not an attempt of the artist to reconcile existence with his vision; it is an attempt to create his own world *in* this world. That which suggests the subject to the artist is the *unlikeness* to what we accept as reality[35]. (Italics KM)

DEFEAT OF THE PERSONAL

In Mansfield's view the artist's responsibility is to bear true witness to his time. He can do so only by purging himself of personal doctrine or prejudice. To Sylvia Lynd, she wrote 'I find my great difficulty in writing is to learn to submit'.[36] The artist must lose himself, according to Mansfield, in order to become radiant. The artistic power must be transformed into the power of vision and Mansfield believed that from such vision there might flow new moral and even political consequences. She wrote:

I believe the only way to *live* as artists under these new conditions in art and life is to put everything to the test for ourselves (...) I think if artists were really thorough and honest they would save the world. It's the lack of those things and the reverse of them that are putting a deadly blight on life[37]. (Italics KM)

In 1919 Mansfield scribbled in a journal: 'At the back of my mind I am so wretched. But all the while I am thinking over my philosophy - the defeat of the personal'.[38] In these years Tsjechov had replaced Wilde as her personal mentor and she had decided that 'Truth is the only thing worth having'.[39] Mansfield's concern with 'truth' had early signalled a new direction in her aesthetics and by her desire to 'defeat the personal' she meant her fiction to be more objective. When quoting from Tsjechov's letters, in her journal, she wrote: 'You may weep and moan over your stories. You may suffer together with your heroes, but I consider one must do this so that the reader does not notice it. The more objective, the stronger will be the effect'.[40] In 1920, when Mansfield noted her 'philosophy' of objectivity, she was not stating a new interest. She was mentioning something that had been important to her during her whole writing-career and would become interrelated with a personal obsession. She believed that she could be a better artist by becoming a 'purer' person.[41]

When she started her writing career she regarded art as the mirror of the world and her own experiences of life. Gradually, however, she attempted to 'purify' herself. In 1921 she wrote in her journal: 'Lord, make me crystal clear for thy light to shine through'.[42] And in 1922 she wrote: 'Life should be like a steady visible light'.[43] What Mansfield wished to achieve was an art that would illuminate the reader, so that the fundamental and universal in human experience would shine through. Mansfield's quest for objectivity is parallelled by her subjective personal vision, for she never wished to write at the expense of emotion, empathetic commitment and involvement. She hoped to broaden the scope of her vision and describe life around her naturally and spontaneously without any constricting self-reference.

INTUITION

As early as 1911, together with John M. Murry, Mansfield commented on an intuitive, subjective selectiveness in the perception of reality:

Reality in the work of art demands true intuition in the artist (...) There is always one (selection), the one fact among a million which is true and therefore the artist's own and part of his personality. Individuality in the work of art is the creation of reality by freedom (...) Art is individual.[44]

An author should not 'show, but render'[45] and recreate 'every drop of life'.[46] Therefore a 'bored'[47] narrator may 'show' his characters and events, but according to Mansfield he should 'render', i.e. he should 'see, feel, think, hear and be full of the sap of life'.[48] According to Mansfield, there should be the (Literary Impressionist's) stress on apperception in the narrator or character's focalisation, in the sense that (they) seem to be 'seeing, smelling, drinking for the first time'.[49] A novel should never be 'less true than life itself'.[50]

When discussing John Galsworthy's *In Chancery*, Mansfield analyses his characters, who 'are so completely life-size'[51]:

the character of James Forsyte (...) comes before us so that we see him, hear him, smell him, know his ways, his tricks, his habits as if he were our grandfather.[52]

EMOTION

In Mansfield's aesthetic views a writer should be in firm control of the narrative design and at the same time express his enthusiasm in writing about life. The narrator should show his feelings, as she proclaimed in one of her Literary Impressionist 'credos':

> Without emotion writing is dead; it becomes a record instead of a revelation, for the sense of it comes from that emotional reaction which the artist felt and was impelled to communicate. To contemplate the object, to let it make its own impression (...) is not enough. There must be an initial emotion felt by the writer, and all that he sees is saturated in that emotional quality. It alone can give incidence and sequence, character and background, a close and intimate unity.[53]

If the narrator remains indifferent and cool[54] the reader will not be carried away.[55] One of the noticeable Literary Impressionist features in Mansfield's aesthetic is the employment of what may be termed an expressive narrator. (See Chapter 4.1) In her enthusiasm over her expressive narrator she praises Joseph Conrad, the Literary Impressionist[56], for the quality of his narrator's evocative emotion. She wrote:

> Mr Joseph Conrad is a remarkable exception (...) This fascinating book revives in us the youthful feeling that we are not so much reading a story of adventure as living in it and through it, absorbing it, making it our own. This feeling is not wholly the result of the method, the style which the author has chosen; it arises more truly from the quality of the emotion in which the book is steeped. What that emotion is it were hard to define; it is, perhaps, a peculiar responsive sensitiveness to the significance of everything, down to the slightest detail that has a place in his vision.[57]

The best reason in the world for writing should be 'Because I am interested'[58] and to convey the author's need to express this. Here is another Literary Impressionist credo of the expressive narrator:

> What it comes to is that we believe that emotion is essential to a work of art; it is that which makes a work of art a unity.[59]

Mansfield claimed that Life is emotion and 'the feasting of our senses'.[60] If there is no emotion, there is no Life, if there is no feeling, no passion. Characters will be flat and images will be cold.[61] 'All must be deeply felt,' the author must 'convey his feeling for life.' In the next review Mansfield discussed E.M. Forster. In a letter she wrote:

E.M. Forster never gets any further than warming the teapot. He's a rare fine hand at that. Feel this teapot. Is it not beautifully warm? Yes, but there ain't going to be no tea.[62]
E.M. Forster does not 'exert the whole of his imaginative power (...), there is a certain leisureliness' and an 'extreme reluctance to (...) commit himself wholly'.[63]

When there is 'observation only'[64] in, e.g. Hugh Walpole's *The Captives*, written with a great deal of determination, but no inspiration, no creativity on the part of the narrator 'we are left absolutely in the air'. The characters are 'not living beings at the end any more than they are at the beginning; they will not, when Mr Walpole's pen is lifted, exist for a moment'.[65] The author

is there as a stranger, as an observer, as someone outside it all. How hard he tries - how painfully he fails! His method is simply to amass observations (...) but we feel that no observation is nearer the truth than another.[66]

There is no subject-object relationship (See Chapter 2) and the mystery of life is not revealed. The reflection of life should be a 'realistic account. We do ask of our author that 'he should have been on the spot and be the witness of every slightest move'.[67] He should lift the veil of 'the mystery of life' but he should not hold back[68] and let himself 'be carried away'.[69] Virginia Woolf, at least in *Night and Day*, also merely recorded, registered observations[70] and failed to present lifelike characters:

specially, when recalling the minor characters, (...) we begin to doubt (...) how much life have they? We have the queer sensation that once the author's pen is removed from them they have neither speech nor motion, and are not to be revived again until she adds another stroke or two or writes another sentence underneath (...) in their case the light seems to shine at them, but not through them.[71]

EMPATHY

A cool, detached view of one's subject was not sufficient for Mansfield. For her it was essential to penetrate one's characters. Feelings and objects must be contemplated first or 'submitted to', until one is truly lost in them.[72] After completing the story "The Stranger" she described the identification she felt with her creation:

I've *been* this man, *been* this woman. I've stood for hours on the

76

Auckland Wharf. I've been out in the stream waiting to be berthed - I've been a seagull hovering at the stern and a hotel porter whistling through his teeth. It isn't as though one sits and watches the spectacle. That would be thrilling enough, God knows. But one *is* the spectacle for the time.[73] (Italics KM)

This 'being inspired', the losing oneself in the passion of writing, what might be called empathy, is one of Mansfield's basic Literary Impressionist aesthetics. When inspiration is lost, when there is no 'possession', no subject-object relationship, a writer is lost. She explained in a letter to Walpole:

You seemed to be determined to shirk nothing (...). You seemed to lose in passion what you gained in sincerity and therefore 'the miracle' didn't happen. I mean the moment when the act of creation takes place - the mysterious change - when you are no longer writing the book, *it* is writing, *it* possesses you'.[74] (Italics KM)

In her letters when commenting on Virginia Woolf's *Night and Day* she also commented upon 'this *utter coldness* and indifference'[75]. (Italics KM). In her review of the same book, she veils herself in images and resorts to metaphor:

To us who love to linger down at the harbour, as it were, watching the new ships being built, the old one returning, and the many putting out to sea, comes the strange sight of NIGHT AND DAY sailing into port serene and resolute on a deliberate wind. The strangeness lies in her aloofness, her air of quiet perfection, her lack of any sign that she has made a perilous voyage - the absence of any scars. Here she lies among the strange shipping - a tribute to civilization for our admiration and wonder (...). In the midst of our admiration it makes us feel old and chill: we had never thought to look upon its like again![76]

The same dominant critical view returns. When referring to G.B. Shaw's review of Butler, she commented on his lack of inspiration. True literature, according to Mansfield, is a product of inspiration, of the artist's empathetic compulsion and not of his strength of will. G.B. Shaw could not impress her as an artist, because he was singularly uninspired:

(...) it's queer he should be so uninspired. There is not the faintest hint of inspiration in that man. This chills me. You know the feeling that a great writer gives you: 'My spirit has been fed and refreshed: it has partaken of something new.' One couldn't possibly feel that about Shaw (...) What it amounts to is that Shaw is anything you like, but he's not an artist (...) Don't you get when you read his plays a sense of extra-ordinary *flatness*? They may be extremely amusing at moments, but you are always laughing *at* and never *with*. Just the same in his prose: You may agree as much as you like, but he is writing *at* not *with*. There's no getting over it: he's a kind of concierge in the house of literature - sits in a glass case, sees everything, knows everything, examines the letters, *cleans the stairs*, but has no part, no part in the life that is going on.[77] (Italics KM)

Mansfield often referred to this talent of showing empathy, also when commenting on her own work or on her reading:

I wish I could begin real creative work. I haven't yet. It's the atmosphere, the (...) tone which is hard to get. And without it nothing is worth doing. (...) It is a difficult thing to explain. Now, Tolstoy only has to touch him (the character, JvG) and he gives out a note and this note is somehow important, persists, is a part of the whole book. But all these other men - they introduce their cooks, aunts, strange gentlemen, and so on, and once the pen is off them they are *gone* ... dropped down a hole. Can one explain this by what you might call - a *covering* atmosphere -?[78] (Italics KM)

It is this empathy when creating the atmosphere that counts most. According to Mansfield, some authors are capable of transmitting their 'possession'. On Dostoyevski she writes:

(...) it's amazing when Dostoyevsky at last turns a soft penetrating and full light upon him (the character Shatov, JvG), how we have managed to gather a great deal of knowledge of his character from the former vague side-lights and shadow impressions.[79]

She insisted on 'becoming' the object or characters:

gather them and play with them and *become them*. When I pass an apple stall I cannot help stopping and staring until I feel that I, myself, am changing into an apple, too, and that at any moment I *can* produce an apple miraculously, out of my own being, like the conjuror produces the egg (...) When I write about ducks I swear that I am a white duck with a round eye, floating on a pond fringed with yellow blobs and taking an occasional dart at the other duck with the round eye, which floats upside down beneath me. In fact the whole process of becoming the duck (what Lawrence would, perhaps, call this consummation with the duck or the apple!) is so thrilling (...) There follows the moment when you are *more* duck, *more* apple (...) than any of these objects could ever possibly be, and so you *create* them anew. (...) that is why I believe in technique, too (...) I do, just because I don't see how art is going to make that divine *spring* into the bounding outline of things if it hasn't passed through the process of trying to *become* these things before recreating them.[80] (Italics KM)

Dickens was one of the few considered by Mansfield, to show his empathy, to have been 'possessed' by the power of inspiration:

There are moments when Dickens is possessed by this power of writing: he is carried away. That is bliss. It certainly is not shared by writers to-day. For instance, the death of Cheedle (in *Our Mutual Friend*, JvG): dawn falling upon the edge of night. One realises exactly the mood of the writer and how he wrote, as it were, for himself (...) He *was* the falling dawn, and he *was* the physician going to Bar.[81] (Italics KM)

EPIPHANY

Once the writer has selected his subject, has absorbed its emotion, so that he may convey a subjective perception to the reader, he still has to decide on the story's structure and its climax(es). For difficulties arise if he compresses too much, or makes too broad a choice of details, when he creates too few or too many climaxes. Compression, selection and surrender are of utmost importance. In a review Mansfield described the author's struggles with a climax:

In the long, slow approach to the 'crisis' he writes well and freely; he takes his time, one has the impression that he feels, here, at this point he is safe, and can afford to let himself go. But when the heart of the story is reached, when there is nothing left to depend upon - to cling to - then he is like a young swimmer who can even swim very well, disport himself unafraid and at ease as long as he knows that the water is not out of his depth. When he discovers that it is - he disappears.[82]

Mansfield's term for the epiphany (See Chapter 3) was the 'blazing moment', 'glimpse' or 'central point of significance'.[83] In one of her reviews she explains why the epiphany should replace plot as an internal ordering principle:

If we are not to look for facts and events in a novel (...) and why should we? (-) We must be very sure of finding those central points of significance transferred to the endeavours and emotions of the human beings portrayed (...) The crisis, then, is the chief of our 'central points of significance' and the endeavours and the emotions are stages on our journey towards or away from it. For without it, the form of the novel, as we see it, is lost. Without it, how are we to appreciate, the importance of one 'spiritual event' rather than another? What is to prevent each being unrelated - complete in itself - if the gradual unfolding in growing, gaining light is not to be followed by one blazing moment?[84]

The epiphany may represent a unifying thematic focus, a climactic revelation (or a failure to achieve a revelation). It is meant to be an aesthetic 'moment of vision' for the reader, and is often equated with a visionary moment in everyday life.[85] In 1920 she wrote:

And yet one has these 'glimpses', before which all that one has ever written (...) The waves (...) and the high foam, how it suspended in the air before it fell (...) What is it that happens in that moment of suspension? It is timeless. In that moment (...) the whole life of the soul is contained. One is flung up - out of life - one is 'held' and then, down, bright, broken, glittering on the rocks, tossed back, part of the ebb and flow.[86]

In many of her short stories that present some kind of change in the central character the narrator builds up towards the moment of revelation by which the disparity between an illusion and reality is often presented in either a positive or a negative sense. The term *epiphany* needs careful consideration now. In English literary criticism it is used in a wide sense, to refer to any experience that stands out in a character's inner life by its concentrated intensity. This aspect of aesthetic theory is elaborated by James Joyce at considerable length, though it has come to extend beyond the Joycean definition as presented in *Stephen Hero*. Stephen's epiphany is characterised by the recognition of the significance of a 'trivial' incident and the emphasis on the spiritual nature of the experience. Here is Stephen's epiphany:

This triviality made him think of collecting many such moments together in a book of epiphanies. By an epiphany he meant a sudden spiritual manifestation whether in the vulgarity of speech or gesture or in a memorable state of the mind itself (...) He believed that it was for the man of letters to record these epiphanies with extreme care, seeing that they themselves are the most delicate and evanescent of moments.[87]

Morris Beja, in *Epiphany in the Modern Novel* (1971) closely follows the Joycean emphasis, extending it by stressing the important relationship between cause and effect in his definition:

a sudden, spiritual manifestation, whether from some object, scene, event, or memorable phase of the mind - the manifestation being out of proportion to the significance or strictly logical relevance of whatever produces it.[88]

The epiphany can be seen as a 'moment of truth' in the character's mind, as described in the text as a brief moment of experience. The 'moment of truth', whether experienced by a fictional character or as a spontaneous 'gift' in life, had considerable weight for Mansfield. The philosophy of Hegel underlies the intuition of harmony within dissonance characteristically assigned to such epiphanic moments. Mansfield had read Hegel at Queen's College, as an early notebook reference shows, and her notes on Vaihinger also indicate familiarity with Hegel's thinking. The Hegelian ideality, when reconciling warring opposites, recurs as one of the themes in letters and journals, with varying degrees of emphasis on (sensory) apperception.[89]

ATMOSPHERE

Mansfield attempted to have the reader experience the entire process of the perception of reality by concentrating on an evocative atmosphere, surrounding the objects or scenes presented, together with the feelings and sensations which are aroused by an experience. Let us first present some of Mansfield's own texts, in which she tries to recreate a prismatically perceived world. In an attempt to create order she often intuitively selected and interpreted her surroundings by presenting concentrated momentary impressions. She attempted to see everything anew, through fresh 'untutored' eyes. Apperception melts with perception in sensory fragments in which the narrator searches for relations, patterns and meanings. Instinctively in her descriptions of nature she struck the Impressionistic note in its evocative, mysterious rendering of an atmosphere.[90] When writing letters in her journal, she often revealed her Impressionistic prismatic sensibility.[91] When portraying the view from her window a world of sensory atmosphere, of seeing and hearing, is evoked:

(...) there is a woman on the opposite side of the river. She sits with her back against a tree, her legs stretched out in front of her, combing her long brown hair. To this side and to that she bends and then, with that charming gesture, she throws her head back and draws the comb all the length of it. If I were near enough I am sure I would hear her singing.[92]

At the age of 27, she had outlined her themes for a new novel. She structured them around sensory Impressionist effects.

Leaning over the bridge I suddenly discovered that one of those boats was exactly what I want my novel to be. Not big, almost grotesque in shape. I mean perhaps heavy with people rather dark and seen strangely as they move in the sharp light and shadow; and I want bright shivering lights in it, and the sound of water. This (...) by way of uplift.[93]

When describing her dreams, she painstakingly made the reader partake of the experience of her perceptive abilities by focusing on the atmosphere and the details of the 'objective illusion' of the picture she created:

Then I dreamed that I went to stay with the sisters Brontë who kept a boarding house called the Brontë Institute - painfully far from the railway station, and all the way there through heather. It was a sober place with linoleum on the stairs. Charlotte met me at the door and said, 'Emily is lying down'. Kot, I found, was also there, taking supper. He broke an orange into a bowl of bread and milk. 'Russian fashion,' he said. 'Try it. It's very good' But I refrained'.[94] (Kot = Koteliansky, the Russian translator friend, JvG)

In December 1915, still recovering from the shock of her brother's death in the war in France, she wrote her Literary Impressionist, sensory memories of New Zealand:

To sit in front of the little wood fire, your hands crossed in your lap and your eyes closed - to fancy you see again upon your eyelids all the dancing beauty of the day, to feel the flame on your throat as you used to imagine you felt the spot of yellow when Bogey held a buttercup under your chin ... when breathing is such a delight that you are almost afraid to breathe - as though a butterfly fanned its wings upon your breast. Still to taste the warm sunlight that melted in your mouth; still to smell the white waxy scent that lay upon the jonquil fields and the wild spicy scent of the rosemary growing in little tufts among the red rocks close to the brim of the sea...
The moon is rising but the reluctant day lingers upon the sea and sky. The sea is dabbled with a pink the colour of unripe

cherries, and in the sky there is a flying yellow light like the wings of canaries. Very stubborn and solid are the trunks of the palm trees. Springing from their tops the stiff green bouquets seem to cut into the evening air and among them, the blue gum trees, tall and slender with sickle-shaped leaves and the drooping branches half blue, half violet. The moon is just over the mountain behind the village. The dogs know she is there; already they begin to howl and bark. The fishermen are shouting and whistling to another as they bring in their boats, some young boys are singing in half-broken voices down by the shore, and there is a noise of children crying, little children with burnt cheeks and sand between their toes being carried home to bed....[95]

She also recorded her plans for the future:

(...) what is it, that I do want to write? (...) Only the form that I would choose has changed utterly. I feel no longer concerned with the same appearance of things (...) the plots of my stories leave me perfectly cold (...). Now, now I want to write recollections of my own country. Yes, I want to write about my country till I simply exhaust my store (...) Oh, I want for one moment to make our undiscovered country leap into the eyes of the Old World. It must be mysterious as though floating. It must take the breath (...) But all must be told with a sense of mystery, a radiance, an afterglow (...). The almond tree, the birds, the little wood (...) the flowers (...) the open window (...): Almost certainly in a kind of special prose (...) No novels, no problem stories, nothing that is not simple, open.[96]

The German word 'Stimmung' (mood and atmosphere), the fusion of the character's consciousness with the world at large, which creates a unity between visual appearance and mental reality becomes all important in Literary Impressionism. For Mansfield the expression of 'Stimmung' grew into a medium by which she condensed one of her Literary Impressionist impulses. By blurring contours and rendering intensity of mood and atmosphere, by illuminating the mysteriousness of all experience, in a fusion of subject and object, she attempted to create an impression of actual perception. She often struggled with the concept of 'Stimmung', because 'Stimmung' should be conveyed indirectly, in oblique images or small details. She wrote:

Suffering ought to be expressed as it is expressed in life - that is, not by the arms and legs, but by the tone and expression not by gesticulation, but by grace. (Quoted from the letters by Tsjechov).[97]

When reading through *The Oxford Book of English Verse* (1915) she compared poetic deficiencies to the lack of a good ear in a musician. Not many of them were exactly on pitch, according to Mansfield. She sometimes compared the overall emotional atmosphere to charm or tenderness in painting or the tone produced by a first-rate musician.[98]

A picture must have charm, music must have tone and literature must have tenderness. For this, only 'delicate perception is not enough; one must find the exact way in which to convey the delicate perception. One must inhabit the other mind and know more of the other mind and steep everything in the light of this secret knowledge'.[99] In other words, the author must have not only sympathy but also empathy. When recording her dreams in her journal, she often made a note of the special atmosphere:

Dreamed of Michael Sadleir. An important dream; its tone was important.[100]

And:

A wonderful pleasant dream about Paris (...) The Doctor and his friends all had the same atmosphere. It was good, kind, quietly happy.[101]

Mansfield also criticised her own work heavily for lacking the correct atmosphere:

Musically speaking, it is not - has not been - in the middle of the note - you know what I mean?[102]

'Can one explain this by what you might call - a *covering* atmosphere?' (Italics KM) she wrote.[103] Without the correct, enveloping emotional atmosphere, she wrote: 'nothing is worth doing', for this delicate adjustment is the fruit of subtle taste.[104] When reviewing E.M. Forster's *Howards End*, Mansfield commented on his very delicate sense of atmosphere.[105] Two months later, she stated that it is difficult to define the atmosphere of a novel:

What do we mean when we speak of the atmosphere of a novel? It is one of those questions exceedingly difficult to fit with an answer. It is one of those questions which, each time we look at them, seems to have grown. At one time 'emotional quality' seemed to cover it, but is that adequate? May not a book have that and yet lack this mysterious covering? Is it the impress of the writer's personality upon his work - the impress of the author's passion -

more than that? (...) For whatever else atmosphere may include, it is the element for which a book lives in its own right.[106]

Writing to William Gerhardi, she included mood and tone in the concept of atmosphere.[107] In a letter to the painter, Dorothy Brett she included 'charm':

Hang it all, Brett - a picture must have charm - or why look at it? It's the quality I call tenderness in writing. It's the tone one gets in a really first chop musician. Without it you can be as solid as a bull and I don't see what's the good.[108]

Character and plot should be enveloped by atmosphere, she wrote.[109] Mansfield extended the term 'covering atmosphere' into 'poet's atmosphere' and saw this as necessary to link the 'moments of being' with the larger structure of the story. She wished to expand and intensify the moment into an 'aesthetic whole':

It is strange how content most writers are to ignore the influence of the weather upon the feelings and the emotions of their characters, or, if they do not ignore it, to treat it, except in its most obvious manifestations - 'she felt happy because the sun was shining' - 'the dull day served but to heighten his depression' - as something of very little importance, something quite separate and apart. But by 'the weather' we do not mean a kind of ocean at our feet, with broad effects of light and shadow, into which we can plunge or not plunge, at will; we mean an external atmosphere which is in harmony or discordant with a state of soul; poet's weather, perhaps we might call it. But why not prose writer's weather, too? Then indeed, as in the stories of Tsjechov we should become aware of the rain pattering on the roof all night long, of the languid, feverish wind, of the moonlit orchard and the first snow, passionately realized, not indeed as analogous to a state of mind, but as linking that mind to the larger whole.[110]

OBLIQUE

An appropriate suppleness, warmth and freshness must be achieved indirectly, Mansfield wrote. The main question is 'how are we going to convey these overtones, half tones, quarter tones, these hesitations, doubts, beginnings, if we go at them *directly*?'[111] (Italics KM) Not many writers seemed to understand 'what the middle of the note is'. 'It's not that they are even 'sharp' or 'flat' - It's something much more subtle - they are not playing on the very *note itself*'.[112] Above all, in

Mansfieldian Literary Impressionism a writer must never 'tell' the reader what he is to feel about his characters. They must be apperceived, seen for the first time not 'shown off'. In a letter she described the need for *oblique* transmission. There must be illumination of an experience first, as, e.g. the experience and influence of the First World War, but the voice should not be too loud nor the gesture too crude:

> But the difference between you and me is (...) I couldn't tell anybody *bang out* about these deserts. They are my secret. I might write about a boy eating strawberries or a woman combing her hair on a windy morning and that is the only way I can ever mention them. But they *must* be there. Nothing less will do.[113] (Italics KM)

Mansfield's technique of systematic allusion, her indirect method of creating a solipsistic visionary perception[114] is explained here. She believed in presenting a profound experience indirectly, by means of apparently trivial incidents, which have significance for what they reveal of a character's inner mood. Feelings are never explained, analysed, but suggested. The expression of emotion must never be unbridled:

> Better a half-truth, beautifully whispered, than a whole solemnly shouted.[115]

The writer should avoid 'the ridiculous excess of painting the lily or throwing a perfume on the violet'.[116] He must govern his emotion, otherwise the reader will not be able to 'see the stars for the fireworks'.[117]

According to Mansfield, an artist is not a propagandist. His business is not to reform, but to reveal - not to impose or propose, but simply to expose.[118]

STRUCTURE

Repeatedly Mansfield refered to the contemporary literary scene, to 'the age of experiments', 'the new fields of experience', 'the uneasy, disintegrating, experimental spirit of the age'[119], which she often described in striking and colourful imagery. The Yeatsian image of the tree is often used to suggest the organic wholeness of the successful work of art:

> If a novel is to have a central idea we imagine that central idea as a lusty growing stem from which the branches spring clothed with

leaves, and the buds become flowers and fruits. We imagine that the author chooses with infinite deliberation the very air in which that tree shall be nourished, and that he is profoundly aware that its coming to perfection depends upon the strength with which the central idea supports its beautiful accumulations.[120]

She focuses on the aesthetic quality of one central idea in composition, selection and interpretation, emphasis on atmosphere, the 'very air in which the tree shall be nourished' and the difficulty of 'accumulations'. For Mansfield the world constituted an indistinct picture, it needed a proper design, 'a whole scheme'.[121] How can one hope to achieve that total, detached vision, which alone can pierce the veil of appearances, if one is not detached? In a Scrapbook, dating from 1922, we found a fragmentary draft for a new short story, accompanied by Mansfield's own comments. These comments are unique as no other notes on her own drafts are still extant. The fragment was intended for a new story on "The Sheridans" and the comments are of a usefully detailed kind, rarely to be found in her secondary writing. The text in the *Scrapbook* reads as follows:

It was late afternoon when Mrs Sheridan, after having paid Heaven knows how many calls, turned towards home.
'Thank Heaven, that's all over!' she sighed, as she clicked the last gate to, and stuffed her little Chinese card-case into her handbag.
But it was not all over. Although she hadn't the faintest desire to remember her afternoon, her mind, evidently, was determined she should not forget it. And so she walked along seeing herself knocking at doors, crossing dim halls into large pale drawing-rooms, hearing herself saying, 'No, she would not have any tea, thank you. Yes, they were all splendidly well. No, they had not seen it yet. The children were going to-night. Yes, fancy, he had arrived. Young and good-looking too! Quite an asset! Oh dear no! She was determined not to allow any of her girls to marry. It was quite unnecessary now-a-days, and such a risk!' And so on and so on.
'What nonsense calling is! What a waste of time! I have never met a single woman yet who even pretended to like it. Why keep it up then? Why not decide once and for all? Mock-orange ...' And Mrs Sheridan woke out of her dream to find herself standing under a beautiful mock-orange bush that grew against the white palings of old Mr Phillips' garden. The little sponge-like fruits-flowers. Which were they? - shone burning - bright in the late afternoon sun.
'They are like little worlds,' she thought, peering up through the large crumpled leaves; and she put out her hand and touched one

gently. 'The feel of things is so strange, so different, one never seems to know a thing until one has felt it - at least that is true of flowers. Roses for instance, - who can smell a rose without kissing it? And pansies, little darlings they are! People don't pay half enough attention to pansies. Now her glove was all brushed with yellow. But it didn't matter. She was glad, even. 'I wish you grew in my garden,' she said regretfully to the mock-orange bush, and she went on, thinking, 'I wonder why I love flowers so much. None of the children inherit it from me. Laura perhaps. But even then it's not the same. She's too young to feel as I do. I love flowers more than people, except my own family, of course. Take this afternoon, for instance. The only thing that really remains is that mock-orange.'

So far Mansfield's unpublished text. Next to it we find Mansfield's comments:

But this is not expanded enough, or rich enough. I think still a description of the hour and place should come first. And the light should fall on the figure of Mrs Sheridan on her way home. Really I can allow myself to write a great deal - to describe it all - the baths, the avenue, the people in the gardens, the Chinaman under the tree in May street. But in that case she won't be conscious of these things. That's bad. They must be seen and felt by her as she wanders home ... that sense of flowing in and out of houses - going and returning - like the tide. To go and not to return. How terrible! The father in his dressing-room - the familiar talk. His using her hair-brush - his passion for things that *wear well*. The children sitting round the table - the light outside, the silver. Her feeling as she sees them all gathered together - her longing for them always to be *there*. Yes, I'm getting nearer all this. I now remember S.W. and see that it must be written with love - real love. All the same, the difficulty is to get it all within *focus* - to introduce that young doctor and bring him continually nearer and nearer until finally he is part of the Sheridan family, until finally he has taken away Meg ... that is by no means easy ....[122] (Italics KM)

In her detailed comments Mansfield described here the narrator's struggle to achieve identity with a character's point-of-view (focalisation) and the traditional, commenting, omniscient narrator in a 'complete' composition. She rejected the narrator's description of a central 'symbol' (the mock-orange for Mrs Sheridan). She wanted to overstress neither the object, nor the scene itself (the afternoon of paying calls), nor the setting (although she hesitated about 'the hour and place'). Instead Mansfield wanted to concentrate on mood and atmosphere. ('The light outside, her feeling, that sense of flowing in and out ... The atmosphere of 'the tide ... going and returning' must surround it all, and must be evoked by Mrs Sheridan's experience. Mansfield preferred a subjective selection and interpretation of a fragmentary experience with a great many accompanying, though randomly selected details (the father, the children), with oblique, indistinct gestures and actions (the father taking not his own, but his wife's hairbrush).

It is only direct experience that counted for Mansfield. Everything must be limited to the actual sensations or impressions of the characters. Here is no mention of any preference for an expansion of the Symbolist's 'conveyance of a concrete symbol and the information that every detail must have a function', as Hanson & Gurr have it.[123] Instead stress is given to the expansion of a Literary Impressionist's 'fleeting moment' into an expressive narrator's description (e.g. 'Heaven knows how many'), in an assumed and apparent objectivity which will finally create an illusion (as it appears that Mrs Sheridan's Meg is taken away by 'the young and good-looking' unknown doctor).[124] In her attempt to be as 'objective' as possible, Mansfield wanted to present the undeveloped consciousness of Mrs Sheridan, and its rather arbitrary associations.

When a writer is unable to relate his/her characters to the larger fabric of the world, of life in art, when a writer deliberately isolates his characters from 'life as we know it', then that writer paints only 'portraits on the wall', Mansfield once commented.[125] It was this failure that was responsible for the 'pettiness of post-war English fiction', and she ascribed this failure to the 'psychological studies' in fiction so popular in her day. Poise, proportion and restraint - these were the *sine qua non* of any piece of writing which aspired to be truly artistic. One must have the ability to select and reject. One must have discrimination, for indiscrimination meant confusion. Therefore, Mansfield cannot be aligned with Dorothy Richardson's fascination with the possibility that experience may be primarily, rather than ultimately or absolutely, indivisible and without structure. She clearly rejected the cultivation of a disproportionate, mental experience in pure streams of consciousness. In reconstructing reality as a stream of impressions, images, running through the mind of one character, Richardson's *Miriam* failed, according to Mansfield, to achieve anything great, because Richardson's presentation of life was unselective.

In order to compress the manifold existence of mankind into a few pages, the writer must maintain a becoming brevity - which excludes everything that is redundant. Unsorted abundance of mental and visual reactions, noted indiscriminately with a deliberate disregard for their relevance to the particular case, will only lead him into insignificance.[126] She wrote that in an ideal work of art:

> (...) there mustn't be one single word out of place, or one word that can be taken out. That's how I *aim* at writing.[127] (Italics KM)

She was a stickler for form. To John M. Murry she wrote:

> I hate the sort of licence that English people give themselves (...) to spread over and flop and roll about.[128]

For example in "Miss Brill", she chose 'not only the length of every sentence', but even the sound of it. She chose the rise and fall of every paragraph to fit the character of Miss Brill, and to fit it on that day at the very moment. After she had written it, she read it aloud 'just as one would play over a musical composition - trying to get it nearer and nearer to the expression of Miss Brill - until it fitted her'.[129] If there is no structure, there is no balance. We will have mere separate 'scraps', 'snippets', 'patches', 'tid-bits', 'oddments'[130], but no unity of structure. A true artist, she felt, satisfies not only the reader's senses but also his imagination. The ideal reader will not be fobbed off with pictures alone - he will demand that someone should discover for him the deeper strangeness or mystery that underlies those pictures, so that his imagination will not be allowed to go starving while his senses are feasted.[131] In a review she wrote:

> It is a very great gift for an author to be able to project himself into the hearts and minds of his characters - but more is needed to make a great creative artist; he must be able, with equal power, to withdraw, to survey what is happening - and from an eminence.[132]

Mansfield appeared to be rather reticent in defining her concrete craft and technique. She nevertheless recognised their great importance. 'I too have a passion for technique', she wrote in a letter to Richard Murry, 'I have a passion for making the thing into a whole, (...) Out of technique is born real style, I believe. There are no short cuts'.[133]

She is not interested in plot. In one of her reviews she wrote:

> The plot, the story is the least important thing. What is important is the message that (...) characters have to deliver.[134]

In another review[135] she complained about the tediousness of plot and externality, again emphasising the significance of 'external atmosphere'.[136] The author should not explain too much and should provide no moral.[137] He should 'capture the basic idea and not recapture it'[138] but should concentrate on one impression.[139] There remains the problem of what can be left out . If the novel is too crowded with details, the reader will no longer recognise the essentials.[140] John M. Murry, too, commenting on her method for designing the structure of her work, stressed the Literary Impressionist focus on the writer's complete visionary situation and its accompanying atmosphere:

> When Katherine was very young she was addicted to short pieces which she romantically called 'Vignettes' or 'cameos' (...) her original bent towards the short story was confirmed and vindicated. Her power of presenting a complete situation or conveying an entire atmosphere, in a transparently simple page or paragraph became remarkable indeed (...)
> Katherine saw and wrote in flashes. Sometimes the flashes were relatively long, sometimes very short indeed. But of steady and equable composition there is no trace in her manuscripts, nor in my memory of her at work. When the full tide of inspiration came, she wrote till she dropped with fatigue - sometimes all through the night (...)[141]

But how much is taken for granted by the reader? What can indeed be left out? Mansfield always stressed the strength of imaginative vision 'the deep breath the author must have taken', as had Couperus in *The Twilight of the Souls*[142], where he did not 'adhere to the old unnecessary technical devices' whereby too many 'accumulations' and unnecessary details were fired at the reader. 'The central idea' should be arranged to produce a complete design, and not be too fragmented[143], as in Gertrude Stein's work. Energy should not be wasted over too many details.[144] Mansfield wanted a 'whole, round, novel, in which the vision is completely real and satisfying'[145] with interrelationships between characters and action. Mansfield often criticised new books under review for lack of design and proportion:

> The novel as a whole lacks proportion. The closing scenes are far too drawn out; they are (...) a grave blemish.[146]

Sometimes she is satisfied with 'a charming composition' because the author 'delights in a sense of order, in composing for each character and scene the surroundings that are appropriate and adequate to it'.[147] For Mansfield, form must be invented. It expresses itself in a pattern, which must be unified. It bestows an intuitive inevitability and animates details in its ordering and illuminating process.

FRAGMENTS

A puzzling omission in Mansfield's comments on novel writing in *Novel and Novelists*, her journals and letters, is that she never mentioned why she had chosen the particular form of the short story. It simply seemed not to have been an issue for her.

In her reviews, however, Mansfield clearly dissociated herself from the usual run of short stories. She was to review several collections and in one review she spoke against short stories being presented as 'digestible snacks'. In another she made an ambiguous reference - the only one in all her writings - to the 'tales' and 'sketches'[148] under review:

> Suppose we put it in the form of a riddle: (...) I am written in prose. I am a great deal shorter than a novel; I may be only one page long, but on the other hand, there is no reason why I should not be thirty. I have a special quality - a something, a something which is immediately, perfectly recognizable. It belongs to me, it is of my essence. In fact, I am given away in the first sentence. I seem almost to stand or fall by it. It is to me what the first phrase of the song is to the singer. Those who know me feel: 'Yes, that is it'. And they are from that moment prepared for what is to follow. Here are, for instance, some examples of me: 'A Trifle from Life', 'About Love', 'The Lady with the Dog'. What am I?[149]

This passage does not contain many keys to her own work. Some reference to Tsjechov's art may be read into it, ("The Lady With the Dog") but Mansfield could not define the 'special quality', the essence which is immediately, perfectly recognisable. In 1920, in her *Scrapbook*, Mansfield confessed that she could not write more than a fragmentary short story about anything in her 'world'.[150] Again she linked herself with Tsjechov:

> I thought a few minutes ago, that I could have written a whole novel about a *liar*. A man who was devoted to his wife, but who *lied*. But I couldn't. I couldn't write a whole novel about *anything*. I suppose I shall write stories about it.[151] (Italics KM)

In 1917 she wrote on the fly-leaf of a volume of Tsjechov's:

> By all the laws of the M. and P.
> This book is bound to belong to me.
> Besides I am sure that you agree
> I am the English Anton T.

On December 12, 1920 she added:

God forgive me, Tsjechov, for my impertinence.[152]

Mansfield often used metaphorical language to describe the 'organic process', the genesis and development of her own work. Commenting on "The Daughters of the Late Colonel", she wrote: 'it just unfolds and opens'.[153] On the form of "Prelude" she wrote: 'it is made up of several fragments, each as separate as flowers on a tree and all contributing to the one effect'.[154] Without form in fiction, Mansfield emphasised, there is only autobiography, the celebration of consciousness in fragmentary moments or mere reportage. Form must intervene into the world of the senses, through a subjective inductive selection and details must be given their place in the whole scheme. Form must be arranged, selected, induced, interpreted and must express experience. Mansfield often mentioned a passion for 'making the thing into a whole', a 'whole round novel'.[155] When reading Tsjechov, she praised his discovery of the perfect form, by which his Literary Impressionism[156] shines through the mysterious life contained in his stories. Her admiration of "The Steppe" is profound.[157]

One of the basic principles for structure that Mansfield always bore in mind is the author's constitution of a clear, yet oblique picture of his vision in the outline of a composition. For Mansfield, outlines may be blurred, but not excessively. When the simplicity of the fragment is 'smothered under a torrent of puffed-up words, which obscured the firm outlines'[158] upon which a story relies, it must be rejected.

Part III:
Chapter 4   AN ANALYSIS OF NARRATIVE
METHODS, THEMES, STRUCTURE, CHARACTERISATION
AND IMAGES IN MANSFIELD'S WORK

As the meaning of many of Mansfield's stories largely resides in the carefully selected narrative methods, the choice of her themes, the deliberately fragmentary organisation of the text, the shadowy characters and the numerous clusters of images a special analytical chapter seems to be called for. In this final discussion, on the 'how?' and 'why?' of her technique, the most important critical attitudes towards the separate subjects will be summarised first. Thereafter an attempt will be made to analyse a great many of Mansfield's stories. Literary Impressionism will be described as a particular mode of presenting a fictional world, as an aesthetic view of reality, which may be expressed by formal characteristics.

Chapter 4.1 NARRATIVE METHODS: RESTRICTION IN
PARALLAX

If the central concept of Literary Impressionism is the fictional rendering of a momentary experience, the qualifying variable is the mind that perceives these sensations. However we must ask ourselves: 'Which mind is it?' In painting it is assumed that what is portrayed is rendered as the painter saw it. In music the general assumption is that the impressions evoked through sound are those of the composer. In fiction this assumption cannot be made, since the story in the text may be presented through some intermediary 'prism', 'perspective', or 'angle of vision', verbalised by the narrator, though not necessarily his own. The narrator often records what is perceived by one of the characters. Following G. Genette, this extra mediation may be called 'focalisation'.[1] A person is capable of both seeing and speaking at the same time and he is also capable of narrating what another person sees, hears, feels or has seen etc. Thus seeing and speaking, focalisation and narration may but need not be attributed to the same person. In principle, focalisation and narration are two distinct activities. If a narrator records not what he himself sees, but what is perceived by a character (focaliser), the effect is a distancing, a supposed objectivity, which makes the illusion of a sensory activity more difficult. The limitation of narrative data to the narrator's projection of the mind of a character is essential to the concept of Literary Impressionism, as it ultimately reveals that reality cannot be fully comprehended by any single human mind.[2] Views of reality in Literary Impressionism are therefore dependent upon the perceiving mind (or minds). It follows that the accuracy of the rendering mind often depends upon the quality of the observer and the limitations his immediate position may place upon him. The awareness that what the perceiver transmits may only be his restricted, sensory impression of the scene is another central proposition in Literary Impressionist aesthetics.

Mansfield's work exhibits a general commitment to the concept of a limited, sensory mind, whether as narrator or character. She experimented with a variety of forms which will be discussed in this chapter. Given the quantity of short stories she wrote in the course of her brief career, there is remarkably little deviation from a basic Literary Impressionist stance.

Although Mansfield began her writing career employing traditional first-person methods, she often used a narrator, who is, as it were, above or superior to the story he narrates. In no sense, does he participate in the story. The term 'omniscience' is perhaps exaggerated, especially for Impressionist and Modernist narrators, although the chief characteristic connoted by it is still relevant, namely, familiarity with the characters' innermost thoughts and feelings. The narrator has knowledge of past, present and future. He is present in locations where characters are supposed to be unaccompanied, and he has knowledge of what happens in several places at the same time. The term 'omniscience' is particularly inhospitable to Impressionist ideas.

Many Anglo-American critics have treated the narrator and the focaliser as if they were interchangeable. One of Mansfield's critics, Yuan She Ye, in his study of Mansfield's point-of-view, also fuses the narrator and the focaliser into an interchangeable system, based on Friedman's classification.

In the criticism of Mansfield's short stories, the study of the narrator has to date been the poor relation. Many Mansfield critics have contradicted each other on this issue. Some of them have alluded to the different kinds of narrators, which Mansfield could create, while others interpreted only the focalisers - characters. Most critics nevertheless agree on Mansfield's achievement in using the extra-diegetic type of narrator, narrating in the third-person, together with multi-personal focalisation, in her major stories "Prelude", "At the Bay" and "The Daughters of the Late Colonel".

In various countries at various periods in the history of literary theory and according to diverging principles, new concepts have been developed in the study of narrative theory. They have often been independent of each other. Work has been done in very different contexts on various components of 'a' theory of narrative.

Anglo-American readers have been presented with narrative studies by e.g. Brooks and Warren (1943), Friedman (1955), Booth (1961),and Romberg (1961), and in 1971 Stanzel (1955) was translated into English. All of these works contain many well-founded insights and have proved more or less useful. The most widely praised, Friedman's typology, Booth's chapter in his well-known book *The Rhetoric of Fiction*, and Stanzel's *Narrative Situations in the Novel*, are based on different criteria, such as perspective, identity and attitude of the narrator and amount of information. For the Austrian Anglist Franz Stanzel, the main criterion is the presence or absence of the narrator in three typical narrative situations (auctorial, I-narrative and personal narrative), which framework was completed by R. Romberg with a fourth type, objective narrative in the behaviourist style (Friedman's seventh type). All these point of view theories have been based mainly on psychological criteria and, as was already noted, two related but different questions have been treated as if inter-changeable: 'who speaks?' (who is the narrator?) and 'who sees?' (who is the focaliser?). The distinction is a theoretically necessary one, formulated in 1972 by G. Genette in an attempt to subsume all the traditional narratological distinctions together into one systematic, theoretical framework. Genette introduced the term 'focalisation' in order to distinguish between 'the vision through which the information is presented on the one hand' and 'the identity of the voice that is verbalising that vision on the other hand.' It is possible, both in reality and in fiction, for one person to speak and to see at the same time and meanwhile express the vision of another person.

It is generally agreed that in Mansfield's "The Garden Party" almost everything is seen through Laura's eyes. Yen Yuan She in *Katherine Mansfield's use of point of view* (1976) claims that Mansfield rightly employs Laura's girlish voice to tell the story in "The Garden Party" which is thoroughly controlled by Laura's point of view. (p. 27) According to Booth any sustained inside view, of whatever depth, temporarily turns the character whose mind is shown into a narrator.[3] If this argument should be accepted, Laura becomes not only a vehicle of focalisation (a focaliser) but also a narrator. Even in passages where the language gets as close as it can be to a translation of Laura's perceptions, verbal communication and non-verbal focalisation remain separate. Let us examine the passage in "The Garden Party", in which Laura goes down to the dead man's cottage:

1   'But we can't possibly have a garden-party with a man dead
2   just outside the front gate.' That really was extravagant,
3   for the little cottages were in a lane to themselves at the
4   very bottom of a steep rise that led up to the house. A

5	broad road ran between. True, they were far too near.
6	They were the greatest possible eyesore, and they had no
7	right to be in that neighbourhood at all. They were little
8	mean dwellings painted a chocolate brown. In the garden
9	patches there was nothing but cabbage stalks, sick hens and
10	tomato cans. The very smoke coming out of their chimneys
11	was poverty-stricken. Little rags and shreds of smoke, so
12	unlike the great silvery plumes that uncurled from the
13	Sheridans' chimneys. Washerwomen lived in the lane and
14	sweeps and a cobbler and a man whose housefront was studded
15	all over with minute bird-cages. Children swarmed. When
16	the Sheridans were little they were forbidden to set foot
17	there because of the revolting language and of what they
18	might catch. But since they were grown up, Laura and Laurie
19	on their prowls sometimes walked through. It was disgusting
20	and sordid. They came out with a shudder. But still one
21	must go everywhere, one must see everything. So through
22	they went. And just think of what the band would sound
23	like to that poor woman, said Laura. (p. 254)

Laura, the main character, the social rebel, intuitively feels that the luxurious garden-party the family is planning, should be cancelled, or at least postponed, when she hears the news of a fatal accident. A worker, living nearby in a small cottage, has been killed. Laura's mother (and Laura's sister José) are opposed to Laura. They will reveal the inequities in class distinction, a conflict made clear in the rest of the narrative. The discussion of the issue is interrupted by the quoted passage, in which, as so often in Mansfield's stories, no clear hint is given of 'who speaks' or 'who sees'. In Genette's terms there is no clear separation between verbal communication and non-verbal focalisation. But we must ask ourselves: 'Whose subjective view about life in the nearby cottages is presented here?' It is *not* the main character Laura, 'who speaks' here. It is not Laura's point-of-view. Franz Stanzel, when discussing the same text in his article 'Teller-Characters and Reflector-Characters in Narrative Theory' (1981), proposes to distinguish between 'teller and reflector-character'.[4] Stanzel recognises, though does not define, the 'concept of a personalized narrator' in his 'teller-character distinction' and advises to make a distinction between different characters.

Stanzel describes his teller-character as follows: his main function is to tell, to narrate, report, communicate, quote witnesses and sources, comment on the story, anticipate the outcome of an action or recapitulate what has happened before the story opens; whereas the reflector-character's main function is to reflect, i.e. to mirror in his consciousness what is going on in the world outside or inside himself.

A reflector-character, according to Stanzel's theory, never narrates in
the sense of verbalising his perceptions, thoughts and feelings. He does
not attempt to communicate his perceptions or thoughts to the reader.
This produces in the reader the illusion of having an unmediated and
direct view of the fictional world, seeing it, through the eyes of the
reflector-character. Stanzel's two categories are based on the Platonic
distinction between diegesis and mimesis.

It may be argued, however, that if Stanzel's theory is accepted, the
critic will not be able to analyse "The Garden Party" narrator's text in
any detail. He will lack the cues, the traces left by the narrator, to
enable him to define the different modes of telling and the functional
quality and special variety of the Mansfieldian narrator. In the same
article in which Stanzel launches his new theory, he also introduces
the possibility of reversing his distinctions: a teller-character may act
temporarily as a reflector-character. This for Stanzel seems a solution
to the complex Mansfieldian text. Let us now examine the example
more closely.

As Stanzel has rightly gathered, the views presented here conform
to the attitude of the greater part of Laura's family. This attitude is
never expressed so poignantly as in this fragment. But it is not through
Laura, temporarily acting as a 'teller-character'. In the passage quoted
above we have a clear example of an extra-diegetic narrator,
presenting temporarily from within and sometimes from without, in
an 'interplay' between narrator and focalisers, the feelings and
thoughts of, alternately, Laura's mother (+José, who always imitates
her mother (e.g. 'chocolate brown' -l. 8), and the Sheridan children,
Laura and her brother Laurie. Sometimes the narrator takes over
entirely, hovering around the characters (l. 20, 21). At first, the
colourful value-ridden language conveys the perceptions of the
prejudiced, narrow-minded, upper-middle class family. But it is not
Mrs Sheridan who speaks. For one thing, the Sheridans are referred to
by their very name (l. 13 and 16). For another, a retrospective view is
presented here by an external narrator, focalising on Laura and
Laurie. They are referred to as 'they' (ll. 17, 18). They are the two
'outsiders' in the Sheridan-family. If Laura herself were the narrator
this would be an impossible procedure. Nor is it Mrs Sheridan
speaking. She will not allow her children to set foot there, and it is not
likely that she knows about Laura and Laurie's prowls.

Besides, various utterances in free indirect discourse (FID) abound
in this fragment. Without any hint of e.g. an introductory verb of
saying, thinking or feeling anywhere in the text we are presented with
the narrator's gist of the story and the Sheridans' prejudiced
commentary (l. 2 - *that really* was *extravagant* (...) *little* cottages (...)
at the *very* bottom (...) *true*, they were *far too near*. They were the
greatest possible eyesore, and they had *no right* to be in *that*

neighbourhood *at all* (...). Mean dwellings (...) a *chocolate* brown (...) *nothing but* (...). The *very* smoke (...) *what they might catch* (...) *it was disgusting and sordid* (emphasis added), continually fusing the narrator's and the characters' speech through slight shifts in focalisation. In the indirect region this 'contaminated'[5] or 'coloured narrative'[6] becomes at one extreme indistinguishable from diegetic narrative, while at the other extreme it converges with FID itself. Here the FID utterances not only suggest actual speech or thought (by Mrs Sheridan and some of her children) but represent a 'résume' by the narrator.

With this 'auctorial' free indirect discourse[7] the view of the character only has a qualified mimetic assent. FID is subordinate in status to the narrator's objective judgement. The examples of FID here, the emotional prejudice in the echoes of words and opinions, is evoked by Laura's revealing statement in l. 1. Verbalisation and rationalisation of FID in this fragment remains firmly in the hands of the narrator. It bears the signature of the characters, though the narrator remains present in the syntax of the passage, in the shape and relationship of the FID utterance.

The shifts between characters and narrator are not indicated by indexes of FID. The words and utterances are 'streaming over' into the narrator's discourse. This 'floating' focalisation, even in FID, seems one of the necessary disguises for the narrator to create his immediacy. In the penultimate, more general commentary (l. 20: But still one must go ...), which is not restricted to anyone of the characters, the narrator extends the significance of the event. Laura and Laurie's prowls are highlighted now in such a way that this utterance applies to humanity at large. The relatively minimal sign of the narrator's presence is made perceptible by the reference to the general 'one'. The narrator seems to disguise himself, abruptly changing focalisation and degree of insight, when circling around the characters.

Stanzel argued that this text must be attributed to a teller-character, who temporarily seems to assume the role of the reflector-character. He makes no distinction between focaliser and narrator. Although Stanzel hints at the functional status of the narrator in Mansfield's work in general, he does not describe this most central concept. He writes: 'Teller-characters acting as reflector-characters are often to be found in Mansfield's stories. Their general characteristic is the withdrawal of 'the personalized narrator' from the story and the prominent role of reflector-characters as agents of narrative transmission. In this way Mansfield's rendering of the Sheridans' lack of consideration gains a poignancy much stronger than could be achieved through a conventional teller-character or through the direct presentation of the social attitudes of the Sheridans, by making one of

99

them, perhaps Mrs Sheridan, utter these sentiments or turn them over in her thoughts, as a reflector-character would'. Stanzel does not recognise the different points of view, or, in Genette's terminology, the variable focalisation. It is clear here that focalisation does not remain constant throughout the text or even within the same paragraph. The focus can be internal and external. We must therefore account for the one who makes these changes in focalisation: *The Narrator*. It is, after all, the extra-diegetic narrator who presents the focalised from within. Let us therefore reconsider the possibilities open to the narrator for presenting the events and the characters he wants to describe.

THE NARRATOR

It is by now generally acknowledged that the narrator's[8] presence in or absence from a text has a crucial effect on a story's structure. The narrator is therefore the most central concept in the analysis of a narrative text.[9] The identity of the narrator, his participation, his perceptibility, and the choices that are implied, all give the text its specific character.

Before the concept of the narrator can be studied it must be constituted as a category, with boundaries and a name, and the theoretical concepts to be used within this study must be defined. In this study then the narrator is defined as the agent (the medium) which decides on the form of the narrative and which produces the linguistic signs within this form, all of which together constitute the narrative. Genre and discourse are included here, so that the concept is more explicit and seems wider than Rimmon's (1983) who with careful vagueness, defines the narrator as 'the agent which at the very least narrates or engages in some activity serving the needs of narration' (p. 88) or Bal's (1985) 'that agent which utters the linguistic signs which constitute the text' (p. 119).

For an author engaged in the act of writing, there is a considerable choice of possibilities. Choices of form (e.g. genre: short story, novel or poetry), and narrative technique (e.g. monologue, dialogue, diegetic or mimetic mode of discourse, focalisation,) are central decisions, quite apart from the narrative content.[10]

What traces are left by the narrator? Does he participate in the narrative and can we perceive him? How do we recognise the narrator? The extent of the narrator's participation in the narrative and the degree of perceptibility of his role are crucial factors in the reader's understanding of and attitude toward the story. The two criteria are not mutually exclusive and allow for cross-combinations between the different types.[11] These two criteria may be used to investigate the role of the narrator in Mansfield's "The Fly". This story presents a so-called, omnipresent, extra-diegetic narrator. He does not participate as a character in the narrative. He is there, he tells the tale. His absence endows him with a high narratorial authority. He is present in locations where characters are supposed to be alone; he is in principle, familiar, with the characters' innermost thoughts and feelings and has knowledge of the characters' past, present and future. As to the narrator's perceptibility a few possible signs are listed by Chatman.[12] Even where a narrator is almost purely covert, several signs of overtness may be presented - in mounting order of perceptibility.[13]

So far only clearly perceptible traces of the narrator have been discussed. The narrator's participation, may, however, be presented by less direct means. Let us therefore pay attention to the modes of discourse he may select and the combination of functions he may hold.

The Platonic distinction between *diegesis* and *mimesis* has persisted throughout discussions on the ways of rendering speech and has served as a point of departure for discussions of 'point of view' in fiction ever since James and Lubbock. The characteristic feature of diegesis is that 'the poet himself is the speaker' and does not even attempt to suggest to us that anyone but himself is speaking. In mimesis, on the other hand, the poet tries to create the illusion that it is not he who is speaking. The distinction between diegesis and mimesis reappears under the names of 'telling' and 'showing'. In Anglo-American criticism, 'telling' is a manner of presentation mediated by the narrator, who talks about events and conversations and sums them up in indirect and free indirect discourse. 'Showing' on the other hand, is the supposedly direct presentation of events and conversations in direct discourse. The narrator seems to be eliminated and the reader is not guided in drawing his own conclusions from what he 'sees' and 'hears'.

To begin with let us review the main points concerning direct discourse, since they are relevant to the direct discourse block in the text of "The Fly". It is obvious that no text or narrative can, in fact, show or imitate the action it conveys. Pure showing, or pure imitation in language is not possible, since language signifies without imitating. Language can only imitate language, and the representation of speech in dialogue comes closest to 'pure' mimesis. All that a dialogue can do is create an illusion of mimesis but through diegesis. There is still a narrator who selects from between the binary oppositions between 'langue' and 'parole', between paradigm and syntagm, between code and message. It is the narrator who 'quotes' or 'transcribes' the character's utterances by selection and combination, substitution and deletion of the character's lexis. All that a narrator can do is create an illusion, a semblance of mimesis. The narrator, though, can never disappear altogether, because in the language communication situation a message is conveyed. The very presence of the message inevitably implies an addresser, producing the message. The truth is that mimesis of words can only be mimesis of words.[14]

How is the illusion of mimesis created in language? By telling in different indirect modes of discourse. Pure diegesis with indirection and condensation says less and does so in a mediated way. 'Telling' is always a presentation clearly mediated by the narrator, who in a more or less diegetic, a more or less indirect manner, talks about, summarises and draws conclusions about events and conversations.

There are various modes of discourse and different degrees of indirectness when representing an actual or inner speech act. Let us therefore turn to the presentation of speech and its various degrees of mimetic illusion on a descending scale of indirectness. Genette, in a preliminary step towards a classification between the different degrees of 'telling' and 'showing' cites only four modes.[15] Another progressive scale with more categories is suggested by McHale (1978).[16] His categories will be reproduced almost verbatim, if slightly summarised, with examples from Mansfield's story, descending from mimesis to diegesis, from a minimum of mediation to a maximum of indirection:

1. *Direct Discourse* (DD) - Although conventionalised or stylised in one way or another, DD creates the illusion of 'pure' mimesis in a 'quotation' from a monologue or dialogue. E.g. "The Fly" (p. 413): 'There was something I wanted to tell you' said old Woodifield.

2. *Free Direct Discourse* - DD without its conventional ortographic cues. E.g. "The Fly" (p. 423): Poor old chap, he's on his last pins, thought the boss. (No quotation marks.)

3. *Free Indirect Discourse* (FID) - Grammatically and mimetically intermediate between indirect and direct discourse. E.g. "The Fly" (p. 427): That was the way to tackle things, that was the right spirit.

4. *Indirect Discourse, mimetic to some degree* - A form of ID, which creates the illusion of 'preserving' or 'imitating' some aspects of the style of an utterance, above and beyond the mere report of its content. E.g. "The Fly" (p. 422) : ... since his ... stroke, the wife and the girls kept him boxed up in the house everyday of the week except Tuesday. (Mansfield's suspension- points).

5. *Indirect Content Paraphrase* - The conventional ID. The paraphrase of the content of a speech event, not imitating but ignoring the style or form of the supposed 'original' utterance. E.g. "The Fly" (p. 416): Time, he had declared then, he had told everybody, could make no difference. (In the non-inverted order this would have been: He had declared then, he had told everybody, that time could make no difference).

6. *Summary, less purely diegetic* - Summary, which to some degree

represents a speech event. It names the topics of conversation. E.g. "The Fly" (p. 425): It had been a terrible shock to him when old Woodifield sprang that remark on him about the boy's grave.

7. *Diegetic Summary* - The bare report of a speech event. No specification is given of what is said or how it is said. Reported speech of this type is on the same level as the report of any non-verbal event. E.g. "The Fly" (p. 422): His talk was over.

When we now return to the text of "The Fly" and the role and functions of the narrator it will be easy to find some instances of DD in dialogue. The observant reader may also recognise some blocks of FID, in the block of indirect modes, in mimetic terms intermediate between DD and ID and often seen as a miniature reflection of mimesis.

At first sight it may seem strange to attribute to a narrator a role other than his most significant one, that of telling a story; but, in fact, we know by now that there are different ways of telling a story. In order to appreciate the distinctiveness of the Mansfieldian narrator as presented in "The Fly", some possible functions will first be summarised, in accordance with the several aspects of narrative in a broad sense. Some of the functions described may exclude the others. Some may include one another. Only the first one, the narrative function is indispensable.

The different functions described by Bühler, Jakobson and Genette may be distributed according to the different aspects to which they are related. The first narrative aspect is the story and connected with it is the *narrative function*. Obviously, the first function of a narrator is to narrate. Without this primary purpose the narrator will lose his status as a narrator. In the next paragraph this function will be subdivided into other functions.[17]

The second aspect is the narrative text. Connected with it is the *directing function*. When the narrator is organising his text he has to shape and edit the story and decide on its internal organisation. He has to mark articulations, and in general, give 'stage-directions' (e.g. inquit-phrases and sequence-signals) and conclude by pulling the diverse threads together. The directing function determines the different modes of discourse and decides on focalisation and mode of telling: on 'Who says what and how'? As contiguity is the dominant principle here, there is a correlation with the referential function.

The third narrative aspect is connected with the overall narrating situation itself, provided - by positing a narrator addressing a reader - we assume that all narrative is subject to the communication paradigm. The function related to this situation is the *communication function*.[18] The two participants in the narrative communication are the narrator and the narratee (reader), present, absent or implied. If the narrator attempts to establish or maintain a contact with the narratee, there are

103

two possibilities: the contact may be verified by the narrator (Jakobson's phatic function) or the narrator may orientate on the reader (Bühler's conative function).

Connected with the narrative function, another three important functions may be distinguished: the *referential*, the *poetic* and the *expressive*. With the referential function (denotative, cognitive) contiguity is the dominant principle, with the narrator reporting on events and characters, when conveying his information in an objective, neutral manner. If the narrator wants to focus on the message as such, to draw attention to the utterance itself, the referential function no longer rules. If the narrator prefers to focus on the message as such, to adorn the message and write in 'poetic language', then the *poetic function* is dominant. In poetry it is one of the dominant determinative functions, but in a narrative text, it can also be described as a subsidiary or accessory constituent. Since the poetic function increases the tangibility of a linguistic sign by enforcing the fundamental dichotomy between the linguistic signs and the object referred to, the narrator draws attention to the utterance as such, within the narrative text. Two poetic types are said to be dominant within the poetic function: metaphor and metonymy.[19]

Finally, a narrator may prefer to express himself more distinctively, more emphatically, in order to persuade the reader. This draws attention to his attitude towards the message. This function, the *expressive function*, not only emphasises the representation of an emotive (or affective), or equally a moral or intellectual, relationship[20], between the sender and the message (narrator and story), but also indicates, in general, the narrator's attitude towards the content of the message. This function may be recognised by acoustic, grammatical or lexical indexes[21] which may 'season' the text. 'Expressiveness' may include everything that transcends the referential function and particularises the 'overtones', such as emphasis, rhythm, euphony, or evocative elements belonging to a particular register (literary, colloquial, slang etc.) or associated with a particular milieu (historical, foreign, provincial, professional etc.).[22]

With these functions in mind we may proceed to examine the narrator's text in "The Fly", with special reference to the relationship between the referential, expressive and poetic functions. For ease of reference these 'functions of the narrator' are here described in terms of the agent of transmission i.e., the referential, expressive and poetic narrator. The study suggests a purposeful, aesthetic attitude towards the many ways of narrating with a preference for the aesthetic 'why?' over the 'how?' The following terminology will be used and illustrated hereafter:

1. the *narrator* (as the basic concept),
2. the *referential narrator*,

3. the *expressive narrator*,
4. the *poetic narrator*.

The many articles (See bibliography) on "The Fly" have provided an example of how an entire body of criticism can ignore the functions of a narrative technique in a text. Not one of the critics writing about the story, has described the narrator, even though, as it will be suggested, the narrative structure seems the main carrier for the meaning that is presented in the story.

The narrator in "The Fly" seems to have three aims. Firstly, he reports on the events and the two characters in the story, Mr Woodifield and the Boss. During old Woodifield's visit to the Boss, the narrator also describes the fly's struggle in a mirror-text. Secondly, he expresses his feelings, his emotive attitude towards the contents of the story, in order to persuade the reader that the story has a message.[23] Thirdly, whenever possible, he wants to 'transcribe' his message in 'poetic prose'. Here is the first line:

'Y' are very snug in here, piped old Mr Woodifield, and he peered out of the great, green-leather armchair by his friend the boss's desk as a baby peers out of its pram.

We start *in medias res*, and the narrator plunges into the dialogue. All three dominant aims are presented in one utterance: the presentation of the dialogue (DD), the declarative, expressive and poetic verb 'piped', by which the narrator immediately suggests that there is something wrong with Woodifield. He is too frail to speak normally. Woodifield is old, and this is indicated seventeen times. In the utterance 'peered' the expressive narrator dominates again. Woodifield seems too small to perceive. In 'out of the' the referential narrator takes over and for the first time hands over to the poetic narrator. The alliteration in 'great - green' emphasises the utterance. An even better example is provided by the metaphor 'as a baby peers out of its pram'. The poetic narrator enforces the expressive narrator in 'piped', 'old', and 'peered'. The rest of the utterance 'leather armchair (...) by his friend the boss's desk' is presented by the referential narrator again. It is obvious from this example that the narrative functions described here are not mutually exclusive, but may reinforce each other.

In conclusion it may be argued that the referential narrator reveals a simple, preferably concrete reality with a dominant denotative function. He has to report on the event and characters and denote place and time.[24] But he is also the objective observer, the neutral narrator.[25] He may give a quick generalised account, compressing and summarising his information.[26] Contiguity is the dominant principle.[27]

A much more interesting aspect of a narrator's discourse is presented by the functions of the expressive and the poetic narrator's. In this text these are relatively dominant and often mutually dependent.[28] The obtrusive expressive narrator in "The Fly" often takes over from the referential narrator, emerging through and even obtruding upon the referential narrator's text. Comments display the expressive and poetic narrator's ironic subjective truths.[29] The obtrusive expressive narrator seems unwilling to let the characters quite out of his grasp, hovering around them[30], describing them most colourfully in expressive details (verbs and predicates). There is a pseudo-detachment (cf. the extra-diegetic aspect) in this expressive narrator. He seems tolerant and rather easy-going, although the ironic flavour of his comments is marked. He seems to live on a more 'colourful' level than his characters. For with all his poignancy and expressiveness[31], the expressive and poetic narrator may at times disconcert the reader, e.g. when cheating the reader's expectations by detachment, in metaphors[32] and metonymy, by the sudden plunge after the blocked epiphany (to be discussed in the section on FID), and in the relationship with the extra-diegetic or commenting status of the narrator. The reader of "The Fly" perceives the fictional world, as presented here mainly through the eyes of the expressive narrator, assisted by the poetic narrator in figurative or ornamental language using metaphors and similes, metonymy and synechdoche.[33] The narrator's concern for contiguity has made the narrative of "The Fly" essentially metonymic in structure, but the meaning of the narrative may be thought to be stressed by the expressive and poetic narrators, albeit in an off-hand manner. The qualifying and functional poetic descriptions clearly reinforce the meaning of the objects described, by means of which the two characters are contrasted. The poetic narrator not only emphasises the utterance itself, but provides the text with a rich metaphoric texture.

In conclusion, it may be argued that the intrusiveness of the expressive and poetic narrators in "The Fly", with their liveliness, imagination, wit and poignancy, enhances the meaning of the narrative. The preponderance of utterances which express the narrator's attitude towards the contents of the utterance and the focus on the utterances themselves both help to present a subjective view in expressive and poetic language. Mansfield never lets a - sensitive - reader forget the presence of a subjective Impressionist narrator expressing his feelings towards the content of the message presented in the narrative. Our example shows that the narrator intrudes discreetly. His subjective, momentary impression of a scene is indirect, elliptical and expressively suggestive. There is generally considerable subtlety in Mansfield's handling of the expressive narrator, as a subjective intermediary, a means of disguise, and when playing on the different angles of vision in a story. This study of Mansfield's use of an expressive narrator has revealed her experimentation with focalisation and her stress on the relativity of any given perspective.

FREE INDIRECT DISCOURSE

Another means of disguise is the technique of free indirect discourse (FID), which enables the narrator to hide behind his leading character. FID is a compromise between direct discourse (dialogue) and indirect discourse. There are several intricate grammatical consequences which cannot be discussed here; only the general form and the functions will be discussed before going on to illustrate Mansfield's use of FID in her short stories. The text of "The Fly" has been chosen as a foothold, since it presents only one main character and an interesting example of an epiphany, which in Literary Impressionism is such an important structural device.

There is, in general, great subtlety in Mansfield's handling of narrators. The obvious function of a narrator is to describe the scene but, as we have seen, there are various other roles that can be performed. Another more intricate role is to formulate and present the mental activity of - usually - a main character. The presumption is that narrative assertions articulate the thoughts of the character. The methodology of text interference with FID may stress the limitation of a sensory perception and a reduced reliability of interpretation.[34]

The 'subversive' function of FID, when offering active resistance to an interpretive strategy by which we might assign Impressionism to a character's vision, also illustrates Mansfield's inner contradiction between her 'technique of empathy' and impersonality, creating indeterminacy, ambiguity, but most of all Impressionist unreliability. The close identification of the narrator's mind with a character has many unreliable manifestations. One of these is the narrator's insistence in rendering sensory impressions without correction, as in the passage of "The Garden Party" describing Laura going down to the poor men's cottages.

Even in the case of visionary perception, for example, in section I of "Prelude", when Linda wants the world to be upside down, reality only exists in the distorted vision of a character:

How absurd they *looked*! Either they ought to be the other way up, or Lottie and Kezia ought to stand on their heads, too. (p. 11, 12) (Emphasis added)

The scene represents one of the simplest forms of unreliability. It is the projection of concise, raw apprehensive data from the mind of a character. It is also possible for the narrator to render subjective, and evidently unreliable thoughts, as in the case in Section V, when Linda again 'sees' something in her imagination:

How often she had *seen* the tassel fringe of her quilt change into a funny procession of dancers with priests attending .... For there were some tassels that did not dance at all but walked stately, bent forward as if praying or chanting. How often the medicine bottles had turned into a row of little men with brown top-hats on; and the washstand jug had a way of sitting in the basin like a fat bird in a round nest.
(p. 27 - Emphasis added)

There is purely judgmental thought in FID, without any inquit-phrase such as 'she thought', in Linda's perception of her husband Stanley:

For she really was fond of him; she loved and admired and respected him tremendously. Oh, better than anyone else in the world. She knew him through and through. He was the soul of truth and decency, and for all his practical experience he was awfully simple, easily pleased and easily hurt .... If only he wouldn't jump at her so, and bark so loudly, and watch her with such eager, loving eyes. He was too strong for her;
(p. 53, 54)

The result of this mode of unreliable narration in "Prelude" is a continuous pattern of bivocal, ambiguous, sometimes distorted judgements by Linda, faithfully projected and shaped by the narrator.
Apart from Linda's dreams, and fantasies, these imaginary thoughts reveal the extent to which Linda's mind, driven by uncertainty, fear of swelling (imaginary or real) and childbirth, reconstructs the data of reality in order to create a context in which her apathy can be seen in its most positive light.[35] The narrator doesn't suggest the bias of Linda's perception. The reader must supply the countering qualifications of Linda's illusions for himself.

MANSFIELD AND FID

Mansfield did not invent FID[36], contrary to what many critics have asserted, nor was she the first writer to employ the technique of FID in short stories. She did not use it only to express the unreliability of her character's thoughts.

In reviewing Mansfield's short stories, chronologically, it will be shown that she does not always use the technique of FID in presenting the inner thoughts and feelings of her character. She also uses Direct Discourse and fuses FID into Indirect Discourse. After the publication of *In a German Pension* (1911), Mansfield began experimenting with dramatic mime, using a rather expressive, empathetic narrator and FID. Reading Jane Austen, one of the first extensive practitioners of FID in the English language, may have influenced this rather haphazard, non-gradual development.

In "The Tiredness of Rosabel", which Murry claims to have been written as early as 1908, Mansfield introduced FID for the first time, but in 1910, in "The Child-Who-Was-Tired", there is none. In another story also written in 1910, "Frau Brechenmacher Attends a Wedding", there is no FID either, but in 1911 in "A Birthday" we do find the technique, together with DD for the dreams and hallucinations of the main character Andreas Binzer. In "The Woman at the Store" (1911), there is again no FID. In "Something Childish but very Natural", (1913), we find DD for the character's intimate thoughts but FID for the reflexive, more problematic and foreboding thoughts. In 1915 in "The Little Governess" Mansfield employs FID for the first time as a vehicle of epiphany. In "A Dill Pickle" (1917) we find some lines of FID, in which Vera, the main character, expresses her doubts, while in "Prelude", published in 1918, there is FID for Linda and Beryl's dreams and fantasies - FID as a vehicle of stream-of-consciousness, bi- and polyvocality and irony, but not as a vehicle of epiphany. Also in 1918, in "Bliss", we find the ideal sequence of ID, FID and DD, in the presentation of Harry's betrayal. In 1920 in "The Man Without a Temperament", there is hardly any FID. In "The Escape" (1920) we find FID only in the introduction, as a vehicle of irony and stream-of-consciousness. In "Miss Brill", written in the same year, we may find some interesting examples of FID, woven into ID, as a vehicle of empathy and stream-of-consciousness. In "The Daughters of the Late Colonel" (1921) FID is used as a vehicle of empathy, irony and stream-of-consciousness again. In "The Garden Party" we find FID for Laura's most intimate thoughts, though in "The Doll's House", written in 1922, there is hardly any FID.

It is evident that FID functions mainly as a vehicle of empathy, irony, stream-of-consciousness, and of bi- and polyvocality. In the analysis of FID in "The Fly", a new first- order function will be described i.e., FID as a vehicle of epiphany. Let us now examine the text of "The Fly".

Because of the brevity of the short story form, Mansfield rarely marks the transitions from ID into FID very clearly, although occasional formal clues may be found in the immediate context e.g., verbs of speech or thought (declared, told, thought, felt, wondering, thinking), which bear crucially upon the perceptibility of a FID utterance immediately preceding the particular FID utterance. The syntax of FID 'permits' the appearance of otherwise inadmissable emotive material e.g., modal auxiliaries such as 'might' (3x), the non-modal conditional 'could' (2x) and 'would', the adverbials expressing doubt 'perhaps' and the deictics (in demonstrative expressions), e.g., 'that' (3x).

In general, FID resembles ID in person and tense, and DD in not being strictly subordinate to a 'higher' verb of saying/thinking, in the word-order of questions and in the admissibility of colloquialisms, which betray the quality of 'something spoken'. Some examples in "The Fly" of 'something spoken' are: 'every man jack of them down to' (p. 426), 'old Macey' (p. 426), and the 'DD' in FID: 'What indeed' and 'For the life of him'. All utterances of FID in "The Fly" present the gist of the boss's stream-of-consciousness, and retain the boss's own personal idiom.

In section I there is no FID. Information is conveyed mainly by ID and DD. In Sections II, III, IV, when the narrator attempts to build up expectation of a revealing moment, the epiphany, we are presented with the six snatches of FID (Presented here in A, B, C, D, E, F).

A - On p. 426 (Section II)
Other men perhaps might recover, might live their loss down, but not he. How was it possible? His boy was an only son (...)
How on earth could he have slaved, denied himself, kept going all those years without the promise for ever before him of the boy's stepping into his shoes and carrying on where he left off?

B - Also on p. 426 (Still in Section II):
No wonder, he had taken to it marvellously. As to his popularity with the staff, every man jack of them down to old Macey couldn't make enough of the boy. And he wasn't in the least spoilt. No, he was just his bright natural self, with the right word for everybody, with that boyish look and his habit of saying, 'Simply splendid!'.

C - Also on p. 426 (Still in Section II):
Six years ago, six years ... How quickly time passed!
It might have happened yesterday (...)
The boy had never looked like that.
(Mansfield's suspension-points).

D - On p. 417 (Section III):
What would it make of that? What indeed!

110

E - On p. 417 (Still in Section III):
That was the way to tackle things; that was the right spirit.
Never say die; it was only question of ...

F - On p. 428 (Still in Section III):
What was it? It was ...
For the life of him he could not remember.
(Mansfield's suspension-points).

In the sections mentioned above a colourful, empathetic, expressive narrator surrounds and even reinforces FID. The narrator seems to submerge himself in the character of the boss and the reader empathetically lives on with the boss.

In A, the first snatch of FID skilfully presents in a true inner monologue the confusion and unreliability of thought and feeling in the boss's mind, yet it is clearly a reduction made by the narrator in presentating the gist of the matter. FID is introduced here by inverted ID and is interrupted by referential narration.

In B, FID presents in the boss's sentimental reverie, his feelings about his son in hindsight, the sort of phrases that would be characteristic of the boss's DD. Again it is a résumé, necessary to reinforce the boss's opinion of his son on the outside world. It clearly bears the stamp of the narrator. FID now concentrates on the irony of the son's death and evokes the empathy of the reader, by establishing a bond of familiarity between the boss and the reader. The impact of the boss's dreams is more cruel now than it would have been in DD or in ID.

In C, in a final 'résumé', FID guides the reader into the present tense again.

In D, in the episode with the fly, the question raised by the boss is answered by the boss's positive comment in the next FID utterance.

In E, FID presents the boss's mechanical and instinctive reaction against his own process of survival in life. The boss and the fly want to be ready for life again.

In F, the dialogue in DD, in the last paragraph, diverts the reader's attention from the information conveyed by the referential narrator. The FID indices in 'he fell to wondering' and in 'he had been thinking', the expressive narrator in FID, in 'What was it? It was ...', make the reader concentrate on the final possibility of a revelation in the boss's inner argument. In a final attempt to persuade the reader, though indirectly, in 'For the life of him' the expressive narrator in FID conveys the message of the narrative: the boss has managed to forget his son.

Summarising the use of FID in "The Fly", we realise that it serves to reveal the boss's deepest and most confused emotions. FID serves as a vehicle of stream-of-consciousness, as an unreliable manifestation of the boss's thoughts. FID is also naturalised as a mode of empathetic identification with the main character. The narrator empathetically identifies with the boss and the identification cannot but affect the reader's response. The reader is easily and quickly plunged into the boss's inward struggle. FID slips effortlessly in and out of the narrator's ID. FID clearly serves a double purpose here, as it is naturalised as a vehicle of bivocality. There is an ambiguous 'dual voice' speaking. On the one hand it evokes the boss's thoughts, *his* words, *his* tone of voice, *his* vivacity; on the other it embeds the boss's statements in the narrative flow and in the narrator's interpretation, since it remains his view of reality, based on his selection and combination of elements. What is so special in "The Fly" is that the expressive narrator keeps hovering around the boss's FID and that there are only short snatches of FID. It seems that the very exuberance of the expressive, sometimes assisted by the poetic, narrator prevents any lavish development of FID. The narrator has so much creativity that what any of the characters may know or feel or see is slight and small compared with the narrator's vision.

The expressive narrator offers FID its optimal habitat and FID caps here the climax of expressive narration. FID - in contrast to DD - eliminates all quotation-marks, setting it apart from the narration. This self-effacement can be achieved in an environment where the narrative presentation adheres most consistently to a character's perspective.

In the final utterance of FID, in F, 'For the life of him he could not remember', FID has a different, second-order, function. Apart from the structural and thematic relationship with the other FID utterances and with the blocked epiphany, FID serves here as a vehicle of irony. The abrupt negative information in the FID utterance not only serves the irony in the utterance itself but also relates back to the interplay between the other discourses preceding F. The narrator's previous identification finally changes into an ironic distanciation from the boss. The narrator embeds the boss's thoughts in his own narrative flow by selecting and inserting 'For the life of him'. It is irony, presented in an indirect and rather ambiguous form. FID, when presenting the gist of the boss's thoughts, may be considered to frame the structure of the three final sections, FID's paradigmatic function as the narrator's short-hand reproduction of the boss's confused stream-of-consciousness. All the FID utterances, taken together, may be naturalised as a kind of supplemented, explanatory, intensive ordering process. By cutting all the FID utterances from the text, FID can be described as a transposition of the thematic message, at the primary level, in an extremely free and indirect mode of discourse. All the FID utterances together present a miniature version of the boss's confusion, an 'explanatory' mirror-text of the complete text.[37]

The psychological context, in which the final negative epiphany is brought about, is one of puzzlement. Structurally and thematically the final ambiguity of the boss's emotional crisis is built up by many factors. The death of the fly, the whirl of thoughts in the boss's series of FID, his subsequent anguish, the 'bossy' disturbance as presented in the final DD ('Bring me some fresh blotting-paper') by the blockage in his thought in 'It was ...' and the abrupt, neutral, quasi-objective, referential narration in 'He took out his handkerchief and passed it inside his collar'. The contrast is most poignant now, because expressive and poetic narration, in terms of epistemological validity, does not claim to present a complete record of events, whereas referential narration does claim completeness and objectivity. The narrator's shift in attitude, from epiphany to irony, brings about the negative realisation in the final DD utterance ('Bring me some fresh blotting-paper (...) and look sharp about it'). The negative epiphany represented in FID in 'For the life of him he could not remember' shatters the reader's expectation and leaves him frustrated.

Another interesting narrative technique, especially relevant in short stories, and closely related to the technique of FID, is that of 'contamination', or overlap with the expressive narrator's discourse, FID and mixture with DD. Here FID seems to cross the inner and outer boundaries, when, for example a character may reflect *on* the sites and happenings, and at the same time reveal his/her thoughts. In the following passage, from Mansfield's "The Escape", we are plunged into the events by the woman's FID, supplemented by the narrator's ID. This is one of the rare 'longer' passages of FID in Mansfield's stories:

1   It was his fault, wholly and solely his fault, that they
2   had missed the train. What if the idiotic hotel people had
3   refused to produce the bill? Wasn't that simply because he
4   hadn't impressed upon the waiter at lunch that they must
5   have it by two o'clock? Any other man would have sat there
6   and refused to move until they handed it over. But no! His
7   exquisite belief in human nature had allowed him to get up
8   and expect one of those idiots to bring it to their room...
9   And then, when the *voiture* did arrive, while they were still
10   (Oh, heavens!) waiting for change, why hadn't he seen to the
11   arrangement of the boxes so that they could, at least, have
12   started the moment the money had come? Had he expected her
13   to go outside, to stand under the awning in the heat and
14   point with her parasol? Very amusing picture of English

15   domestic life. Even when the driver had been told how fast
16   he had to drive he had paid no attention whatsoever-just
17   smiled. 'Oh!', she groaned, 'if she'd been a driver she
18   couldn't have stopped smiling herself at the absurd,
19   ridiculous way he was urged to hurry.' And she sat back and
20   imitated his voice: 'Allez vite, vite' - and begged the
21   driver's pardon for troubling him ...
22   And then the station - unforgettable - with the sight of the
23   jaunty little train shuffling away and those hideous
24   children waving from the windows. 'Oh, why am I made to
25   bear these things? Why am I exposed to them? ...' The
26   glare, the flies, while they waited, and he and the
27   stationmaster put their heads together over the time-table,
28   trying to find this other train, which, of course, they
29   wouldn't catch. The people who'd gathered round, and the
30   woman who'd held up that baby with that awful, awful head ...
31   'Oh, to care as I care - to feel as I feel, and never to be
32   saved anything - never to know for one moment what it was
33   to ... to ...'
34   Her voice had changed. It was shaking now - crying now.
35   She fumbled with her bag, and produced from its little maw a
36   scented handkerchief.
     (p. 196, 197)

The text gives us the woman's thoughts, perceptions and
interpretations and it simultaneously describes the woman and her
husband's departure from the hotel. Here the function of FID seems
to be to render a character's troubled mind, to narrate a fictional event
and to render the woman's blurred, unreliable perception of her
husband. On closer examination we find that, especially after 'But no'
(l. 6) the text oscillates between FID and an expressive narrator's
discourse. Certainly the initial complaint is the woman's FID, but after
l. 9 the expressive narrator has taken over in order to report the
woman's 'narrated perception' and render the event of departure.[38]

The emotive expressions in 'exquisite', 'idiots' and the deictic
'those', the three dots, which often in a Mansfield text seem necessary
to give the reader some rest in a rather breathless, expressive passage,
are followed by more expressive, emotive utterances. The initial 'And
then', the over-emphasised French word for carriage in 'voiture', the
emphatic 'did', the bracketed interjection in DD ('Oh, heavens'), the
sudden inversion in the question 'Why hadn't he ...', the interjected 'at
least', are followed by another rhetorical question, the woman's
opinionated ironic assertion in 'very amusing picture of English
domestic life', the speculative 'Even' and 'whatsoever' - all express the
woman's nervous impatience and indignation in an expressive

114

narrator's report. It is broken up by direct discourse (l. 17-19), interrupted and followed by more expressive narrator's discourse: 'and then', 'unforgettable'; 'those hideous'; 'the glare', 'this', 'of course', 'that awful, awful', 'never', 'for one moment', 'to ...'. In l. 34 the referential, extra-diegetic narrator takes over in narrator's discourse.

THE EXTRA-DIEGETIC NARRATOR

The narrative mode that Mansfield most often employs is an extra-diegetic one. There is an external narrator, who is not a fictional character but 'narrates' the story, focalising on one (or more) main characters. It is the most objective of the narrative devices which Mansfield used. It is, apart from being the natural expression of Literary Impressionism[39], also the one most consistent with Mansfield's artistic goals.

As already discussed, omniscience is inhospitable to Impressionist ideas. Another technique inimical to Literary Impressionism is narrative intrusion, a device often used to provide background, indicate themes, or offer information beyond the knowledge of the characters. The central mind usually perceives, experiences, thinks, dreams, and nothing else. Mansfield believed that didactic art is fatal. She gave her readers only 'a slice out of life' devoid of any overt moral lesson in it. She tried not to point out, but to let the reader find out for himself. This view has been elaborated on in Chapter 3.

Mansfield's method of obliquity implies that important universal data should be rendered as originating from the story itself. There are not many narrative intrusions or even gratuitous judgements in her stories. Whenever there is an external observation, it bears the imprint of the mentality of a character. (As in "The Fly", when the reporting narrator comments on Old Woodifield's visit (p. 412): All the same, we cling to our last pleasures, as the tree clings to its last leaves).

Here and there, unnecessary narrative intrusions may flaw Mansfield's indirect intentions, as in "The Little Governess"[40], although such intrusions are never serious enough to negate the total oblique effect of the stories. Mansfield often merely describes a character's experience. The limitation of sensory information in the restricted vision provides the implicit epistemological condition in nearly all her work. Each character is limited to his own restricted sensory vision and must base all his actions and conclusions upon the limited, subjective information available.

Mansfield's fiction is nearly always written in accordance with these restricted Impressionist concepts. There is a 'constant interpenetration of sensation and consciousness, and rendition is used to present stimuli to the sensory faculties while point-of-view functions as the translator of sensations into consciousness'.[41] What her fiction loses by narrative restriction it usually gains in intensity. S.L. Weingart has commented in *The Form and Meaning of the Impressionist Novel* (1964) that 'The more limited the point of view, the more intense is the recapitulation of stimuli, wherein lies the strategy of the Impressionist' (p. 26).

Mansfield's fiction abounds in examples of restricted and yet intense narrative perspectives. One of the most dramatic presentations of this method may be found in "Bliss", in which the extra-diegetic narrator largely focuses on and identifies with the main character. In "Bliss" we are given Bertha Young's selected and limited vision as she fails to perceive the true condition into which her marriage has fallen. Being blindfolded by blissful illusion, she pretends to be a semi-intellectual and acts the literary hostess to pseudo-aesthetes. Bertha mistakenly perceives their showy eccentricities as signs of genius.[42] There is no token of friendship, no ultimate sign from Pearl Fulton. Bertha expects and does not receive. She wakes up to the betrayal by her 'special friend' and her husband. Bertha's apprehensive data are always mingled with interpretive distortions. She has the ignorance and lack of perception of a child; she has not matured mentally. The narrator's first indications are given when Bertha feels she cannot express her blissful feelings, in 'It's not what I mean, because-' (p. 92 - 2x). Being ignorant and in her mistaken interpretation of reality she 'knew' that something must happen 'infallibly' (p. 92) in her interpretation of reality. Apprehensive data are mingled with sensory interpretive distortions. Ironically ,her friends are presented as 'very sound'. When Bertha asks Harry, whether Pearl Fulton has something more to offer apart from her mysterious sensuousness, he, of course,in his vulgar, down-to-earth manner, denies it. Bertha, ignorant as she is, does not contradict him, although she does not agree with him; 'not yet, at any rate.' (p. 95). Bertha has very little perception and doesn't know how to judge people and her husband.

Overwhelmed by the scent of the jonquils and the warmth of the room, she decides to take a look at the pear tree. The emphasis is here on Bertha's perception. No clarifying information is introduced. Sensory details increase the vividness of the scene. Of all the guests, the remote and mysterious Pearl Fulton is Bertha's greatest joy. Ignorant and immature, Bertha does not doubt her perceptive faculties for a moment. She really believes that Pearl Fulton will give her some 'sign' (p. 101) of a mysterious 'bond' between them. When Pearl Fulton asks her to see the garden she thinks the sign will finally come. Bertha shows her the flowering pear tree. The two women stand shoulder to shoulder and observe the tree emerging from the darkness:

116

And the two women stood side by side looking at the slender, flowering tree. Although it was so still it seemed, like the flame of a candle, to stretch up, to point, to quiver in the bright air, to grow taller and taller as they gazed - almost to touch the rim of the round, silver moon.

How long did they stand there? Both, as it were, caught in that circle of unearthly light, understanding each other perfectly, creatures of another world, and wondering what they were to do in this one with all this blissful treasure that burned in their bosoms and dropped, in silver flowers, from their hair and hands?

For ever - for a moment? And did Miss Fulton murmur: 'Yes. Just *that*.'Or did Bertha dream it? (p. 102) (Italics KM)

This vague sensory passage does not enlighten the reader as to the nature of the mystic communion; its emphasis is on problems of perception and interpretation: 'it seemed', 'as it were', they are 'wondering'. Visual data become indistinct and even Bertha herself is not sure of the reality of the situation. ('Or did Bertha dream it?'). Early in the story Bertha, in her naive and limited sensory perception, has regarded the flowering pear tree as a 'symbol of her life'. Now, with the desire to possess some mystical bond with Pearl Fulton, she invites Pearl to see into the sanctuary of her blissful mood[43] and her marriage. Ironically, in her naivety, it is Bertha herself who has introduced Pearl Fulton to her husband and urged him to be friendly to her. Her blissful immaturity, her lack of perception, have blinded her to reality. She does not know how to guard her flowering tree, nor her bliss, nor her marriage. Bertha mingles apprehensive data with interpretive distortions. For Bertha, appearances are not deceptive and what Bertha and Pearl have in common is nothing mystic but the love of Harry.

"Bliss" is artistically and ideologically a study in the limitation of mental perception, rendered from the mind of an immature and naive woman. At one of the most critical moments of the story, when Bertha and Pearl Fulton are looking at the pear tree, the reader is not informed of what goes on in either of their minds. Because of the sharply restricted narrative perspective, the reader is - at first - not aware of the incongruent and contradictory thoughts of the two women, or the irony of the situation.

There are many other examples in Mansfield's work of sharply restricted perspectives in an Impressionist mode, where a character's mental constriction of vision demonstrates complex problems with the reception and interpretation of sensory data. In "Miss Brill" it is the main character's lack of self-knowledge, her wealth of self-delusion and her vanity that will shock and hurt her. The selective, sharply restricted narrative perspective in "Miss Brill" involves the limited intelligence of one main character. The confrontation of reality and Miss Brill's perceptual blindness spells the character's downfall. At the end of the story she is an enlightened, though sadder person.

Miss Brill's awareness[44] hovers on the borderline between knowledge and ignorance; she is not completely unaware of her true condition, but her sense of vanity sways her to the side of ignorance and self-delusion.[45] Miss Brill's reality is that she is single, middle-aged and lonely. She talks to herself and to the dead fur. The narrator expresses Miss Brill's moment of awareness, her epiphany, without correction or compensation. The effect is one of psychological immediacy, uncluttered by expository intrusions. The subjective presentation of the sensory and interpretive experience of a character is delimited and unreliable. The obvious implication of the narrative projection of data from the mind of a character, without any compensatory comment by the narrator, is the potential for unreliable assertions. This is, in fact, the standard fictional situation in most of Mansfield's short stories. We find it in "Prelude" and "At the Bay", where the narrator restricts access to narrative information to the mind of some characters, to their sensory apprehensions and associated thoughts and feelings.

In typical Impressionist manner, the characters' experiences are discontinuous and fragmented and result in short stories composed of brief units. These scenes do not always relate directly to juxtaposed episodes, nor do they always develop the same themes. The different characters' views of reality, of life around them, are limited, one more than the other. The children, in their innocence, cannot interpret the events around them. The adults distort and transform the data they receive. In short, their views of things are limited, highly individual, unreliable and, to a greater or lesser degree, subjectively distorted. Yet a momentary projection of the working of their minds becomes a dramatically Impressionist depiction of how life may appear to an ordinary family.

No reading of Mansfield's work can be complete without dealing with the significance of perception in these works as both a methodological and thematic component. In this sense, the narrative method of "Prelude" and "At the Bay" is a rendering of the various characters' apprehension and their thoughts. The capacity to *see* themselves more clearly in their lives presents the unifying and informing theme.

PARALLAX : RESTRICTION AND IRONY

Beyond these narrative methodologies, there are a few other strategies that may play a role in individual scenes. One of them is narrative irony, which is present in Mansfield's fiction from the first. In the *In A German Pension* stories, and even in "In a Café",written at the age of nineteen, one of the most remarkable qualities is the ironic perspective.

Naive and sensory perspectives have a propensity for error. Characters in Mansfield's stories often continue to believe things in the face of direct experience. One method involves narrative qualification, when some character or a scene is described as 'it seems'. On other occasions with typical Impressionist restrictions, the narrator may present erroneous interpretations without narrative judgement.

This essentially is Mansfield's method of narrative irony. In "The Daughters of the Late Colonel" the irony is not so much the product of events, or the conversations and thoughts the two daughters have, but the manner in which these events, conversations, and thoughts are viewed by the characters. The narrator projects the distorted 'non-judgements' of the characters without qualification. The irony is generated by the reader's progressive awareness that these views are subjective and unreliable. The two subjective perspectives are ironically contrasted with each other throughout the twelve fragments of the story.[46]

Although not so ubiquitous as pure narrative irony at an extra-diegetic level, this narrative method is often used by Mansfield with a thematic function, when she subtly contrasts the different perspectives. This device is called narrational 'parallax', i.e. the device of rendering the story from more than one point of view in variable parallactic focalisation[47]. The opportunities for variation on the parallactic method are numerous. They centre on two basic patterns: the juxtaposition of two or more restricted perspectives, and the contrasting of a restricted perspective with that of an extra-diegetic or omnipresent narrator. Other variations may include first-person perspectives recorded at different times, as for example, in "Poison".

The underlying characteristic of this method is the relativistic philosophy that reality is a function of perspective. How a given event or situation is perceived is qualified by the age, intelligence, mood, angle of vision etc. of the viewer. When a scene is narrated from contrasting perspectives this will reveal not only a greater complexity of reality for the reader, but reveal also contrasting views, values and thoughts of the perceivers as well. That Mansfield used various multiple perspectives in many of her works has not been an obscure point in Mansfieldian scholarship, although the implications of the device have not yet been fully explored. Most critics relate the device to subject-matter or characterisation in isolation or describe it merely as 'an experiment' not fitting in with a 'symbolist' account of her development.[48]

Mansfield's ironic use of parallax to suggest that man's experience of the world is multifaceted also marks the particular modulation into a selective, restricted perspective, which is Impressionistic in concept. She employs this technique haphazardly, beginning with "How Pearl Button was Kidnapped" (1910) and ending with "Miss Brill" (1920). There is no consistent development. The method depends on a single device: the restricting of the perspective and knowledge of a focaliser-character into a broadening, more objective narrator's one. He is not emotionally detached from the scene, but capable of perceiving it from a great distance. It often involves an initiation, a sudden awareness or enlightenment (epiphany) of some profound significance. The imposition of narrative distance on a scene of intense emotional concern on the part of the participant(s) creates an irony of perspective which often suggests the isolation of individual human beings, their lack of consequence in the universal flux of life, their diminutive significance as seen from a superior vantage point and their defiant private inflation of the significance of their own lives and the events that surround them. One of the best examples of this method can be found in "The Little Governess", where the nameless, inexperienced young governess is made aware of her fellow-travellers, of herself, and reality outside her. At the end of the story she is isolated from everyone because of her own inconsistent behaviour. She feels hopelessly insignificant and deflated by events.

"Miss Brill", as we have seen, also employs ironic narrative juxtaposition, contrasting Miss Brill's preoccupation with a detached narrator's perspective. Miss Brill's search for knowledge is involuntary and, for better or worse, she is momentarily forced to quit her shell of self-delusion. The narrator first elevates the character to the pinnacle of comfortable delusion, by means of fantasies, dreams or distorted visions and then throws him/her into deep despair. The narrator, extra-diegetic and detached, leaves Miss Brill heart-broken at the end.

Mansfield often follows this formula of ironic narrational parallax. It is in the narrative juxtaposition of perspectives that Mansfield's basically Impressionist achievement lies. The method may be seen as the fundamental source of Mansfield's irony. Mansfield's view of reality is ephemeral and evanescent, constantly shifting its meaning and continually defying precise definition.

A congruence can be established between the ontological assumptions underlying Mansfield's fiction and the device of narrational parallax, when narrating from more than one perspective. As many critics have agreed the stories in narrational parallax are her greatest. They attempt to epitomise the complicated and multifarious world within a narrow space from a variety of positions in order to create an image of an Impressionist atomistic modern world.

Apart from the juxtapositional parallactic method of using more than two perspectives, the stories "Psychology" and "The Daughters of the Late Colonel" are worth mentioning, because here only two equally important perspectives are contrasted with each other and sometimes even combined into a hazy, oblique one.[49] The contrasting or juxtaposed perspectives are often roughly similar in their degree of limitation and reliability. In "Prelude" and "At the Bay", Linda's and Beryl's visions are both deluded, in their fantasies and distorted views, although they themselves regard their visions as invested with superior wisdom or social or marital respectability. No perspective is authentic or authoritative, but through the narrator's ironic modulation between various contradictory perspectives the image of the world is confused and blurred.

The world is depicted as fragmentary, momentary. It lacks a centre. The narrator is merely a medium through which reality flows into words. Mansfield's ironic use of juxtaposition and contrast suggests that man's experience of the world is multi-faceted and that is what marks this particular modulation as Impressionist in concept. In "At the Bay", ironic narrative juxtaposition is employed, contrasting the preoccupations of the different characters, Kezia, Beryl, Linda, Mrs Fairfield, Stanley, and Jonathan with the minor ones. Juxtaposed to their restricted views are the narrative intrusions, the detached philosophical and pastoral framing by the narrator, and occasional general narrative comments. As Yen has argued:

the author's intention is not to focus the material in a certain single character and thus achieve unity of vision. She centers the material upon all characters and thus obtains a number of visions which exist not in a hierarchy but in an anarchy. The very sectioning of the stories indicates the author's intentions of avoiding characterization. Each section is a piece of coloured glass, and all the pieces exist together not in subordination but in juxtaposition. Out of each piece comes a shaft of light, the point of view of a character. (p. 195)

The effect of these 'shafts of light' by means of 'the coloured glass' suggest the different moments of great intensity, varying in significance according to the perspective from which they are seen. The reader is led to consider the preoccupations of the different characters, sometimes from both an oblique abstract view and sometimes from one which identifies closely with the characters' situations. This is one of the impersonal and objective ways in which Mansfield was able to reconcile intrusive narratorial passages with the restrictive assumptions of Literary Impressionism.

Perhaps nowhere else is Mansfield's use of a juxtapositional

121

parallactic method as clearly illustrated as in "At the Bay". Here we have a stringent control of various narrative perspectives.[50] There is a swift juxtaposition of scenes, with a frequent use of terse dialogue, an almost total adherence to extra-diegetic narrative distance, which, together with the use of unusual images, conveys the incredibility of man's plight in an indifferent universe. Mansfield's use of narrative parallax as an Impressionist method reveals her experimentation with point of view and her stress on the relativity of perspective.

THE HOMO-DIEGETIC NARRATOR

Relatively few works are written in the homo-diegetic method and they often manipulate access to fictive data in an Impressionist manner. One of the most revealing works is "Je ne Parle Pas Francais", a written rather than spoken dramatic monologue, with its ironic revelations of a distorted personality. The character's opinion of himself is often inconsistent with his perverse revelations. His dark, perturbed soul is clearly revealed in the tonal urgency, for example, in the last sentence where assertive words are heavily stressed and repeatedly punctuated in order to create an atmosphere of despair. The fox-terrier, Duquette, the homo-diegetic narrator, constantly attempts to detach himself from his emotions, which he reveals in momentary, lyrical and poetic fragments. Duquette's slow transformation in outlook - the indirect awakening of his conscience - is shaped around the revelation springing from a cued moment or 'geste'. It is a direct measure of his inner change, his slowly developed epiphany. Despite his own assertions to the contrary, Duquette is unable to distinguish between his own fictional illusions and reality.[51] He cannot communicate normally with himself and his memories are vaguely inconsistent. He affirms his distortions in a series of misunderstandings and blurred communications.

"Je ne Parle Pas Francais" is a carefully framed anecdote, though framed by a distorted narrator and displayed in fractured misalignment. Duquette, one of the major Literary Impressionist homo-diegetic narrators in Mansfield's work, reveals his distorted, sensory vision as follows:

How can one look the part and not be the part? Or be the part and not look it? Isn't looking - being? Or being - looking? At any rate who is to say that it is not (...) (p. 75)

For Duquette the surrounding world is not well ordered. In his conceit and in his blurred perception he creates an indistinct and distorted picture of and around himself, made up of confused and irresistible impressions. Human experience for him is fragmented; even the human soul is taken to pieces. Here is Duquette's vision of people:

> I don't believe in the human soul, I never have. I believe that people are like portmanteaux - packed with certain things, started going, thrown about, tossed away, dumped down, lost and found, half emptied suddenly, or squeezed fatter than ever, until finally the Ultimate Porter swings them on to the Ultimate Train and away they rattle ... (p. 60)

All his distorted expressions are referred to as being his own. There are only a few comments of compensatory interpretation. For example, when confessing indirectly that he doesn't grasp the meaning of his awakening in the dirty café, he says: 'Life seems to be opposed to granting you these entrances, seems indeed to be engaged in snatching them from you and making them impossible, keeping you in the wings until it is too late, in fact (...)' (p. 62). For Duquette, life is a flood of ever changing, distorted impressions, which can be grasped only intuitively:

> When a thing's gone, it's gone. It's over and done with. Let it go then! Ignore it, and comfort yourself, (...) with the thought that you never do recover the same thing that you lose. It's always a new thing. The moment it leaves you it's changed. Why, that's even true of a hat you chase after; And I don't mean superficially - I mean profoundly speaking .... I've made it a rule of my life never to regret and never to look back. Regret is an appalling waste of energy (...) You can't get it into shape; you can't build on it; it's only good for wallowing in. (p. 65)

Occasionally - most indirectly - Duquette's ratiocinatory remarks reveal his limited perception. For example, his repeated ironical intrusions, in which he attempts to confirm to the reader the accuracy of his statements 'I feel sure of that' (p. 65); 'But no, that was real!' (p. 69); 'How profound those (Dick's) songs are !' (p. 70). When seeing Mouse for the first time, Duquette imagines her to be Dick's mother. Also Dick has changed according to Duquette. (p. 77) But in Duquette's vision, he confesses that Mouse must be very beautiful, as far as he can make her out in the dark in the 'occasional flashing glimpses'. Duquette, an author, who is going to make a name as a writer about the submerged woıld, most clearly and ironically reveals himself in the titles of his books: *False Coins, Wrong Doors*, and *Left Umbrellas*. (pp. 67, 71, 78). "Je ne Parle Pas Francais" is a most effective story that demonstrates one of the ways in which Mansfield could adapt a homo-diegetic narrator to the needs of distorted perception and indirect revelation of identity.

When facing the problem of interpreting reality, the other homo-diegetic narrators, in "The Woman at the Store", "An Indiscreet Journey", "Late at night", "The Lady's Maid" and "The Canary" are not given such a complex development. Many of these stories manipulate access to fictive data in an Impressionistic manner, as one of them, the incomplete, but most interesting, "A Married Man's Story", will reveal.

In this uniquely Impressionist story the homo-diegetic narrator is also unaware of the limitations of his impaired vision and of the significance of these constraints. The story has not received a great deal of critical attention, but it seems of no little import in assessing Mansfield's consciousness of the technique of a homo-diegetic narrator as an impaired, distorted perceiver of his own life and the world around him. Mansfield's homo-diegetic narrators often live in a condition of flux and development, changing subtly as they move through the psychological experience at the core of the story. Mansfield's narrator in "A Married Man's Story" is essentially congruent with the basic concepts of Literary Impressionism. His narrative method is fragmentary, parallactic, seemingly objective, dramatic and indirectly suggestive. He seems to be plunged into a world beyond his comprehension and his sensations provide an inductive means to knowledge. Mansfield shows how the anonymous married man is conditioned by his social environment and is ultimately prone to distortion and misinterpretation. In a sense, Mansfield's homo-diegetic narrative stories are finally character-studies: narratives in which the psychology of an individual personality and the way in which it perceives reality is the central issue.

"A Married Man's Story" is written in a form of interior monologue, ironically revealing the distorted personality of an anonymous man, whose mother has been murdered by his father. The narrative concentrates on the unconscious and most indirect revelations of his mind, all rendered by a homo-diegetic narrator, who is often revealing the psychological central issues of Literary Impressionism in general: 'Who am I?' and 'What is happening now?' (p. 444, 447), and through his own uncertainty, his restricted and blurred view, demonstrating his fallibility as a narrator. The narrator-focaliser is an adult married man, presenting what is focalised, his youth and his blurred views of the world, from within, through the filter of his own feelings and thoughts. His knowledge is by definition restricted, as he himself is part of the world represented. He cannot know everything about his youth, and he certainly does not. Everything is blurred in his deranged vision of himself and the world around him:

(...) and beyond the fence, the gleaming road with the two hoarse little gutters singing against each other, and the wavering reflections of the lamps, like fishes' tails. While I am here, I am there, lifting my face to the dim sky, and it seems to me it must be raining all over the world - that the whole world is drenched, is sounding with a soft, quick patter or hard, steady drumming, or gurgling and something that is like sobbing and laughing mingled together, and that light, playful splashing that is of water falling into still lakes and flowing rivers. And all at one and the same moment I am arriving in a strange city, slipping under the hood of the cab while the driver whips the cover off the breathing horse, (...) (p. 433)

Language seems too complex as a means of expression to reveal all his emotions:

That about the wolves won't do. Curious! Before I wrote it down, while it was still in my head, I was delighted with it. It seemed to express, and more, to suggest, just what I wanted to say. But written, I can smell the falseness immediately and the ... source of the smell is in that word fleet.
(p. 438)

Tell me! Tell me! Why is it so difficult to write simply - and not simply only but *sotto voce* if you know what I mean? That is how I long to write. No fine effects - no bravura. But just the plain truth, as only a liar can tell it. (p. 438) (Italics KM)

The disparity between illusion and reality cannot be solved. There remain far too many questions, raised and answered by himself, the answers breeding new questions. Forty-five questions are raised in the course of the narrative. The narrator cannot answer them all, although he tries hard. He feels restricted in his solipsism, limited by his own subjective impressions:

this sensation (yes, it is even a sensation) of how extraordinarily *shell-like* we are as we are - little creatures, peering c᷉ ᷉ of the sentry-box at the gate, ogling through our glass case at the entry, wan little servants, who never can say for certain, even, if the master is out or in .... (p. 437) (Italics KM)

The narrator's experience is fragmented into the eight sections of the story. In Impressionist terms, these fragments *are* his experience. The narrator's first image of momentary glances are vague and indistinct in his unreliable account. Most of the time he leaves it to the reader to create a coherent and meaningful picture out of his memories and experiences. He often addresses the reader directly, posing his many questions, constantly wondering about the concept of experience itself, as a valid external touchstone or point of reference for the reader and the narrator.[52] The communication of experience, as he attempts to discover his own identity, is severed by himself, in his preference for being shell-like, solipsistic, and bottled up. Not answering his wife's repeated and important questions, he escapes into his Impressionist dreams, full of blurred, flowing synaesthetic and concatenated images, as in the passage quoted above. (p. 433) At the same time the narrator wants to confront the 'everyday little lies' he formulates himself, with his own subjective truth:

The Truth is, that though one might suspect her of strong maternal feelings, my wife doesn't seem to me the type of woman who bears children in her own body. There's an immense difference! (...) She hasn't the sign of it.
(pp. 434-435)

Paradoxically portraying his wife 'as an aunt and not a mother' immediately after her first appearance as 'an immense *mother and child* (p. 433) (Italics KM) at the beginning of the story, he immediately adds: 'But of course I may be wrong'. After his long meditation on his wife and on marriage, he exclaims again: 'But I don't know, I don't know' (p. 437). Commenting on his own writing, he confesses again that he cannot express what he feels: 'I can smell the falseness immediately (...)' (p. 438), as he is continually poised on the knife-edge between his truthfulness of impression and the danger of slickness or falseness. He is playing with his subjective, blurred impressions, memories and fantasies, though he wants to express 'everything, everything' - 'but how?' The first set of images he creates is often rejected as unsatisfactory, because it conveys only 'the traces of my feeling'. He introduces a new set: 'Yes, perhaps that is nearer what I mean'. (p. 434) The narrator realises that even the most direct feelings cannot be expressed with simplicity, they require careful and patient manipulation. The secret bonds of marriage cannot be expressed either, as 'they can't disclose it even if they want to' (p. 436).

The narrator faces cognitive problems, which are also revealed indirectly. The way in which the narrator apprehends reality around him, when describing his quest for identity, closely approximates to common human experience. His portrait of himself contains all the distortions, reactions and limitations which are needed to make him seem 'real'. The homo-diegetic narrator is revealing his thoughts. Because of the restriction of narrative data the narrator must adopt a stance in which he seems to have no prior knowledge of himself. We do not know his name, only his nickname, given to him by his pestering classmates: 'Gregory Powder', a descriptive epithet which also has a thematic function.[53]

If the virtue of an Impressionist narrator is 'objectivity', its weakness is a limitation of scope. Consistent with the Impressionist tendencies in Mansfield's first-person narrator, 'Gregory Powder' is a common, limited, homo-diegetic narrator, active as a formulator of his own blurred visions, and thereby distorting his own limited experience. He conforms to his limited views and reconstructs them on the basis of fantasies, dreams and fears. In a sense the most distorted recorder of sensations, like the narrator of this story, makes the best Literary Impressionist narrator: when focusing on the process of interpreting the past and his presence, revealing the sensory limitations; when grappling with his reality, his confusion and distortion. An Impressionist approach to the unreliable narrator reveals a great deal about his blurred visions. In Section I, trying to escape from the present moment, although his window is blinded by shutters (p. 433), he is slipping under the hood of the cab (p. 433), and it is raining, so that he cannot see very clearly. He, nevertheless, imagines himself travelling outside. He is rushing through the world by land and by sea. In the same section his initial vision of his wife in the *mother and child* image is contrasted with his later puzzling, distorted 'truthful' vision, where he describes his wife in the kitchen, even though he is not there. He cannot see her, but imagines her 'standing in the middle of the kitchen' (p. 435).

In Section II, when his wife has apparently brought him some tea, he describes his own visionary youthful experience as 'Dimly- dimly-' and confesses: 'or so it has seemed to me' and 'I don't know, I don't know'. Solipsistically , sensationally, and shell-like, when 'peering out of the sentry-box', he 'never can say for certain, even, if the master is out or in' (p. 437).

At the end of Section II he can't see properly either, as 'Every line, every fold breathes fatigue. The mirror is quenched; the ash whitens; only my sly lamp burns on.'(p. 438) In this section the same unreliability is illustrated when he is brooding over his wife's eyes. He shakes off any responsibility for these 'trustful, bewildered eyes (...) like the eyes of a cow that is being driven along the road.' It must be her 'natural expression' because, in his distorted impression, his wife's eyes were just the same when she was a girl at school, on 'a little old photograph.'

In Section V he still believes that his wife and he were an ideally suited pair. Describing his father as he appears in his impaired memory, the disparity between his view of reality and illusion is quite evident. He is once again a tiny little boy, as he visualises his father, when 'the stair-rail was higher than my head' and he 'peered through'. Through the multi-coloured glass he sees his father. His 'bold head was scarlet, then it was yellow' and he dreams that he was 'living inside one of father's big coloured bottles' (p. 440).

Describing this last memory of his mother alive, he perceives her, staring out of the window at brightly coloured circus figures. Though affirming to the reader that his vague image of the murder episode 'has remained solid in his memory', he reveals his impaired childlike vision of his father: 'I stared (...) so long that' he is cut off at the waist by the counter'. The 'five-penny pick-me-up', too, the little glass of bluish stuff sold by his father the chemist, remains for him a mysterious concoction: 'God knows what it was made of'. Just as his memory is blurred and distorted, so is his vision of the outside world and of himself. He is, truly living in a bottle, and in a fragmented existence. His bottled world is of his father's making. He feels now and again 'like a plant in a cupboard', 'when the sun shone, a careless hand thrust me out on the window-sill, and a careless hand whipped me in again - and that was all.' That is why, he prefers the dark (p. 443). He confesses that he doesn't remember 'everything' about his childhood very clearly: 'Do you remember your childhood? ... I certainly don't. The dark stretches, the blanks, are much bigger than the bright glimpses.' (p. 442)

He gives away the greatest clue to his unreliability. He wonders about 'what happened in the darkness' and cherishes his not overtly concrete but crumbled recollections 'the star-shaped flake of soot on a leaf of the poor-looking plant', the dead bird put in his pocket by his classmates, his father's pestle, and his mother's cushion with 'Sweet Repose' sewn on it (p. 443). These recollections are as few and restricted as is his vision of his mother's death, an 'episode' revealed in Section III. It is a 'puzzling' scene and he writes: 'I know no more than I did then, whether I dreamed them or whether they really occurred'. He was only thirteen at the time, and fast asleep when his mother came into his room and 'whispered to him' that his father had poisoned her. And 'I said, or think I said, is that you Mother?' When seeing her in the moonlight and seeing 'how queer she looked', he confesses: 'I think she smiled' and 'I thought I heard the door shut' (p. 444) and 'everything became confused'. 'Did that visit happen? Was it a dream? Why did she come to tell me? And her expression ... was that real? I believed it fully the afternoon of the funeral.'(p. 445) He begins imagining his father in the shape of a big black bottle, with 'Deadly Poison' on it, and from now on names his father 'DP' (Section VI). He fantasises about the only bond he has, with the moon, and the 'green star' and 'the sly creeper' (p. 446). In a final revealing image he 'breaks off' the white peaks of wax that rose above the wall and floated them on 'his lake of memories'. He sees everything anew, though still in his blurred visionary images: 'I saw it all, but not as I had seen before' in his own bottled-up, cupboard-like, little world.

Imaginative data have replaced sensory data with a clarity that make Gregory Powder resolve to accept his solipsism, because he feels 'accepted and claimed' (p. 447). He now confesses that he has never known the world and the reader realises that he will never know it. His subjective reality is still a function of interpretation for him, within his own mind. Analysed perception is subject to the distortions of his memory and fantasy.

The Literary Impressionist emphasis on the narrator's mood is manifested by the descriptions of the total atmosphere around the narrator, contrasting the initial 'Stimmung' in Section I, when describing his wife and child at the fireside, with the later cold, dark, lonely mood when the narrator at the end of his extended period of retrospection returns from the past to a perceived and new present. This contrast is also underlined by the use of differing sentence length. The bulk of the narrator's emotional crisis is expressed in very short sentences, while, fewer but very striking extraordinarily lengthy ones, are used in the presentation of nostalgic moods. The very short sentences create an impression, a 'Stimmung', in which the narrator seems to be discursive, quizzical and desperate. He stops himself on every utterance, scrutinises his mind, tortures himself with his own deficiencies and thereby questions his own authenticity and identity. Here, as elsewhere in Mansfield's work, human comprehension is shown as subject to error and distortion. The main character's analysed perception is subject to distortion of memory.

In conclusion, the diversity of Mansfield's narrative methods has suggested experimentation with a variety of modes. As an exploration of the narrative methods of her short stories has revealed, she rarely employed any of her strategies with absolute consistency and artistic integrity. Although she started off with traditional first-person methods, the overall tendency throughout her work is to restrict sources of information, and to create juxtapositions of points of view, so ironically suggesting that the interpretations of the principal character(s) may be limited and erroneous. Mansfield's subjective intensity often requires the rendition of a sharp, expressive narrator, in relatively brief momentary fragments of sensation, and numerous atmospheric episodes full of 'Stimmung'. A single episode will often be opened in *in medias res*, either in DD or ID or in a sensory descriptive passage, often rendered before the narrator moves into the main narrative in which he records dialogue, describes some action and the thoughts from within the scene. In the process, the narrative perspective often becomes identified with the mind of a single character, resulting in an immediate apprehensional awareness of the fictional world of the character. On a more immediate level, it is evident that Mansfield was able to achieve the illusion of a sensory reality being apprehended by a character. There is, however, a point on the continuum of Impressionist narrative modulation at which the narrative mind becomes so closely identified with the mind of a character, often in FID, as to begin recording the flow of thought without any apparent reformulation by the narrator. In this centrifugal process outlines become hazy and blurred, blending narrator and character into a single oblique angle of vision.

The restriction to a third-person identification with the mind of a character reveals the extent to which individual human beings may only partly comprehend fragmentary truths about the world around them, may delude themselves about their restricted knowledge, and may therefore live with a continuous matrix of illusion, distortion or self-serving reconstructions of empirical data.

Mansfield's narrative methodology, as suggested for example by "At the Bay", is to present an Impressionist epistemology of a world in which the appearance of reality is constantly in flux, in a kinetic world of light and shadow, of sensory multiplicity, of confusion and uncertainty. The reader's mind is usually exposed first to the narrator and then, as the narrator's perspective is fused with that of a character, identified with that character and drawn into perspective. The resultant emphasis is on a psychological reality rather than external reality itself.

Mansfield's narrative methods are a good deal more complex than has generally been assumed, especially by those readers who have regarded the narrators of her works as Mansfield herself, and by those readers and critics who have focused on thematic issues only. Narrative restriction, limitations on sensory data, distorted interpretations, modulations among differing perspectives, these are Mansfield's basic methods of presentation in her best works. Her narrative methods are diverse, suggestive of a formulation of human reality remarkably modern and existential for the 1915s, and fundamental to the central ideas and aesthetics of Literary Impressionism.

Mansfield writes of childhood joys, fears of adolescent pleasures and pains, of adult aspirations and frustrations and of the memories and final knowledge of the aged. Her short stories often suggest a situation in which, in the end, the individual is basically alone and insignificant. Characters are usually unable to comprehend much beyond their own personal world, however beautiful the natural surroundings and its 'Stimmung' and however strong the impulse to resist a passive outlook upon life. From this perspective, a character's view of life is necessarily subjective, solipsistic, tentative and qualified by preoccupation. As a result, Mansfield's reality is arbitrary, fragmentary, momentary, ambivalent, and complex.

As the epistemological nature of Mansfield's narrative methods suggests, her truth is elusive and transient, and the search for truth is likely to yield only flashes of insight. Viewing 'truth' or reality from several angles may enhance the verisimilitude of the picture of life without resolving the isolation and restriction of each of the viewers. Isolation, delusion, cognitive restrictions, fantasies, hallucinations, dreams and fears and the difficulties of apprehensive youth all qualify and restrict the potential for knowledge and thereby for thematic clarity. Therefore, it is argued, if the restrictive, ironic and selective 'parallactic'[1] method is Mansfield's fundamental mode, then the underlying meaning, the sum of thematic motifs resides in Impressionist ideas.

One of the first critics of Mansfield's work, H.E. Bates, criticised her for writing monotonous stories, with repetitive characters and situations.[2] The statements made by later critics belie this charge.[3] Sylvia Berkman argues that 'it is often difficult to define a precise theme in her stories'. She concludes that Mansfield's themes are essentially those of the writers of her generation: 'a preoccupation with loneliness and frustration, with sexual maladjustment, with purposeless suffering, with the falseness, ostentation and sterility of modern sophisticated life, with denial of emotional fulfilment to all classes of men. Put this broadly, this statement comprehends the early thematic substance of T.S. Eliot. Again, implicit in her work, appearing and disappearing like a winding thread, is a dispersed expression of the great Proustian theme: that in the shift and flux of time, through the invasion of other values, other demands, other interests, no human relationship remains unchanged; at the moment of its consummation it is being altered, to be lost until reanimated from the past.' The total pattern, she writes, 'emerges as a dichotomy'.[4] Another later critic, S. Daly, makes a, rather limited, list of recurrent subjects: 'isolated women, overbearing businessmen, fathers, adolescents'.[5]

However, a variety of more or less direct themes, which persist in her work over time, may now be listed. The first is expressed in her distaste of bourgeois life. From the Decadent influence she inherited a tradition of hatred for the stuffier sides of Victorian and Edwardian life.[6] Mansfield's criticism is also directed at several other recurrent targets, for example, the (German) greedy preoccupation with food[7] or, especially in the earlier stories, a stuffy, stereotyped ideal of domesticity, man-chasing, admiration for numbers of babies, the work-a-day aspects of marriage, the terrors involved in childbirth and a sort of prurient glory in the sexual side of marriage.[8] The family circle, too, is almost always presented unfavourably. Some are accorded a gross, satirical treatment, while others, like the Brechenmachers or the family in "The Child Who Was Tired", are presented directly and harshly.[9] This critical attitude lingers, but is somewhat modified in "A Picnic" (1917). Another characteristic is her attitude towards childbirth. The Frau's pregnancy in "The Child Who Was Tired" is made to seem repulsive.[10] In *The Aloe*, "Prelude" and "At the Bay" a critical attitude can be found in Linda's combined hatred for her husband and her family and her fear of childbirth. But here Mansfield's treatment of the theme is different: there is no touch of satire or innuendo.[11] Other targets, particularly in the early German stories, are sycophancy and chauvinism.[12]

Mansfield's second theme - the one for which she is best known - is the world of the child, presented in stories mainly after 1915. In the later children stories there is no bitterness, no criticism. "Her First Ball", "The Voyage", "At the Bay", "The Garden Party", "The Doll's House", "The Young Girl" and "Taking the Veil" are all presented sympathetically, with a touch of humour.

A third theme Mansfield often dealt with might be termed 'the wish for individuality' - in the complex varying relationships between individuals in marriage or in friendship.[13] In love, as Mansfield has it, there are countless pitfalls. There is emotional variability in "The Swing of the Pendulum", "Psychology", "Taking the Veil" and "The Singing Lesson".[14] The fourth theme, related to the third one, dealt with a stress on a solitary, spiritual life. It is the solitude of the lonely that is presented.[15]

Mansfield's fifth theme, the one to which her critics mostly refer, is often summed up by the phrase 'the snail underneath the leaf', by which she meant the corruption of the world, or 'The Ugliness of Life'. To Murry she described the theme in her so-called 'kick offs':

I've two 'kick offs' in the writing game. *One* is joy - real joy - (...) and that sort of writing I could only do in just that state of being in some perfectly blissful way *at peace*. Then something

132

delicate and lovely seems to open before my eyes, like a flower without thought of a frost or a cold breath - knowing that all about it is warm and tender and 'ready'. And *that* I try, ever so humbly, to express.

The other 'kick off' is my old original one, and (had I not known love) it would have been my all. Not hate or destruction (both are beneath contempt as real motives) but an *extremely* deep sense of hopelessness, of everything doomed to disaster, almost wilfully, stupidly, like the almond tree and 'pas de nougat pour le noel'. There! as I took out a cigarette paper I got it exactly - *a cry against corruption* - that is absolutely the nail on the head. Not a protest - a *cry*, and I mean corruption in the widest sense of the word, of course.[16] (Italics KM)

By the widest sense she meant all that is evil, all that betrays beauty and goodness. The image of snails often crops up in her stories, and is usually connected with unpleasantness.[17] In many of the *In a German Pension* stories she attacked varieties of corruption or 'corrupt' individuals.[18]

Among the most frequent varieties of corruption was the theme of betrayal, either of others or of oneself.[19] The betrayal of others is dealt with, directly and indirectly. In "The Little Governess" the waiter at the hotel destroys the character's chances of getting the job, in "Bliss" Miss Fulton betrays Bertha's love, and the boy and the girl in the park ridicule Miss Brill's illusion. 'The Snail under the Leaf' theme also has a more general aspect in its emphasis on the evil of the universe, the basic cruelty of life, as a part of the general make-up of humanity. In the later stories, the handling of theme grows darker and more despairing.[20]

Related with the 'snail under the leaf' theme is the sixth one, the juxtaposition of life with death.[21] In *The Aloe* and "Prelude" it is dealt with among other issues. From early 1920 onwards the death theme is either directly or indirectly present in many of her greatest stories.[22] Connected with the latter theme we detected another one: Time, its flight and brevity and the nostalgia of distance in time.[23] It is especially after 1917 that Mansfield attempted to crystallise her feeling of nostalgia for New Zealand, in which the memory of her people and her country combines the sorrow of separation with a mixture of joy and beauty.[24]

Finally, Mansfield's greatest, most universal theme is that dealing with 'the question of life'. In her greatest stories one may find the same protest as described in her earlier satirical attacks against the sadness in life when questioning the meaning of it all.[25] Mansfield often blends this last theme with an atmosphere of beauty or of nature: the pear tree in "Bliss", the trees in "The Escape", "Weak

Heart", *The Aloe*, "Prelude", "At the Bay". She mingled the sense of beauty and happy moments with the complex issue of the question and meaning of life. Man is seen in his joy of life but there is always the question, as raised in the phrase, 'pulled by the sun' but 'drawn to what?'.[26]

When we attempt to define a basic recurring situation in Mansfield's stories, it may be argued that the dominant themes in her short stories are derived from man's delusion ('the snail under the leaf' theme) and from man's isolation, in the solitary, solipsistic processes of her characters. The basic indirect themes in Mansfield's short stories often appear as sensory limitations in the truth-illusion conflict, or as epiphanies that bring characters to a possible new level of perception and a deeper state of comprehension. Mansfield's short stories are replete with these concepts in striking and often tragic formulations. The lack of a wider, less sensory view of reality, in for example Linda, Beryl, and Kezia in "Prelude", may cause (unnecessary) fear and anxiety and a wish to escape. This argument requires a definition of reality in Literary Impressionist terms.

In Realism natural phenomena are generally described as they are commonly understood to be, whereas in Literary Impressionism a simulation of a sensory experience is presented with little additional information. As a result, characters notice relatively little about the world around them. They perceive the world in momentary, fragmentary experiences. They seem to know little, and thereby distort and restrict their sensations and confuse the entire epistemological process.[27] From the beginning of "Prelude" to the end, the main characters are unable to sustain any realistic conception of themselves. Their minds resort to fantasies and uncertainties about themselves. Their mental conflicts find expression in illusions in a restricted sensory vision. Linda's and Beryl's underlying problem is not simply their effort to escape from everyday life, as one critic has argued[28], but rather to perceive and interpret themselves and discover their true identities. Their views are less than complete. They present sensory, confused, false and incomplete data, inspiring a sense of isolation. Linda, for example, with her 'watchful eyes', is 'waiting for someone to come, watching for something to happen that just did not happen'.[29] Linda's attempts to see more clearly are comprised by her imaginary illusions. She can only fantasise about life and her (day)dreams are essentially deductive, deriving from an illusory picture of life.

One of Mansfield's major themes is the theme of illusion, of a faulty interpretation of an experience. Illusion, as the distortion of either apprehended data or comprehensive analysis, is central to Literary Impressionist fiction. The difficulty of discussing illusion in Mansfield's short stories is that it is everywhere. Almost every character expresses an interpretation of reality that deviates in some degree from 'the norm' the short story itself presents. Mansfield's stories constitute a continuing record of the inability of the human mind to interpret reality and to sustain a verifiable grasp on the self. The disparity between illusion and reality, in fact, accounts for the basic tone at the heart of her fiction.[30] The stories follow a regular pattern with the 'positive' theme dominant until the climax, where it comes into decisive conflict and is superseded by the negative theme. Illusion and deception exist at virtually all levels, often varying from simple misinterpretations of empirical data to grand distortions of self-perception.[31]

The many qualifying terms of uncertainty in a Mansfieldian text, such as 'to seem', 'as if', 'as though', 'as it were', 'in a kind of', 'rather like', 'like someone', 'as one might say (imagine)', 'it reminds of', and 'makes you think of', often indicate the illusion of proximity or a variable intensity.[32] There is a stress on the deluding tricks of the eye, which may suggest the unreliability of empirical data. Visual phenomena are characteristically problematic. In the first section of "At the Bay", for example, we find a distortion of proximity in the early foggy morning at sea, in the hills, the bungalows, the paddocks, the dew drops, the birds, the sea, which are all immersed in the blurring primeval light. They are distorted when seen from a distance.

Similar errors of perception, and of interpretation, occur throughout Mansfield's fiction. In one sense or another, nearly every main character in Mansfield's short stories suffers from the reality-illusion-disparity problem and from his or her limited experience. Delusion in Mansfield's fictional world affects both matters of fact and matters of judgement. These concerns are evident in many stories.[33]

Reliable data are difficult to find in Mansfield's short stories and reliable interpretations of data are even rarer. Mansfield's reality is elusive, shifting and impenetrable. Save for those few instances in the stories, in which the character experiences a moment of awareness, there is very little accurate 'interpretation of reality'. Misinterpretation, distortion, misplaced emphasis, and illusion dominate human understanding.

Illusion is also universal in the stories about children. The children, playing out their interpretation of adult behaviour, often indulge in fantasy. If the children reveal the social pretensions of their parents through their imitative fancy, so too they portray the common illusions of adult life.

One of the most cruel examples of self-delusion in children is the wishful distortion of perception in the famous decapitation scene in "Prelude". The children are to be initiated into and confronted with a shocking, but simple, everyday happening: death. Pip has been given a duck to hold, but at the sight of death he throws life away and shouts: 'I saw it, I saw it!' But the exact revelation for him is unfathomable. Isabel is only seeing 'The Blood! The Blood!'. Rags is overwhelmed by the experience and Kezia, too is initially dumb-founded. But when Pat puts the headless duck on the ground and lets it waddle like a live duck with its dead-yet-alive body, Kezia cries out: 'Put head back! Put head back!'. She cannot accept what she sees. She does not want to be initiated into the reality of life.

These epistemological themes, directly related to Literary Impressionist methods of narration (See Chapter 4.1), are common in Mansfield's short stories. Nearly all the major short stories find their underlying meaning within the variables of illusion/reality and awareness. Beyond the sensory perceptual incapacities of many of Mansfield's characters, however, there is a compensating epiphanic pattern of growth. The continuing and developing emphasis lies on moments of a 'glimpse' with cognitive implications. The shock effect of a negative experience frequently results in a modification of a character's assessment of his or her significance. Such is the case, for example, in "Sun and Moon".[34] What is consistent throughout Mansfield's work in moments of awareness, when 'new eyes' or a fresh perception are given to a character, is the sensation of a complete feeling of the sudden awareness of acceptance and of insignificance.[35] Ordinarily, the main characters in Literary Impressionism experience the feeling of awareness and insignificance as a stage in their growth. They customarily go on to a moment of reflection of such depth and sensitivity that these moments alone imply a refutation of their previous role and lack of importance. These epiphanic moments are frequent in Mansfield's fiction, particularly in her finest short stories.[36]

The theme of relative insignificance in its various formulations is widespread in Mansfield's later fiction and is related to the themes of isolation and alienation. Naturalistic fiction tends to stress the impotence of human beings, their lack of stature, the hopelessness of their condition and the futility of their reactions to their circumstances. Literary Impressionist fiction develops a modified version of this concept based on perceptual isolation. The theme of isolation is also dominant in Mansfield's short stories, as we have discussed in the survey of themes. Since reality is in flux, it will be perceived differently by each individual, and only fragments of its complexity will ever be revealed. Human knowledge is inadequate in confronting the problems of the world. But the emphasis is not only on the relative insignificance of the individual, but also on how and why a character's perceptual separation may engender a sense of isolation and alienation.[37] That is why Mansfield's latest short stories have a close association with the existential elements in later and

Modernist works, such as those by Virginia Woolf, T.S. Eliot and James Joyce.

The theme of an indifferent universe is usually underlined by human action in Mansfield's stories. It is not an indifferent Nature, that is expressed, as in Naturalist determinist literature, but it is dramatically articulated in evocations of atmosphere. Often nature is seen as a great companion. It is the corrupting human force in man's existence, 'the snail under the leaf' that destroys.

Mansfield's fiction describes a dramatic revelation of isolation to the mind of the character. Isolation is not only reconcilable with Literary Impressionist concepts, it is in many ways, intrinsic to them.[38] The adherence to restricted narrative methods, the focus on individual perspectives, his relative uniqueness, the quality of only his sensations and only his mental reflections, all stress the isolation of the individual.

Contrary to Romantic solipsism, in which the individual is often ennobled through isolation, in Mansfield's stories characters seem most often impoverished by their alienation, and are sometimes driven to desperate acts by it.[39] Isolation and alienation in Mansfield's fiction often prompts aberrant psychological states in which a character is not understood by his surroundings.[40] This happens especially when these conditions are exacerbated by stress. In "Ole Underwood", "The Woman at the Store", "Life of Ma Parker", and "Marriage a la Mode" the characters meet with significant problems in interpreting reality. Often in Mansfield's stories these mental distortions develop from an acute sense of isolation and remoteness.[41]

Although there are many examples, perhaps the most dramatic and best-known is the story entitled "Life of Ma Parker", in which Ma Parker's hard and lonely life is drawn into final focus. She is left desolate in an indifferent outside world. In a sense, the 'cry against corruption' theme represents the extension of a basic Literary Impressionist concept to its negative ultimate potential. Unlike Naturalistic characters, who seldom realise much about their destiny in life, or Realist characters, whose anguish often derives from an ethical conflict, Literary Impressionist characters do sense the isolation of their empirical solipsism. In Mansfield's fiction it is the indifference of the surrounding world, the indifference of the total universe, and a character's irreducible loneliness and alienation from other people that is expressed. It is in these despairing moments that the most profound feelings of Literary Impressionist fiction are presented. Mansfield's sense of protest against the conditions that life has meted out can only be expressed in 'a cry'. Whether the controlling agent in this circumstance is perceived as God, Fate, chance, deterministic social and economic forces, or the vagaries of genetic accident, in Mansfield's fiction the individual will always be helpless before it.

As indicated in the survey, a number of other themes run through Mansfield's short stories, but all of them are finally secondary to fundamental epistemological concerns. One of these, the class system as a deterrent to friendship or romance, is social in nature, e.g. in "The Doll's House", and "The Garden Party". In essence the minor themes provide a secondary level of concern in her fiction and are subordinate to individualistic, solipsistic and ontological concerns.

Nature as a physical presence and as a concept is a complex topic. In general, the perception of nature as hostile or benevolent or indifferent is an indicator of important philosophic issues. Nature may be the innocent victim of human actions, and the pastoral and mythical undertones may give a Romantic cast to the first section in "At the Bay", but frequently in Mansfield's fiction Nature is seen as a beautiful and serene phenomenon amid the calamaties of human strife. In Mansfield's fiction it presents a poignant motif when contrasted with the corruption of human action and behaviour, when an individual human being must probe his identity or personal value. Nature is often used in 'imagistic correlatives' (see Chapter 4.5) to evoke a special atmosphere, in order to create an Impressionist 'Stimmung'.

When viewed as a coherent body, Mansfield's short stories have as their underlying themes the concepts of empiricism, epistemology and evanescent reality, all central to Literary Impressionism. Her treatment of a character's empirical process in a fragmentary, ordinary, everyday-life setting, suggests both limitations of knowledge and the potential for a sudden 'glimpse' of insight in moments of recognition. These moments are expressed imagistically and metaphorically in visual, everyday terms. Mansfield has implemented Literary Impressionist ideas and invoked them beyond apprehensional and intellectual states into psychological and everyday, atmospheric conditions. In her short stories she explores the cognitive process of forming generalisations about ordinary life from an isolated experience, the problems of comprehending inadequately perceived phenomena and the enigma of formulating a sense of reality or the self. On the basis of an everyday experience, which has become fused, blurred with fantasies, dreams, hallucinations and fears, all of these problems have distorted memory and impaired a character's perceptions.

Mansfield created fictional impressions of real life around her. She gave her themes a fictional expression that attempted to define reality as viewed by one or more central characters. She also chose to emphasise the problems of conceiving it. In her main work the stress is on the freedom and the individuality of characters, in defining their realities. This condition may lead to empirical solipsism, to a sense of an indifferent world and 'a cry against corruption', in despair at the human condition.

An Impressionist painting must be viewed from a certain distance and every observer may derive his own theme. It is often difficult to define the most important element in an Impressionist composition. Likewise in Mansfield's stories it remains difficult to define 'precise' themes. They are not often stated directly, but obliquely. Although in a complex body of short stories, such as Mansfield's, there are certain to be variations and ideological contradictions, Mansfield's themes are consistent in encompassing the fundamental ontological issues of Literary Impressionism. By only suggesting or exposing everyday consequences, Mansfield develops the philosophical and artistic norms indirectly and casually. This places rather severe limits on the expository development of theme and its range of aesthetic devices. She presents her reality with the inevitable ommissions. Characters and settings are suggested, rather than defined. A few strokes must capture the mood of the characters and the minute 'objective' details. An elaborate finishing touch is eschewed in an attempt to achieve the narrator's subjective, fragmentary impression of the world.

It is clearly beyond the scope of this study to produce a general poetics of the short story, but in view of Mansfield's emphasis on structure the first part of this chapter is meant as an introduction to the fragmentary, episodic composition of her short stories.

Relatively little critical attention has been paid to the structure of the short story. Until recently almost all theoretical writing has come from practioners themselves.[1] In 1968, however, T.O. Beachcroft analysed and surveyed the English short story and traced its history. She isn't much concerned with theoretical issues. Another study, by Ian Reid (1977), appeared in the *Critical Idiom* series. He describes the state of short story criticism and offers definitions of the central terms, short story and novella. How long is short and what is the short story's relationship with the novel? Russian Formalist critics paid a good deal of attention to the short story and their structuralist heirs have also addressed the genre, Todorov (1977), for example, in *Poétique de la Prose.*[2] When discussing genre, he points out that any critic must make a distinction between the theoretical and the actual (historical) genre of the work to be discussed. There is a dynamic distinction between theory and the actual work under discussion, which continually modifies each other, as the critic wanders between 'a continual coming and going between the descriptions of facts and the abstractions of theory'.[3] Valerie Shaw in *The Short Story: A Critical Introduction* (1983) highlights the basic types of narrative in terms of theme and the technical concerns which influence any short story-writer's decision to shape a brief narrative. She studies the various aspects of short story writing, illustrated by specific statements, drawn from a range of periods and countries. In Chapter 8 'The Splintering Frame' Shaw describes the breakthrough of the short story at the beginning of this century and its relationship with other literary genres. Clare Hanson in *Short Stories and Short Fictions*, 1880-1980, (1985) distinguishes between two major types of short stories from the early 20th century: on the one hand, the 'plotty' tale and on the other, plotless short fiction which paved the way for the emergence of Modernist fiction in the early years of this century. Hanson also distinguishes 'the free story' from Modernist short fiction, the Impressionist form, which followed 'the free story' in chronological terms.[4]

The problem of defining the genre of the short story remains complex as many of the above-mentioned critics restrict themselves to only one or certain types of short story, or they concentrate only on the form of the folk-tale, which is not directly related to contemporary short fiction.[5] Another complication is that to most readers the phrase 'short story' suggests the popular story type of women's magazines, a kind of sub-species of the genre resembling the folk-tale more than modern prose fiction, having more rigid rules of construction and content and appealing to a different audience. Most readers expect from a popular short story a tightly plotted narrative, together with suspense or fantasy and possibly a surprise-ending.

When attempting to define the short story there is always the problem of its adjacency to the longer form, the novel. Other genres such as tragedy and comedy may be opposed to each other, by discussing themes, plots, forms, or when opposing drama in general to the novel, by its medium of presentation and its audience, but a literary short story is always, most awkwardly, next to the novel, overlapping, imitating or interpenetrating.

In attempting to place Mansfield's work correctly, it is clear that one has to formulate two separate categories of the short story in early 20th century literature. Firstly, there emerged from the 19th century the conventional tale-telling story, the linear descendant of the Gothic tale: for example, Dickens' and Hardy's stories. Secondly, there appeared a different category of, what Hanson terms 'short prose fiction', i.e. the new 'plotless' story, concentrating on inner mood and subjective impression rather than on external events. This type must include a degree of narrative, but is almost 'plotless'. It is highly flexible varying in length from one page to one hundred, but cannot be categorised by its length, but rather by certain regularly recurring common qualities. The writers of these short stories distrusted the 'plotty' well-wrought tale for a variety of reasons. They argued that the pleasing shape and coherence of the traditional short story represented a falsification of the heterogeneous nature of experience. These stories relied on a too ready-made and facile identification of causal relationship. The achieved and rounded finality of the tale was distrusted. The term 'story' in this sense seemed to convey the misleading notion of something finished, absolute and wholly understood. The plotless short story on the other hand seemed to arise naturally from the intellectual climate of its time. In a world where evolutionary theory had produced a sharp sense of man's insignificance in a changing man-centred universe, the only alternative seemed to be a retreat within oneself and a reflection of the compensating powers of the imagination.[6]

As early as 1873 Walter Pater had signalled a 'retreat into subjectivity'[7] and the years which followed saw a movement towards subjective reflection with great emphasis on the value of the passing moment. Impressionism in general produced new forms in literature, the prose poem and the psychological sketch.[8] The vogue for the prose poem with its enthusiasm for the 'purple patch'[9] in longer writing was symptomatic. To express 'everything to the last extremity, to fix the

141

last fine shade of mood and feeling' was the aim of a whole school of writers in the 1880's and 1890's. Most important was that these writers were interested in prose in preference to poetry. Prose was chosen now, as it was seen as a more inconclusive, promiscuous medium, by definition better suited to express feeling, all the nuances in reflection, comparison and shading in language.

The interest in unstructured prose, though with a strong underlying aesthetic design, prepared the way for the Literary Impressionist short story, which Hanson termed 'the psychological sketch', with the introduction of a more directed and mediated sensibility.[10] These stories tend to deal with an apparently trivial incident which has significance only for what it reveals of a character's inner mood or state of mind. Often the subject of the story is a major change of feeling, but this may be conveyed obliquely, through patterns of images and contrasting narrative methods. Themes are not stated directly. The use of direct discourse and free indirect discourse, in which a more direct and colloquial register of language can be used, marks an important stage in the formal development of the English short story. A clear effort is made to fuse narrator and character through the adoption of a freer, fresher idiom for inner speech.[11] Retreating into the inner consciousness to convey 'mood', the emphasis was laid on a single moment of intense or significant experience, on a 'moment of being' or epiphany, the flash of insight which is outside time and space.

The questions to be asked therefore are: 'What was so new, so special in Mansfield's writing?' and 'How can we relate Mansfield's structural predilections to her Literary Impressionist impulses?' One of the few critics to have hinted at the Literary Impressionist impulse is Vincent O'Sullivan, who has related Mansfield's Impressionism to Walter Pater's aesthetics, to her fictionalisation of memories and responses to her family, her perception of people in New Zealand and England, to Impressionism in painting, to the question of 'how to handle light in a writer's movement of time'[12] and to contemporary cinematic development.[13] O'Sullivan's arguments on Mansfield's innovations may have triggered another contemporary critic, Gillian Boddy, who wrote in 1988:

Like an Impressionist painter she worked to convey the light and the shade, the overall impression or mood; details were altered, outlines blurred and places, people or occasions merged into a composite picture. (...) people were shaped and manipulated to fit the impression she wished to create.[14]

In an attempt to analyse the structure of Mansfield's short stories in general, it is argued that of all the aesthetic elements of Literary

Impressionism, structural organisation serves as the most graphic indication of its fragmentary nature. As in painting and music, the basic unit is a single moment of experience, what the French painters called a 'flash of perception' and Debussy and Ravel translated into fragmentary musical compositions.[15] The concept resulted in disconnected fictional episodes, brief scenes that require unique organisation in order to give the short story a satisfying artistic order. (See Chapter 3.3 on Structure and Fragments)

If structural organisation is dominated by (an arbitrary) juxtaposition of scenes and characters, sub-themes, narrative methods, imagery for emphasis, and the arrangement of episodes into patterns, any other selection of these different items will provide a different design. Episodic progression will therefore be the controlling idea, when consolidating the design into an artistic arrangement of fragmentary experiences to produce an aesthetically satisfying unity.

Many critics have admitted the precision of Mansfield's sharp sensory descriptions, without recognising or acknowledging the aesthetic basis for using brief scenes and without comprehending the ways in which these fragmentary units were organised into larger patterns exhibiting considerable balance and control. An important implication is that many of Mansfield's stories were written in 'a flash', as J.M. Murry has argued. Mansfield's fictional predilection was for brief episodes and one implication of this method may have been epistemological. Rather than describing a continuum of action Mansfield portrayed events as abbreviated units of apprehension, as flashes of perception. As a result, Mansfield's canon consists of short and long stories in which brief scenes record the impressions of the central characters. Even the longer short stories, "Prelude", "At the Bay" and "The Daughters of the Late Colonel", are basically episodic in structure, fragmentary and discontinuous, while Mansfield's shortest short stories are composed of fragmentary, sometimes numbered sections, complete sketches within themselves, depicting interrupted moments, linked in meaningful progression.[16] The succession of episodes is not always teleological, as there is a tendency for periphrasis and there are digressive episodes only tangentially related to the central event. Often, however, these digressive scenes provide significant juxtapositions of, for example, setting, characters and ideas.

The structural use of setting, as an integral part of a Mansfieldian story, often helps develop a theme and provides an insight into the characters. For example, the juxtaposition of the interior scenes in "Sun and Moon" reveals the two different perceptions of the reality versus illusion theme.[17] Mansfield also juxtaposes both interior and exterior settings, as for example in "How Pearl Button was Kidnapped", where the houses of boxes are contrasted with the open sea. In other stories, Mansfield juxtaposes tumultuous inner emotions with outer composure, which in turn is reflected in the setting. "Bliss" has become a famous example, but there are many more examples, of which "Frau Brechenmacher Attends a Wedding", "The Tiredness of Rosabel" and "The Daughters of the Late Colonel" are but a few. In a number of stories Mansfield used sharp changes in interior settings to illustrate changes in the main character's mood. In "The Singing Lesson" the actions of Miss Meadows are reflected in the setting.[18]

Another way in which Mansfield frequently uses setting as a functional structural element in her stories is the juxtaposition of nature and the character's emotions. Even in her early stories she introduced nature as a parallel, as in "The Woman at the Store", where the heat, dust, wind and slate blue sky of the New Zealand bush country affect not only the woman and her child but also the travellers. The wind, pumice dust and tussock grass have turned a beautiful woman into a desperate one, whose appearance reflects her emotional state. In many stories Mansfield selects a family and its domestic setting. Next she selects a macrocosmic 'objective' setting in which to place the family, and finally she cuts into a highly specific time to describe this family, giving only their inner thoughts and remarks of the moment. The crisis is in the microcosm. This insertion of a microcosmic setting within a macrocosmic one lends universality and reality to the story.[19] In "The Garden Party" the luxuriousness of the life the Sheridans live is juxtaposed with the ugly life and home of the dead workman's family. The contrasting setting provides Mansfield with ample background to work out the juxtaposition she so often expressed in her journal, 'the snail under the leaf', which destroys the beauty of life.

Events are often juxtaposed in order to give a story a structural unity. Some events are composed of a series of juxtaposed incidents, often without any transition or explanation.[20] In many of the stories meaning is derived in part from the juxtaposition of characters.[21] Often the character's attitudes or moods are juxtaposed to give structural unity to a story. A character's feelings may be revealed by juxtaposition against scenes, objects or backdrops.[22]

Ideas are also juxtaposed, most often in the appearance versus reality concept. Fancy is juxtaposed with fact, the dream with reality. Beauty is juxtaposed with ugliness, stasis with action, the serious with the absurd. In "The Man Without a Temperament", for example, reality is juxtaposed with memory, sensuality with sterility, summer with winter, illness with health, clock time with a more permanent and enduring time.

Mansfield was deeply concerned with the arrangement of fiction. What seems to have developed as a principle of organisation is in a sense a paradoxical aesthetic. Her aim was to adhere to the episode as

144

the basic unit of her short stories and yet create a unity of structure, theme, image, narrative method and detail without an overall plot, to fuse all the separate units into an artistic whole. As her work developed, she achieved sophistication of design by means of a number of patterns. Within 'a slice of life' setting, she worked obliquely through implication, through contrasting or foreboding imagistic correlatives, through juxtaposition of setting, events, characters, ideas and narrative methods, through her skill with dialogue, and by moving from 'the outside towards the inside'.[23]

Especially in the longer short stories, which are divided into different sections, Mansfield employed what may be termed, an oblique 'enclosure'-technique (see Mansfield's comment on Tsjechov's technique of 'enclosing' in "The Steppe", mentioned in Chapter 3). This is most obvious in her stories built around an epiphany. She 'encloses' the disparate scenes in the stories between opening and closing sections of related content. She uses seemingly arbitrary, though particular, details, which give coherence to an episodic story. Perhaps the clearest evidence of Mansfield's meticulous craftsmanship is the fact that many of her major plotless stories are basically 'epiphanic' in structure, with some revelation either in the centre or at the very end. All the episodic scenes are enclosed by unifying or contrasting but corroborative events in interior and exterior settings, imagistic correlatives, chronological time and small details. For example, the final section of "The Daughters of the Late Colonel", serves to unify the short story artistically and thematically. It concludes the action, character development and patterns of imagery of the earlier sections and brings a coherent meaning to the story, enclosing the impotent sisters' life in the passage in the final section, as a parenthesis, as if it were inserted. It is only a parenthetical remark, but it sums up their whole life:

> There had been this other life, running out, bringing things home in bags, getting things on approval, discussing them with Jug, and taking them back to get more things on approval and arranging father's trays and trying not to annoy father. (p. 284)

Here is Constantia looking back at her life, using the same overwhelming number of present participles as in the introductory passage in the first section:

> The week after was one of the busiest weeks of their lives. Even when they went to bed it was only their bodies that lay down and rested; their minds went on, thinking things out. Talking things over, wondering, deciding, trying to remember where ... (p. 262)

Both passages betray the same futility in the midst of busy action. The numerous present participles convey the bustling activity which overwhelms the two sisters: thinking, talking, wondering, deciding, trying. The one piling upon another creates the impression of constant motion, yet the very nature of the present participles indicates in itself that the activities are futile - they will be momentarily taken up, suspended and then forgotten. In terms of images too the final section echoes that at the beginning. The passage in the first section reveals Constantia's impotence:

Constantia lay like a statue, her hands by her sides, her feet just overlapping each other, the sheet up to her chin. She stared at the ceiling. (p. 262)

A passage in the final section suggests the sacrifice of Constantia's life:

she remembers the times she had come in here, crept out of her bed in her nightgown when the moon was full, and laid on the floor with her arms outstretched, as though she was crucified. (p. 284)

In a spiritual sense there is no more life in their bodies, they have been sacrificed, their minds petrified and fossilised. Near the end the two daughters realise it is already far too late to change their lives, of which discovery, Mansfield observed in a letter:

All was meant, of course, to lead up to that last paragraph, when my two flowerless ones turned with that timid gesture to the sun. 'Perhaps now ....' and after that, it seemed to me, they died as surely as father was dead.[24]

This careful arrangement of fragments is further enhanced by Mansfield's use of time, which the two daughters visibly fritter away. Examining the story's outward structure, it is evident that the suspension of the chronology of the two daughters' condition is reflected by the story's twelve-part sectioning.[25] The final shift in section 12 encloses all the other sections. It concludes the action and provides a coherent final meaning to the spatio-temporal arrangement reflecting the daughters' self-division. The disruption of chronology allowed Mansfield to present the two parts of each daughter's personality in a parallactic manner. (See Chapter 4.1). If she had followed chronology, the story would have been deprived of the humour so inherent in the juxtaposition. Mansfield also used the enclosure technique in a variable pattern, in which passages of Impressionistic description begin and end the story. She employed this device in many of her finest stories. Perhaps the subtlety of her organisational pattern is evidenced by the fact that very few readers over the decades have realised how tightly ordered her fiction actually is. The prototype of the enclosure technique is in "At the Bay", where themes, characters and settings of the 12 sections are structurally enclosed, presenting the different characters in their activities, thoughts, fears, fantasies and dreams, from dawn to dusk. The enclosure-technique functions structurally and thematically.

Each of the sections in "At the Bay" are juxtaposed, by different points of view, imagistic patterns and all the sections co-exist, not in subordination but in juxtaposition. All the various sections, with all the different perceptions of life, like pieces of coloured glass pierced by various shafts of light, form the episodes in the lives of the Burnells and the Trouts. Life is just as random as that. The enclosure-technique is used as a unifying force. There are other examples of Mansfield's use of the enclosure-technique as an ordering principle, of which some deserve specific comment. Perhaps the best of these is "The Wind Blows" in which the controlling imagistic correlative of the wind enforces the meaning and the contrasting atmospheres of the story and encloses the epiphany.[26]

Another method by which Mansfield gives fragmentary scenes a sense of unity is the use of small apparently casual details. "Spring Pictures", for example, demonstrates this.[27] Many of the accumulated details recur throughout the story, serving to unify later sections with the opening one. These apparently casual details not only give the story a cinematic quality but establish a pattern of internal reference that creates unity in a basically fragmentary Impressionistic story. As this story shows, the general effect of Mansfield's use of unifying details is to give coherence to the basic fragmentary units that comprise her fiction. If, for the Impressionist, experience consists of quasi-unrelated fragments, of flashes of perception, we should also expect to find a quasi-arbitrariness in the presentation of the smallest components, the single detail. Although both Naturalist and Impressionist writers may pay a great deal of attention to details there is a difference in their use of it. Where the Naturalist tends to be comprehensive and complete, the Impressionist is highly selective. Where the Naturalist tends to give equal emphasis to a large number of details, Mansfield singles out the first detail that catches the narrator's eye, the main impression on the particular occasion, and has the detail completely dominate the scene. Sometimes details of sense impressions are used to create a vivid scene, as for example in the first section of "Spring Pictures", where all five senses are evoked. Further on the details are juxtaposed in other scenes, but the images presented do not form patterns. Details selected to convey the impression of a scene or character often seem insignificant, puzzling and inconsequential compared with the momentousness of the action and scene presented. The Literary Impressionist's attitude to experience as a succession of detached and momentary impressions is presented in these instances. The Impressionist narrator does not introduce order where there is none. Mansfield often presents an effect and leaves the reader deduce the unmentioned and sometimes illogical cause. Impressions only gradually gain in meaning.[28] Sometimes the short stories begin with dialogue in the manner of a stage play.[29] More often they begin with some stage setting direction[30] or they open within the consciousness of a character.

The *in medias res* openings with the conjunction 'and' - as a typical Literary Impressionist device - must also be mentioned here.[31] Life is seen as a sequence of impressions, devoid of beginnings and endings. The conjunction 'and' may connect everything in concatenation of the unknown past and the beginning of the story.[32] All the abrupt *in medias res* beginnings involving empirical or sensory data reflect the Literary Impressionist fragmentary view of life as made up of discontinuous units of experience, whereas the revealing ironic and open endings (with: ...) may often provide an extra level of meaning for the preceding events.[33] The ironic deflation of man in many conclusions of Mansfield's stories often emphasises the disparity between illusion and reality. The sense of insignificance and loss (similar to many of Anton Tsjechov's endings), ironically presented, is the tonal and atmospheric corrolary of Mansfield's basic themes and an oblique method of conclusion for most of her stories.

Finally, to return to Mansfield's manner of structuring her short stories in general, it may be argued that the most frequent design is a modification of the 'enclosure-story'. The story opens *in medias res* beginning (sensory description + action) and concludes with an ironic event or comment. The sensory evocation of a scene at the beginning of the story has the effect of involving the reader directly in the scene by presenting the direct impression of a character at the location. The absence of introductory background information and motivation or explanation for the initial scene has the effect of intensifying the reader's interest in more sensory details from which he may derive an understanding of the situation. The reader is often plunged immediately into the narrative situation.[34] The oblique and abrupt introduction of empirical data and characters in discontinuous experiences, in flashes of perception, reflects the Literary Impressionist fragmentary concept of life. Flashes of perception exhibit important organisational patterns in juxtaposition or symmetry. They may unify references in order to create a structural balance between the adherence to the episode, and the one single significant scene, or epiphany. The unity of setting, events, characters and ideas in narrative methods, themes, images, in juxtaposition or symmetry, attest to Mansfield's artistic control of structure.

Mansfield's methods of characterisation have been described in rather vague, ambiguous and contrasting terms. They have not been explored with the vigour accorded to the study of other dimensions of her writing. Pritchett's comment, attempting to define characterisation in Mansfield's work, is typical. Commenting on her characters in general, he writes: 'Who are these people, who are their neighbours? What is the world they belong to ? (...) They drop out of the sky, and fill the little canvas'.[1] Pritchett nevertheless admits that there is a clarity of insight into them: 'Can one find a more precise portrait of a play-acting, adolescent girl than Beryl in "At the Bay" or a more terrifying notion of what it may be like to be a cynical woman of a certain age than Mrs Kember in the same story? - We see through all these people, one by one as they will never see through themselves. And Stanley Burnell, the back-slapping, go-getting business man with his awful energy and his hopelessly egotistical remorse (...) she did get that key character, the business man'.[2] Another critic, Berkman, argues that Mansfield presents 'a highly particularized character' (when comparing with Joyce's Gabriel Conroy in "The Dead"), though her characters are 'not necessarily (...) always deeper'.[3] Berkman also comments that the 'fullness of character portrayal is achieved because the characters have space in which to grow'.[4] On this aspect Magalaner is more explicit. She argues: 'in "Prelude" and "At the Bay" the delineation of the major characters, though often remarkable in the short space at the author's disposal, is less impressive than her power to present the separate characters in their interrelationship'.[5]

Over the years the concept of character has changed in literary criticism. New conceptions of change and diversity have replaced the notion of stability in the traditional, for example, Realist concept. The Realist argument insisted that characters acquire, in the course of an action a kind of independence from the events which they experience and that they can be usefully discussed or outlined in isolation from their context. In Naturalism, a character is more likely to be representative of a type, to be an unindividualised character. These characters are created in order to demonstrate the driving nature of deterministic forces, whether genetic or environmental. Their individual capabilities or limitations can have little effect on their destinies. Ethical choices for the Naturalist characters, usually trapped by environmental or genetic forces, are essentially irreconcilable with the themes of their stories. Matters of cognitive growth are of little significance for them.[6] A Naturalist character, in both role and method, is therefore not difficult to distinguish from a Realist or an Impressionist one.

Another argument, the 'purist' one[7] - nowadays in the ascendancy - points out that characters do not exist at all, except in so far as they are a part of the images and events which bear and move them, and that any effort to extract them from their context and discuss them as if they are real human beings is a misunderstanding of literature. These different views must be borne in mind when we attempt to describe Mansfield's method of characterisation.

Mansfield's dramatic revelation of character through dialogue and free indirect discourse (as opposed to an expository description of them) the oblique use of tag names in titles and in the text in order to identify them, and the character's emergence from a kinetic portrait, require a critical approach different from the Realist, Naturalist or 'purist' one. These techniques are not only central to Mansfield's methods of characterisation but also basic to the aesthetics of Literary Impressionism. Empirical relativism at the core of Literary Impressionism has a direct bearing on the kinds of characters portrayed by Mansfield and on the way in which she presents them. Long passages of background information are eliminated and what remains is a dramatic presentation through dialogue, free indirect discourse and action. Unless they are moulded into a narrative focus, revealing their own thoughts, many characters are described from the outside only. The reader barely knows their names and they are only vaguely sketched in. There is often no effort at all to say where they come from. They simply flit across the picture, or shift from one posture to another in a moving composition. Many figures make only brief appearances and do not remain in focus long enough for even cursory analysis.

Mansfield pretended to present characters without prior knowledge. On the basis of dramatic revelation, she imposed sharp limitations on the depth of all but major figures. For protagonists, however, Literary Impressionist methods, unlike Realist ones, allow a good deal more depth, though, since an expressive narrative identification with the characters allows the representation of thought as well as action and dialogue. In "The Garden Party" the reader has access not only to Laura's actions but also to her apperceptions of the world, of the people around her, of herself, her fears and insecurity. As the story progresses, a great deal is indirectly revealed about Laura. Her perceptions are not stated in narrative assertions but implied and obliquely suggested by the ambiguous alteration in the way Laura perceives the world.

As the characterisation of Kezia in "Prelude" suggests, Literary Impressionist characters are frequently engaged in new, different, unfamiliar actions and realisations. An Impressionist character generally faces a cognitive rather than a moral dilemma, and establishing the character's background and history is, therefore, of

150

little importance. 'Positive' characters are generally those who grow and develop new ideas.[8] This is why there are many young people and children in Mansfield's work, of interest to her because they still have the potential for change. As in Modernism, characters are reflected in each other's thoughts. They would hardly recognise themselves as they are presented, coloured and changed by different points-of-view. In "Prelude" Stanley is seen by his wife by turns as a turkey or a Newfoundland dog.

Comparing the characterisation in "Prelude" with that in Virginia Woolf's *To the Lighthouse*, it is evident that the characters face a cognitive problem. The constantly shifting perspective gives the reader a series of shocks, as one perspective shifts to another. In "Prelude", Stanley's view of women is offensive. In *To the Lighthouse*, the reader shares Tansley's pleasure in being with Mrs Ramsay.[9] But Mrs Ramsay's response to him seems rather blunt after his experience of happiness: 'Odious little man, thought Mrs Ramsay, why go on saying that?'.[10] Both works focus on perception, on ways characters see each other, and it is no accident that windows and mirrors recur in each. Mrs Ramsay is not described by the narrator; she is presented from many perspectives. In the first section, called 'The Window', she is a dark shape for Lily's picture and an image of vulnerability for Mr Ramsay.[11] She, looking out at the light-house, exhausted by protecting Mr Ramsay from his own vulnerability, escapes the pressures of domestic life and becomes 'a wedge-shaped core of darkness' to Lily Briscoe.[12] Mr Ramsay in *To the Lighthouse* and Kezia in "Prelude" are literally mirrored. The other characters are reflected by other minds and no one view seems an objective or 'correct' one. "Prelude" is full of fleeting images signalled by words like 'looked', 'seemed', and 'as if'. Reality in "Prelude" only exists as momentarily perceived by the characters, as it seems to them at a particular moment. Kezia sees the aloe as old and withered; her mother sees it as cruel, invincible, and as a means of escape and she lies about the blossom period.[13] Characters in "Prelude" have a solipsistic, momentary, fragmentary view of reality. There is continual irony as different characters misunderstand each other, fail to communicate or remain trapped in solipsistic isolation from each other.

We have to be similarly alert to tone and changes in point of view in *To the Lighthouse*. On publication of the novel some reviewers complained that the characters in *To the Lighthouse* were insubstantial and Virginia Woolf received complaints that 'the story isn't complete'.[14] Characters are fleeting. The reader must make links and interpret himself. However, comparing characterisation in *To the Lighthouse* and in "Prelude", some differences are also to be found. Firstly, we must bear in mind that Mansfield deliberately selected the

151

short story as a mode of artistic expression. Mansfield attempts to express her vision in a word, a few lines, whereas Woolf usually strings out her arguments and detailed intellectual discussions into lengthy conjectures. For Woolf it takes much longer to get to the point, if she ever gets to it at all. The reader, like the characters, only half-comprehends and is compelled to guess and piece together a character's view from images and half-finished thoughts. Secondly, Mansfield uses more dialogue in her attempt to create a more lively picture and atmosphere around her characters. Woolf focused on the Modernist relativist philosophy itself and used the character's individual critical mind as a point of departure when rendering the evolution and movements of her characters' intellectual considerations. Woolf saw characters and life in general as a flux and wanted only 'to record the atoms as they fall upon the mind'.[15] Woolf's characters change their views without motive, and present an unending, shifting perspective on events, for there is no fixed reality for them. Reality is questionable and meretricious. Values are tentative. Woolf, the Modernist, abandoned the idea of character as a fixed and fully knowable identity. In its stead, she presented a floating, ever-changing essence, a seemingly external individual, developing though - but rarely to be felt or apprehended by - the other characters. Thirdly, Mansfield's characters are not very mobile in their thoughts, Mansfield's intellectual range is more limited than Woolf's. Mansfield's characters only momentarily feel and perceive in a flash. They remain encapsuled in their solipsism. A Modernist character first 'thinks', or 'is aware of', and 'conscious of', then he may feel detached and, only thirdly will he perceive, observe or imagine.[16] Mansfield's characters are Modernist only in their isolation, in their uncertainty and in their struggles to comprehend themselves and the world they live in.

Mansfield's adherence to Literary Impressionist narrative methods compelled a number of devices, which must now be discussed. One of her techniques is the use of a descriptive epithet when identifying her characters. The narrator in Mansfield's stories is often perceptive, but has no prior knowledge of characters or of the situation or the meaning of events. The *in medias res* beginning of many of her stories allows for no extra information. The narrator attempts to capture impressions *in statu nascendi*; he depicts the outer world not as it is, but as it appears, via the senses rather than the intellect.[17] As a result, he must identify people on the basis of their appearance, size, age, voice, or any descriptive dimension, using a large number of adjectives and adverbs.

Apart from the anonymous characters who are only 'he' or 'she'[18], there are also characters who are described in terms only of rank[19] or nationality[20], or with ironic epithets.[21] In narrative terms, all these descriptive epithets result from the restriction of knowledge to what a person, newly introduced to the scene would be able to perceive about these people and their circumstances. Mansfield's short stories usually present little beyond what a character can see, hear, remember, dream or fantasise. What is outside the character's experience is not described. It does not exist. Mansfield's use of epithets is a logical feature of an epistomologically Impressionist method of narration, which implies initial apprehension of character.

At times, as in her earlier *In a German Pension* stories, there is a tendency to stereotype, but most often the epithets reveal dominant traits which may have a thematic function or relate to both occupation and psychological preoccupation. Mansfield was often able to present important concepts of role, personality and thematic function through this device, as the use of tag names implies a judgement of character, by the narrator based on observable traits.

She also used a method of presenting characters through action and dialogue. This method, according to Kronegger the most purely Literary Impressionist one[22], requires a significant response and analysis by the reader. There is no record of earlier information, little initial definition, and no reference apart from specific actions and statements. Characters seem suggestive of real human beings, but the method of revelation precludes full development. As a result there is a great deal of justification for Berkman's contention that Mansfield's characters are no 'deeper' than Joyce's. Berkman's argument has some bearing on the methodological and philosophical condition which Literary Impressionism generally implies. It is applicable to minor characters, who are often introduced as a contrast, as a fixed point against which to develop the main characters. Mansfield often uses the narrator as a generalising formulator, but she also found means to provide information in terms of what characters themselves could observe on the spot. In "The Fly" the minor character old Woodifield is established through dialogue, through the narrator's exposition and in imagistic correlatives. At the beginning of the story we read:

> ... piped old Mr. Woodifield and he peered out of the great, green-leather armchair by his friend's the boss's desk as a baby peers out of his pram ... Since he had retired since his ... stroke the wife and the girls kept him boxed up in the house ... All the same we cling to our last pleasures as the tree clings to his last leaves. So there sat old Woodifield ... (p. 412)

The narrative method here reveals omnipresence and exposition, although these facts about Woodifield's weekly outing suggest the character's own account ('the' wife, 'the' girls).
Typical of Mansfield's method is, in this short story , that the narrator is active as a formulator of the observations of another character:

153

'Poor old chap, he's on his last pins, thought the Boss'.[23] Most characteristic is Mansfield's ironic, intrusive, expressive manner when describing minor characters, speech or actions, and quickly setting the scene. For example, alluding to Beryl's flirtations and Stanley's bossiness in "Prelude":

> Beryl, sipping tea, her elbows on the table, smiled over the cup at him. She wore an unfamiliar pink pinafore; the sleeves of her blouse were rolled up to her shoulders showing her lovely freckled arms, and she had let her hair fall down her back in a long pigtail. 'How long do you think it will take to get straight - couple of weeks - eh?' he chaffed 'Good heavens, no,' said Beryl airily. (p. 20)

If the objective of a Literary Impressionist manner of characterisation is supposed 'objectivity' in a subjective narrator's perception, one of its drawbacks is a limitation of scope. Especially within the confines of a short story, full-fledged characterisation is precluded by the inevitable condensation, narrow perspective and verbal and imagistic economy the genre requires. Kronegger, who supports a broad concept of Literary Impressionism, links the Literary Impressionist lack of 'stable'[24] characterisation with the absence of plot and the characters' solipsism:

> Since the definition of character is inseparable from a novel's plot, character cannot exist in a formless novel. The most solid characters, such as Fréderic and Mme Arnoux of Flaubert's *l'Education Sentimentale*, Joyce's Stephen Dedalus, Virginia Woolf's Mrs Ramsay, Rilke's Malte, and Gide's Nathanaël, seem at times to melt away into a mere atmosphere. Even when they are given sharp perceptions, their character remains enclosed in a sort of envelope, it comes rarely into contact with others, and remains isolated.[25]

Mansfield wanted to celebrate the union of the main character with the world at large (See Chapter 2). Strangely enough, this union is òften consummated by vision alone and not by participation. Characters perceive images which appear for an instant and then vanish. Vision may elicit a choice between remaining passive or becoming active. Mansfield's main characters undergo passively the basic dichotomy of life. They first reflect their joy of life. In the end they may be led to inevitable disaster, succumbing to despair. They may seem imprisoned in a vision of loneliness, solipsistic heaviness and enclosure. Their states of consciousness wax and wane. They perceive fragmentary flashes of instantaneous experience. Often the

154

main character's consciousness finds reflection in images of intoxication by nature, silence, dissolution and immobility, failure, paralysis and inertia, fantasy and unfulfilled dreams. Mansfield's characters seem to be conceived under the ambiguous signs of motion and stasis, of flight and fall, in a response to their contradictionary need to escape from their solipsistic self and yet seek refuge in dissolution within it. What is called into question is the value of both the reality of the (outside) world, of appearances and the self. At the early stage of their experience, Literary Impressionist characters seem to be rather optimistic about their becoming sensitive slates on which impressions can be written without their volitional effort[26], but in due course man's stable framework and bounds crumble away. The Literary Impressionist's main characters are also to some degree crumbling, multiple personalities with multiple faces, seen in different fragmentary situations, known by hearsay and through their fragmentary selves. Mansfield's main figures are shadowy and have limited potential to become representatives of a mythical or complex human strife. But they are mimetic, they do not dissolve into textuality. They may be equated with real people, but in Impressionist terms. For a brief period of time they may be known to the reader as they approximate actual personalities, who have penetrated into their inner lives. They are seen mainly from the outside, they do not resort to intellectual hypotheses, and their minds remain opaque. The way in which Mansfield's characters apprehend reality closely approximates the common human experience. All the limitations necessary to make them seem real are there in the representation of the sensory surface of human life. Mansfield's characters live in a condition of flux, in a fleeting moment; they may change subtly but do not really 'develop'.[27] Mansfield exhibited a predilection for children as characters, as innocent victims, stressing their sensations in the process of interpreting experience. She showed that, Laura, for example, is conditioned by societal norms and is ultimately prone to distorting and misinterpretating her experience. Mansfield's major stories are in a limited sense, in the last analysis, stories about character, narratives in which the unique psychology of an individual, though shadowy, personality is the main issue. As Margaret Drabble writes, 'Some of her stories, and this is no mean tribute, one never forgets.' She mentions Miss Brill and the silent 'Lil and our Else' (...), 'the sentimentality, the devastating loneliness, the courage, the hope and the cruelty, all the ingredients are there'.[28]

The quality of her characterisation has sustained interest in Mansfield's work, because of the sensation it conveys of penetrating into the inner life of characters. Her methods of characterisation are essentially congruent with the basic concepts of Literary Impressionism. They are seemingly objective, dramatic and descriptive and her characters, though shadowy, are momentarily reflective, sentient and actively involved in the process of identifying themselves in their world.

In the genre of the short story, the poetic image does not generally play an important part. In Mansfield's short stories, however, the striking use of imagery does require an examination, and this cannot stop with the evaluation of its contents. The function within the composition also needs to be discussed, since one of the important unifying devices in Mansfield's fiction is imagery, in its whirling clusters, chains and patterns. These imagistic groups occur frequently and evoke a variety of effects, from significant thematic suggestions to subtle humour and sharp ironic contrasts.[1] The numerous images of light and dark, for example, in "Prelude" may be linked with the characters' apperception. Light, which can change the shape of things so mysteriously, is caught (and personified) by Mansfield in many different shapes and forms. Nature images often link a character's close harmony with man in the pictorial evocation of a particular atmosphere or help convey an epiphany. In similar fashion, contrasting patterns of images often generate a thematic layer of meaning.[2] Patterns of imagery emerge increasingly from the body of Mansfield's work. In her earlier work *In a German Pension* (1911) there are found 96 pages with 94 comparisons and 45 metaphors, while "At the Bay" (1921) contains 40 pages with 101 comparisons and 88 metaphors.

The term imagery, however, is an ambiguous one in modern criticism and needs to be discussed before going further. Three uses of the word are especially current.

Firstly, imagery (i.e. images taken collectively) is used to signify all the objects and qualities of sense perception referred to in a poetic text, whether by literal description, by allusion, or in the analogues (the vehicles) used in its similes and metaphors. Imagery in this broad sense includes the literal objects the poetic text refers to. J.A. Cuddon in *A Dictionary of Literary Terms* (1977) states that imagery as a general term covers 'any use of language in order to represent objects, actions, feelings, thoughts, ideas, states of mind and any sensory or extra-sensory experience'.[3] Cuddon distinguishes between literal, perceptual and conceptual images. If there is no figurative language he speaks of a literal image, which may or may not convey a visual image. If a meaning other than the referential one is stated, and if the image refers to a perceptual experience, he speaks of a perceptual image. If the image can hardly be visualised, but the reader is given an idea of an image, for example in 'castle of God', he speaks of a conceptual image. Cuddon embraces a wide and sometimes a too elastic view when he states that 'many images, but by no means all, are conveyed by figurative language. 'It is often the case that an image is not exclusively one thing or another, images may overlap, intermingle and combine. Secondly, imagery is used, more narrowly, to signify narrative descriptions of visible objects and scenes, especially if the description is vivid and particularised. Thirdly, and most commonly in recent criticism, 'imagery' is used to signify figurative language only, in the form of metaphors and similes. Recent criticism has gone beyond older and affective criticism in stressing imagery only in this sense, as the essential component in poetry, and as a major clue to poetic meaning, structure and effect in a poetic text. Carolyne Spurgeon, in her influential book *Shakepeare's Imagery and what it tells us* (1935) made accounts of the subjects of this type of imagery. She also studied the frequent occurrence in Shakespeare's plays of 'image clusters', recurrent groupings of metaphors and similes, and presented evidence that a number of individual plays have characteristic image motifs. Many critics have joined Spurgeon's conscientious search for images, image patterns, and thematic imagery in various works of literature. One of her disciples in Germany, Bertha Haferkamp, has presented a most valuable study of Mansfield's imagery.[4] She uses the results as clues to Mansfield's personal experience, her interests and temperament. Mansfield's images are analysed in terms of her figurative language, metaphors and similes only. Adopting Spurgeon's concept of 'every kind of picture drawn in every kind of way in the form of simile and metaphor - in their widest sense'[5] this study will be continued. Spurgeon's concept seems a safe starting-point for the study of Mansfield's mass and variety of images, which often fuse to form a medley of complex thematical and atmospheric language pictures.

Before discussing her various forms of imagery we must first differentiate between Mansfield's mature work and the early sketches of *In a German Pension* (1911), with their more individualised imagery. In these journalistic travelogues, which she did not wish to republish in 1920, because they were 'immature' and 'a lie'[6], the narrator often uses imagistic language to express a repulsion for the characters. In the early stories the narrator seems estranged from nature. The loud tones and sharp contrasts dominate. There is no atmospheric transparency in imagistic patterns, which is so evident in Mansfield's later imagery. In *In a German Pension* imagery seems to originate not from any inner structural necessity, but to be introduced more or less at random.

VAGUE, OBLIQUE

Mansfield's complex and varied forms of images range from the simple metaphor to complex imagistic creations, combining several forms of imagery. Haferkamp argues that the preference for undefined, vague, at first sight rather random, but striking images, echoes the writer's inner insecurity. Mansfield cannot achieve a complete vision, there is 'no clarity when perceiving the characters she presents', nor can she grasp reality or the world at large.[7] Mansfield's images differ in intensity. It is remarkable how often a pictorial image is weakened or enlarged. When Mansfield applies the indirect method a large variety of possible forms of comparison are used and oblique images are presented.[8] These images leave the impression of a suggestive vagueness, a feeling of indirection, of insufficiency, as if the narrator wants to leave a gap between a subjective impression and an objective presentation of the experience to be described and compared.

> (...) something which is like longing, and yet it is not longing. Or regret - it is more like regret. (p. 429)

When using expressions like 'it seemed to him', as mentioned above, Mansfield deliberately attributes the comparison in question to a subjective, restricted point of view, stressing its relative aspect. In the occasional correction or rejection of comparisons the narrator again underlines their subjective nature. The Literary Impressionist seeks to depict the world as it seems to be, as it appears at a particular moment, in order to catch the impression in *statu nascendi* within a susceptible consciousness. Mansfield expresses the unexpected, meant to produce a sense of spontaneity.[9]

CONCATENATION

Little touches are placed side by side and, as we shall see, concatenation prevails in Manfield's imagery. One of her methods is to heighten the pictorial atmosphere, by accumulations of comparisons for the same object. The images are swollen and blown up by extra additions:

> (...) Every note was a sigh, a sob, a groan of awful mournfulness. (p. 346)
> (...) how extraordinary shell-like we are as we are - little creatures, peering out of the sentry-box, ogling through our glass case at the entry, wan little servants, who never can say for certain, even, if the master is out or in (...). (p. 437)

Some images require a constant change of scenery.[10] Normally the imagery is derived from closely related areas. If pictures are non-related, they are mostly coordinated by the conjunctions 'or', 'and', by which a certain concatenated 'Stimmung' is evoked.[11] When expanding images in this way, the narrator sometimes fuses comparisons and metaphors into complex compositions, which push the compared object (the tenor) into the background:

> Taller houses, pink and yellow, glided by, fast asleep behind the green eyelids, and guarded by the poplar trees that quivered in the blue air as if on tiptoe, listening. (p. 182)

In the referential field Mansfield sometimes finds difficulty in phrasing sensory impressions, which are anyway not easily put into words. She applies the indirect method again when using the vague 'something', or 'I felt as though'. All the emphasis of the referential tenor is shifted into an Impressionist pictorial or moving atmosphere:

> There were glimpses, moments, breathing spaces of calm, but all the rest of the time it was like living in a house that couldn't be cured of the habit of catching fire, or a ship that got wrecked every day. (p. 222)

Often this concatenated 'Stimmung' is created by stressing a variety of separate aspects instead of just one. A pictorial atmosphere is created by means of imagistic fusion:[12]

> For the special thrilling quality of their friendship was in their complete surrender. Like two open cities in the midst of some vast plain their two minds lay open to each other. (p. 112)

In the comparisons, Mansfield's narrator often presents as many additions as desired, by using strings of adjectives and relative participles. The stylistic markers are the omnipotent, omnipresent comma, hyphens, and the conjunctions 'or', 'and', which may coordinate anything.[13]

> I believe that people are like portmanteaux-packed with certain things, started going, thrown about, tossed away, dumped down, lost and found, half emptied suddenly, or squeezed fatter than ever, until finally the Ultimate Porter swings them on to the Ultimate Train and away they rattle (...). (p. 60)

It is especially in images that express the narrator's emotion that we find repetitions:

160

(...) A dark porch, half hidden by a passion-vine, that drooped sorrowful, mournful, as though it understood. (p. 374)

The repetition of sound images must also be mentioned here. The emotional and expressive narrator often focuses on the pictorial atmosphere in the comparison.[14]

She looked as though she was going to bow down, to bow down to the ground, before her generous Father and beg his forgiveness (...). (p. 504)

FUSION

In an important article on Literary Impressionism, F. Busch writes that the Literary Impressionist is not troubled by cause and effect, which is a matter of the intellect. Mansfield's narrator, in accordance with the Literary Impressionist's tendency to reverse the order of cause and effect (since it is the effect that must produce the suggestive impression), often provides the vehicle before the tenor is mentioned. The pictorial atmosphere is again heightened.

Fat, good-natured, and smiling, they stuffed away the little newspaper they were reading, (...). (p. 401)

The same tendency to fuse subject and object is found in the Literary Impressionist creation of 'Stimmung', which creates a fusion of referential and pictorial images and enhances meaning. Expressions like 'to turn into', 'to become', 'to be part of' frequently occur.[15]

They (the sparrows) turned into little boys. (p. 663)
They (the same sparrows) 're little boys. (p. 663)

Sometimes the 'fused' surroundings may be objectivised and expressed physically:

(...) as though you'd suddenly swallowed a bright piece of that late afternoon sun (...). (p. 91)
(...) was the air always like this? Little faint winds were playing chase in at the tops of the windows, out at the doors. (p. 249)
(...) it seemed to her that kisses, voices, tinkling spoons, laughter, the smell of crushed grass, were somehow inside her. (p. 259)

The metaphors may be fused into referential narrative. In "Je ne Parle pas Francais" we read on p.71: 'you little perfumed fox-terrier of a Frenchman'. Further down we read: 'I (was) more like a little fox-terrier than ever' (...) and on p. 74 we read: 'away the little fox-terrier flew'.[16] In the major, recurring images in Mansfield's stories, the birds, trees, and insects[17], the objects are often introduced by means of a precise comparison. In the story "Bliss" the flowering pear-tree is first presented in narrative description:

> At the far end, against the wall, there was a tall slender pear tree in fullest, richest bloom; it stood perfect, as though becalmed against the jade-green sky. (p. 96)

The beauty of the pear-tree is slightly blemished by the appearance of the two cats, creeping through the flower-bed: one grey pregnant cat, and a black one, following like a shadow. The flowering tree appears to be a symbol of Bertha's life. The image of the cat appears once more after Bertha's shattering discovery of her husband's unfaithfulness. Finally, of the flowering tree it is said that:

> the pear tree was as lovely as ever and as full of flower and as still. (p. 105)

The examples mentioned above, may serve to demonstrate that Mansfield's imagistic patterns are important in that they suggest various levels of meaning not always inherent in the action of the story, create ironic contrasts and support themes with rhetorical figures.

As for the images of man, it is a remarkable feature that grown-up people are often compared with children and children with grown-ups, often revealing contrasting joyful or painful emotions. Sad tones often dominate the scene, sometimes conveying a feeling of claustrophobia, when characters feel as if they are in prison or hospital, or like actors performing on a stage. People appear like actors, wearing masks.[18]

Beryl says in "Prelude": 'I'm always acting a part' (...).[19] Characters seem to be estranged from their original destiny. Linda, the mother, hates being one. Old people look like babies[20], men are as sensitive as women, and women behave like men.[21] When man is compared to animals and beasts, insects, water-creatures or birds, disagreeable emotions are revealed. The animal images, in all their different nuances, encompass the whole range of human emotions and feelings. Disappointment and pessimism are revealed: the helpless insect, the preying spider, the cunning snake, the escaping rabbit, they all represent a cruel or suffering aspect of mankind. Birds in Mansfield's stories, involved almost half of the animal comparisons, do not express liberty or happiness. Comparisons with inanimate nature reveal a painful feeling of imprisonment and the sensation of being unwillingly driven along. Only plants express blissful harmony. Dying nature, flowers and the blown leaf appear to be closely related to man. Even beautiful flowers are described ironically.[22]

> She (...) began to sing like a pansy. (p. 149)
> 'You smell like a petunia'. (p. 486)
> (...) a number of ladies, apparently languid as the (...) flowers (p. 602)
> Policemen are as thick as violets everywhere. (p. 635)

It is not only mankind and nature that are compared, we also find a great variety of images describing material surroundings, pictures, garments, and household objects. Mechanical figures, in pictures, masks, caricatures, statues[23] present the largest group among them, all emphasising the narrator's subjective perception of the world. Mansfield's narrator perceives the world as a huge theatre, in which everyone is playing the wrong part.

SYNECDOCHE

In the comparisons involving garments, utensils or personal belongings a synecdoche is often used to reveal one important characteristic or a first impression in an outward appearance.[24]

> And now an ermine toque and a gentleman in grey met just in front of her. (p. 333)

Individual limbs may represent entire human beings. Feet, hands, fingers, heads, hair (particularly women's hair), arms, often coupled with an adjective, may express the extra meaning. The indirect oblique picture creates a mixture of cause and effect. The human voice may represent the speaking character. As an indirect indication the narrator selects and implies, partly by means of different adjectival effects, partly by means of different verbal metaphors. The voices are often subdued, softly vanishing, usually in low key, in a dreamy echo, longing or trembling and dying away.[25] Less frequently, though in a similar manner, the human face is compared[26] with the eye, a smile or expression revealing a 'Stimmung' around the characters. It is often sadness, disappointment, or grief that is revealed in these images. A vague longing for fulfilment is expressed through Mansfield's comparisons, with mankind appearing powerless in the grip of emotions. This tenor of thwarted hope may have a life of its own: as it may grow, breathe and be paralysed. Emotions may choke a character, but also leave him again.[27]

163

NATURE

Throughout Mansfield's work the reader feels that it is in nature that the narrator and characters seek understanding and companionship. They attempt to become one with nature, to identify with plants, animals and inanimate atmospheric forces. All Mansfield's nature images portray a wish for unblemished emotional harmony.[28] Only the plants or bushes, in some instances, suggest the sadness we already encountered in the comparisons involving people. There is also the urge to create an atmosphere of overwhelming joy, apart from the feeling of loneliness and sadness.

> a freesia (...) the delicate flower leaned over, swung, shook (...) it fluttered still as though it were laughing. Happy careless flower! (p. 421)

As in the interplay of light and shadow, contours seem to be constantly blurred or quite frequently, softly flowing. Flowers, bushes and trees are portrayed as a moving wave, a shower or a fountain, brought to life, as a movement of colour or light[29]:

> (...) the slender, flowering tree. Although it was so still it seemed, like the flame of a candle, to stretch up, to point, to quiver in the bright air, to grow taller and taller as they gazed - almost to touch the rim of the round, silver moon. (p. 102)

OBJECTS

It is not only people or nature that are compared. Mansfield also knows how to describe the domestic setting of her stories: elegant appartments, fashionable clothes, ribbons and silk stockings.[30] Where one particular garment is picked out, it is usually to characterise the wearer: the ladies' garments especially evoke sarcastic, mocking and cruel comparisons. They may attract the reader, or it may be suggested that they are unsuitable for the character, expressing the narrator's contempt for the person who wears them. Buildings, rooms, pieces of furniture, household objects are also used in comparisons.[31] Sometimes they are personified and share the character's emotions. It is movement or change that characterises Mansfield's descriptions of material or household objects. She often presents them as living beings in anthropomorphic imagery which creates an atmosphere of unexpected restlessness and unease. A depressing or claustrophobic atmosphere may be suggested by the size or lack of size of a room. Vehicles may move towards distant, never-to-be-reached destinations.

164

The prevailing themes of shattering of illusions or the disparity between reality and the narrator's momentary truth may be introduced by images like 'a dead kitten', 'a hanged man' or 'broken wing', in a fused emotional atmosphere. In Literary Impressionist fiction Man and his surroundings are fused into one:

(...) she plunged the teapot into the bowl and held it under the water even after it had stopped bubbling, as if it too was a man and drowning was too good for them. (p. 213)
(...) (The) shop was perched on a little hillock (...) It had two big windows for eyes, a broad veranda for a hat, and the sign on the roof (...) was like a little card stuck rakishly in the hat crown. (p. 228)
On the veranda there hung a long string of bathingdresses, clinging together as though they'd just been rescued from the sea rather than waiting to go in. (p. 229)
She walked over to the mantelpiece to her favourite Buddha. And the stone and gilt image, whose smile always gave her such a queer feeling, almost a pain and yet a pleasant pain, seemed (...) to be more than smiling. He knew something; he had a secret. (p. 282)

SENSORY EXPERIENCES IN BLURRING OUTLINES

Mansfield's short stories derive their meaning from a narrator's projection in language of the thoughts and sensory experience of one or more principal characters. These are 'impressions' in a fundamental sense, and they often reveal the limitations of the character(s) and the psychological apperception of reality. Images may evoke a sense of fictional realism for the reader, who is given the illusion of experiencing visual, auditory, tactile, olfactory and kinaesthetic sensations on the same level as the fictional character. Mansfield's narrator often appeals to the senses through a large amount of synaesthetic imagery. Different sensory experiences are mixed. A peculiarity of her style is the materialisation of phenomena of light and sound. Light may be seen as a liquid, e.g., in "Miss Brill" - 'like white wine splashed' (p. 330); music may be visualised as a ribbon, ('... a fellow ... draws ribbons - long, twisted, streaming ribbons - of tune out of a fiddle') (p. 364) or as a wave, ('He was tossed away on a great wave of music that came flying') (p. 515). As Busch points out, for the Literary Impressionist there is no such thing as a semantic field. Everything may be fused into an impression.[33] Light in Mansfield's short stories is caught and personified. It is endowed with the gift of seeing and feeling.[34] Light is also fused into drops and roses, whereas drops turn into bright or shining luminous dots, trees are fused into flames and blue moonlight. Appearances are deceptive. Things are not what they seem.[35]

The firm outlines of objects and characters dissolve. Contours blurr into pictorial descriptions. The image of darkness is related to that of light and here again we find the fusion, the interplay of light and shadow, the fading and dissolving of contours.[36]

> Although it was so still it seemed, like the flame of a candle, to stretch up, to quiver in the bright air, to grow taller and taller as they gazed - almost to touch the rim of the round, silver moon. (p. 102)
> ... the day had faded; the gorgeous sunset had blazed and died. And now the quick dark came racing over the sea, over the sand-hills, up the paddock. (p. 234)
> ... even the stars were conspirators too. So bright was the moon that the flowers were bright as by day; the shadow of the nasturtiums, exquisite lily-like leaves and wide-open flowers, lay across the silvery veranda. The manuka tree, bent by the southerly winds, was like a bird on one leg stretching out a wing. (p. 242)
> Out of the smudgy little window you could see an immense expanse of sad-looking sky, and whenever there were clouds they looked very worn, old clouds, frayed at the edges, with holes in them, or dark stains like tea. (p. 303)

Apart from the images of light, shadows and darkness[37] acoustic images are also important. Mansfield creates a dreamlike fluorescent atmosphere, in which all sharp outlines become blurred. The fusion of sensory impressions is increased by the use of synaesthesia of all sorts: 'Cold, blue light' (p. 182), 'Silent (...) or unholy splendour' (p. 237), 'sickening smell of warm humanity' (p. 524). Usually in this fused sensory experience a character turns away from reality and becomes one with nature around him.[38] Often the light and sound transference is so complete that by the end of an imagistic impression it is not clear if the phenomena described are lights in the distance or muted sounds. Mansfield's short stories are alive with Literary Impressionist verbal evocations of experience at almost every level. The acuity and/or obscurity of the images defines the character's awareness and places him within a scene.

COLOURS

The intensification of sensory data results in a heavy emphasis on images of colour. These images pervade Mansfield's work and contribute values from the purely descriptive to subtle evocations of mood. Basically, the colour images fall into two categories: those related to the visual experience of the perceiving character(s) and those which express in colour the atmospheric mood or the mental state of the character(s). The first category relates to Mansfield's narrative method of presenting data drawn from the sensations of her characters. A direct link between Mansfield's colours and those of Impressionism in painting is her use of subdued colours in a manner resembling the Impressionist's law of subjective compensatory colour, which left the process of blending these tints and hues to the eye of the viewer. Although Busch has gone too far in insisting that Mansfield's prose is to be paralleled with the technique of pointillism in painting, there is no doubt a painterly quality to her descriptive prose. In virtually any of her short stories and also in her journals and scrapbooks, Mansfield displays an Impressionist intensity in colour descriptions. These 'verbal paintings' occur throughout Mansfield's fiction and create a vibrant setting for the action of the story.[39] Colour images may express a particular 'Stimmung' together with an evocation of the mental state of the characters. Mansfield uses colour images in a manner that transcends their purely descriptive function. She provokes a colourful 'Stimmung' in which the action can be perceived. She uses purple, green, and gentle colours - mild yellows, greys, blues, and variations of light and shadow throughout her work for tonal, atmospheric as well as visual effect.

ACTION

As this survey of different patterns of imagery in Mansfield's total work reveals, she used patterns of imagery to give her short stories a fictional coherence and suggest layers of meaning. In many of Mansfield's short stories the Imagistic patterns are more complex and require more elaborate exegesis than they have received in traditional or Symbolist readings. Some of Mansfield's imagistic patterns seem to be introduced, because they - indirectly - emphasise a character-trait which is also displayed and exemplified by means of the character's direct speech or action. Though the image may have a purely narrative function - on the axis of a temporal narrative organisation - it may also extend or exemplify the meaning of a previous image. Mansfield preferred to write fiction with an emphasis on a fragmentary momentary psychological experience with little action, but with numerous images which convey obliquely some possible thematic motif, movement or action.

In "The Garden Party", for example, the images of hats are incorporated in the action of the story, not only functionally but also with respect to moral values.[40] The contrasting imagery in "The Fly" describing the boss and his friend Woodifield not only suggests an important theme, it also corroborates the physical action in the story, the killing of the fly. In the first episode in "The Fly" Woodifield and the boss are contrasted in using imagistic patterns. Old Woodifield, though five years younger, is nearing his grave. He's 'boxed up' and looks 'like a baby in his pram' but still likes to go out as 'he clings' to his 'last pleasures as the tree clings to its last leaves'. He 'pipes', 'peers', has 'shuffling footsteps' is 'frail' and 'old' (stated seventeen times) and 'on his last pins'. The Boss, on the other hand, though described in less imagistic language, is still 'at the helm', 'going strong', rolls in his chair, and 'flips' the *Financial Times*, interested as he is in his business and life. The Boss has a strong lust for life and shows a great capacity to survive. The imagery that defines the environment is remarkably positive, and equally rich in suggestions of the boss's energy, his strength, warmth and generosity. Indeed the implication, especially through contrasting comparisons with old Woodifield, is that the Boss has an unageing vitality. He seems to be immune to life's ravages and this suggests an important theme. The very effect of the description of the room and the boss's subsequent conversation with Woodifield is to establish a dichotomy between the two men as well as to portray them naturally in a realistic social context. Mortality, already implied by the contrasting images, is directly conveyed by the striking verbal metaphor of the boss's son in his grave: 'It was exactly as though the earth had opened and he had seen the boy lying there with Woodifield's girls staring down at him'. This *momento mori* together with his son's photograph make him forget the six years, although his mental grasp has weakened. But the Boss has built up not only his thriving business but also an effective defence mechanism. There are no tears to shed. By sheer accident the boss finds a fly in the inkwell and unconsciously picks it out, watching the struggling fly brushing off the ink in order to survive, the Boss finds in its fight for life an analogy with his own will to survive. The introductory, contrasting images have generated a sense of the boss's zest for life, which is also evident in the action. Killing the fly he paradoxically wishes it to weather adversity, increasingly identifying himself with the courageous little insect in the animal images: 'like a minute little cat', 'the little beggar' and 'he's a plucky little devil.' Time and his zest for life ('for the life of him') have healed the wound in his heart.

The images reveal the true nature of the Boss and inform and extend the meaning of the action in the short story. With Mansfield's method of narrative restraint, which eschews expository comments, the boss's final oblivion is expressed in the referential narrator's discourse, but the full weight of the boss's fight for survival is expressed by imagistic patterns. This sophistication of imagistic treatment was a device that Mansfield used in many of her short stories. In 1981 Clare Hanson & Andrew Gurr summarise the two main problems in criticism[41] of "The Fly" so far. The first, according to them, is that the theoretical insights of structural analysis have not been pursued or developed.[42] An analysis of Mansfield's fictional technique is required, which Hanson & Gurr do not present. The two authors only discuss some of the details, which may function on both narrative and symbolic levels. The second problem for Hanson & Gurr is that "The Fly" 'lacks the fullness and richness of implication of Mansfield's finest work'. They compare "The Fly" with the form of "The Wind Blows" and *The Aloe* without realising that structurally the three stories are completely different.

A Symbolist interpretation is fraught with difficulties on a number of levels, thematic, and structural as well as literal, all generated by the initial supposition that the fly or the Boss image *must* function as a symbol. This assumption has apparently led many critics to a Symbolist interpretation of other stories by Mansfield. It is argued that the image of the fly, or of the main character, the Boss, is fundamentally not a symbol, nor are the other images in the story symbolical. They do not reach outward to other planes of values. They do not shape the story into an allegory or archetypal construct. Rather, together with all the other chains, the patterns of images build up 'imagistic correlatives' within the story, in order to corroborate a character's action or his psychological state at a given moment. As in numerous other examples, the ultimate meaning of the images is to be found within the narrative and not outside or in mythological structures. (See the discussion on the image of the aloe later in this chapter).

CHARACTERISATION

Mansfield used imagery in a variety of manners. One of these is to establish character, a basic problem in Literary Impressionism. Direct expository comment is usually limited. The qualification that an objective narrative stance imposes upon imagery is that the image is generally the product of a character's perception only and is hence just as potentially unreliable as any other assertion by the narrator. For example, in "A Cup of Tea" we are told by the narrator that Rosemary is not exactly beautiful. That she is very insecure is only revealed by her speech and her action, when she throws the pretty woman out again. Beatrice in "Poison" is described as a heavenly beauty, not because she is, but because that is how she appeared to the narrator at the time.

Sometimes the images are more reliable in establishing aspects of

169

a character, however temporary. For example, in "The Escape", the woman in all her narcissism is characterised by images thematic in themselves - (powder puff, rouge stick, a bundle of letters, pills like seeds, a broken cigarette, a mirror, white ivory tablets of notepaper). Spiritual and marital death is powerfully evoked through the image of the dust that settles on their clothes like the finest ash (p. 198). Or in the imagery in "The Daughters of the Late Colonel", when in the first section, the two ineffectual personalities begin to emerge in a conversation in which none of the questions is really answered or solved. The first section abounds in images which serve mainly to shape the characters. At Constantia's suggestion that their father's top hat be given to the porter, Josephine only imagines: 'and now the porter's head (...), popped out like a candle, under father's hat (...)'. At Constantia's proposal that they should have their dressing-gowns dyed black, Josephine imagines themselves as two black cats creeping off to the bathroom. Josephine in the opening section assumes a foetal position ('arched her spine, pulled up her knees, folded her arms so that her fists came under her ears') and Constantia resembles a corpse already, an image which is stated again in the final section.

Given the wide variety of Mansfield's figures and the diversity of their effects, it is difficult to posit a single artistic ideology that explains them all. Contrary to conventional critical doctrine, which assumes that Mansfield was a Symbolist, the most revealing approach to the figures is from an Impressionist perspective. Such an interpretation, congruent with Mansfield's restrictive narrative methods, her indirect presentation of characters, her focus on atmospheric 'Stimmung' , and the technique of empathy (See Ch. 3) explains much of the source and meaning of the sensory imagery, including the colour images that pervades Mansfield's work. Further it suggests that few if any of Mansfield's figures are genuinely 'symbols' deriving their values from established associations. More often the atmospheric devices are better understood as images and metaphors which project a character's psychological state, expressing feelings undramatised in action, and 'objectivise' meaning, mood and atmosphere in the manner of Imagistic poetry. Since all of these matters are complex and elusive, it is perhaps best to discuss some of them individually. The first paragraphs of the short story "Bank Holiday", often neglected by the critics, serves as a colourful example. The story is a plotless description of the haphazard whirling movements of some anonymous people enjoying a day off on Bank Holiday. It opens with a static picture of the band. The musicians are perceived as individual objects of curiosity, not in terms of their actual physical movements.[43]

Mansfield's mixing of sensations, merging of individuals and surroundings, when enforcing a dissolution of characters into an

170

identification of the separate selves with a larger reality, is visualised by synaesthesia and turned into an existential question frozen in a moment of suffusion. Virtually any descriptive passage may reveal a sensational vitality, as the famous first passage of the opening of "At the Bay" illustrates. In a brilliantly evocative Impressionist passage, indicative of Mansfield's descriptions at their best, there is light, shadow and colour, many blurred contours, a variety of natural sounds and movements, animals and people, a mixing of different sensations, the passage of time, and a sense of coherent design in the concluding movement of the shepherd rounding the bend. ('Then pushing, nudging, hurrying, the sheep rounded the bend and the shepherd followed after out of sight' (p. 207).

There are other strains of imagery as well, many of them thematically significant. Mansfield's individual figures and images are often ironic, projecting a character's erroneous interpretation of events. They rarely function in the manner of traditional images. When characters are compared with animals or beasts, the images do not cast them in the role of these animals but ironically suggest human estrangement, dehumanisation and degrading primitive behaviour. When material objects are compared they are sometimes personified and share the character's emotions in a fused emotional atmosphere. They often function as an objective 'imagistic correlative'. Hence Hanson & Gurr may encounter hermeneutic problems when regarding 'the lamp' as a symbol of light, of art, as the central reality[44] in "The Doll's House" because their analysis takes no account of the fact that the lamp in "The Doll's House", is a sham, an illusion. ('It was even filled already for lighting, though, of course, you couldn't light it.' (p. 394) and 'you couldn't tell it from a real one' (p. 397)). In "The Doll's House" the imagery must be seen in its proper perspective, as a thematic structuring principle to reveal the story's main theme: the revelation of social discrimination and injustice. The imagistic patterns (e.g. in 'the door was like a slab of toffee)' when describing the doll's house (very big, awful smell, big lumps of paint, the hook was stuck fast), the very stiff dolls ('as though they had fainted') are all thematically significant. They reinforce the basic theme by implication. Else is 'a white little owl' and it is only Else who seems to understand that the rich people's 'little teeny lamp' is a sham and fake. Mansfield's imagery is faithful to Pound's dictum for poetry; that the poet should reject discursive analysis in favour of the poetic image - 'that which presents an intellectual and emotional complex in an instant of time'.[45]

Mansfield often uses imagery to reveal rather than discuss or explain the mental lives of her characters. Her images often encapsulate the full impact of one particular short story, particularly in a concluding or ironic paragraph. Examples include, as we have

171

seen, 'the broken wing' image for Robert Salesby, or Mrs Raddick's boredom in "The Young Girl" ('she was as bored as though heaven had been full of casinos with snuffy old saints for croupiers and crowns to play with') (p. 295); Raoul Duquette's quasi-submissiveness in "Je ne Parle Pas Francais" ('and the faithful fox terrier carried it across to him and laid it at his feet, as it were') (p. 84) and many more examples.[46] Sometimes Mansfield uses an 'imagistic correlative' as a concluding image for a short story, focusing the meaning of the preceding action in a vivid, sensory figure. This is a device, often described as an Impressionist technique of compression. At the conclusion of "Bliss", for example, the narrator provides a final descriptive passage to focus the reader's thoughts and feelings[47]: 'But the pear tree was as lovely as ever and as full of flower and as still.' (p. 135)

IMAGES OR SYMBOLS ?

Related to Mansfield's use of colour images are the figures that in traditional criticism, were described as symbols. Symbols generally point outside a work to meanings established by supernatural or historical concepts. It is argued here that Mansfield's figures may best be called 'imagistic correlatives'[48] because they express internal meanings drawn from the minds of the characters, which may be individual, may have associational meanings, and may pertain to one fragmentary experience only. The same image, used in a different context, a different fragment with a different perspective and character(s), may have different functions and values. An example is the aloe in "Prelude" and in "The Man Without a Temperament". This image does not draw on a spiritual or supernatural plane for its meaning, as Clare Hanson has it[49]. The image does not attribute a symbolist significance to a character, either in the case of Linda in "Prelude" or of Robert Salesby in "The Man Without a Temperament". The aloe in "The Man Without a Temperament" has a personal value for his invalid wife. It refers to a purely personal meaning, established by a small fragmentary vision, which may be compared with the other guest's visions, evoked in contrasting ironic imagistic patterns. In "The Man without a Temperament" (originally called 'The Exile') Robert's alienation from everyone, from the other guests at the pension, the servants, the local children and the old women washing their linen, is contrasted with his day-dreams of being at home with his literary friends in England. Robert without his natural surroundings is a man without a self, momentarily capable of sustaining a pose only in a secondary, a nursing role. In his alien role he cannot but lose his temperament. The images underline Robert's exile, and his loss of ego.

172

The signet ring registers his nervousness over his loss of identity, his roots or marital ties in these new surroundings and his new role as a nurse. For his invalid wife, Robert is all the life she has. At night she is laid out like a white corpse, and by contrast he is 'like a bird with a broken wing, that tries to fly and sinks again and again struggles'. But in his wife's desperate devotion he is envisaged as and identified with the aloe tree. The flowers are already melting away: 'Out of the thick, fleshy leaves of a cactus there rose an aloe stem loaded with pale flowers that looked as though they had been cut out of butter; light flashed upon the lifted spears of the palms.' (p. 135) His wife's momentary vision is contrasted with those of the other guests, the outsiders with the derogatory nicknames: The Two Topknots, the American woman, the Honeymoon Couple, the General and the Countess. Since Robert Salesby contemptuously ignores his fellow guests at the pension, they pay him back in kind. The Two Topknots remark to themselves that 'he is not a man but an *ox*', (Italics KM) the General feels too superior to look at him, but the Countess (and the driver), sniggering, confirm the alienation already shown in the contemptuous maid servant and the frightened children. All these momentary visions, some expressed in imagistic language, are in evident contrast with his wife's sentimental obsession in which she refers to the aloe tree: 'She looked up at him. She thought he looked pale - but wonderfully handsome with that great tropical tree behind him with its long, spiked thorns', which all refer inward to meanings already established and enforced by, for example, the narrative 'Stimmung', atmospheric descriptions evoked by nature, colour, and household objects. The images momentarily refer inward to different, contrasting personal values as generated by the thoughts, and feelings of some major characters. The image of the aloe in "The Man Without a Temperament", loaded with pale flowers that looked 'as though they had been cut out of butter', presents the narrator's momentary subjective vision, to be contrasted by his invalid wife's obsessive perception.

The aloe here does not represent 'life itself ... holding within itself the possibility of the rare flowering which justifies existence' as Hanson argues. The image of the aloe tree is used here evocatively. It comments on internal matters and gives internal structural coherence to this short story. Rather than drawing new associations into the narrative, it suggests different, contrasting layers of meaning, through the narrator's and the wife's totally different perception of the aloe.

The aloe also has an ironic function. It projects the wife's erroneous interpretation of reality, in her sentimental possessiveness. It projects the wife's psychological state and expresses feelings which cannot be dramatised in action. The wife's emotional reaction is objectified in an image, related to her feelings and to the meaning of the description of her mistaken perception. The aloe and the wife's reaction to it, express layers of feeling and thought which Mansfield could never state directly, only obliquely. She needed imagery to evoke the mental life of her characters. Hanson's methodological short-cut from the image of the aloe in "Prelude" to Robert Salesby in "The Man Without a Temperament" cannot be made.

An Impressionist reading of Mansfield's short stories may reveal a good deal about the function of her imagery, as a consideration of "Prelude" may serve to demonstrate. If the narrative method of this story is perceived as rendering the fragmentary experiences, thoughts, feelings, dreams and fantasies of the many different characters in the twelve fragments, then the images within the story become components of psychological revelation. They describe not only the manner in which Linda, Stanley, Beryl, Mrs Fairfield, the children Kezia and Lottie perceive the external world, but also reveal the quality of the mind at that moment. Imagistic patterns portray the different psychological states of the characters, of the innocent children, (for example Kezia) of the initiated woman (Beryl), the afflicted mother (Linda), the reconciled grandmother (Mrs Fairfield), and the energetic businessman (Stanley). Their interrelationship is characterised by isolation and loneliness. Their worlds are silent and fragmentary. Very rarely do the characters conduct any meaningful communication with one another. Linda seldom talks to anybody. She spends her days dreaming and ruminating in secret. Beryl is a little more communicative, but keeps her intimate thoughts to herself. Kezia is most of the time entirely alone. Mrs Fairfield, the grandmother, lives in memories of the past. Only Stanley, bumptious and crude, does not seem to have an inner mental life. Truly meaningful communication occurs only between Mrs Fairfield and Kezia when they talk about death.

A most revealing moment comes when Mrs Fairfield and her daughter Linda are linked by perceiving the aloe under the moonlight. There is a variety of restricted visions in various perspectives and if the narrative method of "Prelude" is perceived as rendering the thoughts, feelings, experiences, daydreams and fantasies of the different characters, then the images within the story become components of psychological revelation. The images describe and suggest not only the way in which the different characters perceive the external world but also the quality of their minds at any given moment. Imagistic patterns change according to the different psychological states, motivations, desires and thoughts of the characters.

Let us now examine the images used in relation to Linda, Kezia, and Mrs Fairfield more closely, as they are the only characters that perceive the aloe. In the first fragment, the imagery reveals the narrator's and Linda's vision of the Burnells' departure to their new house. There's not an inch of room for Lottie and Kezia. The two children have to be left behind to be picked up later. Instead 'the absolute necessities' (p. 11) are transported. The irony of the situation causes Linda to laugh with a laugh bordering on the hysterical. In Linda's vision even the children 'ought to stand on their heads!'. But Mrs Josephs, the neighbour, 'like a huge warm black silk tea-cosy', comes to the rescue by taking temporary care of the children. The narrator articulates Linda's thoughts and her vision of the outside world. Linda is pregnant yet appears to hate her children. She looks upon them as pieces of furniture. The imagery reveals Linda's grappling with reality and her confusion. The fragment already gives the reader a premonition of Linda's discontent with her life. In the second fragment, the narrator focuses on Kezia. Her perspective is articulated in atmospheric blurred contours. There are 'long pencil rays of sunlight' and 'the wavy shadow of a bush outside danced on the gold line'. Kezia sees 'a little Chinese Lottie through the multi-coloured glass-window'. She sees everything tinted by the glass. Kezia's analytical power is still that of a child, unable to tell appearance from reality. The blue lawn and the yellow lawn observed through different coloured panes of glass are two different lawns. The white Lottie becomes Chinese when her vision of the yellow Lottie conflicts with Kezia's everyday vision of her sister. Her mind is momentarily off balance and she needs to restore her normal vision by looking through the ordinary window.

Characterisation progresses in a leisurely accumulative manner. The narrator moves within and without the characters in order to present a complete, though fragmented, momentary view. When Kezia lingers in the deserted house her mood and atmosphere are fused into sensory impressions, into an atmospheric 'Stimmung'. Kezia's fear is skilfully caught in the images of the chasing animal. The contrasting images in this fragment have revealed Kezia's delicate sensibility and her fear of imaginary monsters in the dark.[50]

In the third fragment, Kezia's perceptory powers are again tested. The world around her seems out of proportion.[51] Through Kezia's imaginative eye we see 'hundreds of parrots (but the parrots were only on the wall paper (...) (who) persisted in flying past Kezia' (p. 18). In a further reinforcement of the pattern of images, Kezia's fear of animal attack is again revealed. ('I often dream that animals rush at me - even camels (...) their heads swell e-enormous.' (p. 17)

At the end of the fourth fragment, we meet Linda again. When she says good night to Stanley ('Mr Businessman') 'her faint faraway voice seemed to come from a deep well' and 'her faint voice from the deep well' said 'Yes, clasp me'. (p. 23).

In the fifth fragment, as in an Impressionist painting, the primeval beauty of the sound of the creek and the kingfisher are personified in a dreamlike world. In Linda's dream her father shows her 'a ball of fluff', which begins to swell until it changes into a tiny bird. The bird again swells and changes into a baby which Linda has to hold in her apron. This dream is very significant. It not only links Linda with Kezia's fear of swelling animals, it presents Linda's swelling syndrome for the first time in great detail. The field, the grass, the fluffy ball, the bird, all suggest the early morning and the innocent beginnings. But out of this primeval world comes the baby, a product which Linda deeply detests. Out of the very stuff of primeval innocence, the essence of life is presented to Linda. Unwillingly, she is caught up in the chain of events. The imagistic pattern of swelling animals is expanded by another one. It appears that the image of Linda's father has fused with that of her husband (p. 24). The fusion of the two images creates a paradox: love and hatred exist side by side in her mind. She both loves and hates Stanley. She is repelled by his vigour, watching him from the clouds doing his exercises, he is 'bending and squatting like a frog' and looks 'like a turkey'. (p. 25)

Love-making again involves a paradox. Still in bed, she is mentally preoccupied with it. Anthropomorphic and synaesthetic images project Linda's swelling syndrome again. Whatever she touches seems to come alive, especially when she is preoccupied with sex. She unconsciously re-creates the moments of life in imagistic patterns. In her imagination she struggles with the notion of the imagistic strains of her perception, of sex, swelling and coming alive, as *'they'* fill the air. She feels that under her steady gaze everything in her room comes alive. When *'they'* are there, Linda is petrified. *'They'* have hurt Linda. (Italics KM) She wants to rebel or escape. At the same time she is attracted by the mysterious swelling. Linda, the paradox, is discontented with life. What she consciously wishes is not what she unconsciously desires and lives up to. The swelling and coming alive imagery manifests her fear of again being pregnant and her confused sense of reality. It also points towards her 'split personality' - the conflict between having sex and the consequence of having children.

This antithesis is supported by other strains of imagery. Nature is described as tranquil, as serene, and fertile 'like a fat bird in a round nest'. Yet nature is feared. It excludes Linda.[52] Animal images further deflate her imaginary conception of life, especially when they involve ordinary animals which may grow out of proportion and swell. There are frogs (Stanley), a turkey (Stanley) and birds. Nothing reveals more clearly the process of the projection of her mind than does the image of the tiny ball of fluff (a bird), which becomes a baby and smiles knowingly at her. All these images are essentially vehicles of psychological revelation. They take the place of expository assertions of mental states. They reveal indirectly the thoughts and feelings that lead to Linda's imaginary escape on the aloe.

At the end of the fifth fragment, the synaesthetic strains of images portray Linda's paradox, which is the paradox of the disparity between illusion and reality.

In the sixth fragment, Linda is asked to go and look after Kezia, but doesn't. Kezia at this moment is wandering all by herself in the huge garden round the house. The contrasting images also underscore the antithesis in nature. There are two distinct sides of the garden: the side which is full of exquisite flowers (p. 32, 33) and that which is frightening and no garden at all.[53] In her wandering, Kezia comes upon the aloe tree. First we see the aloe through Kezia's wondering eyes:

> Nothing grew on the top except one huge plant with thick, grey-green, thorny leaves, and out of the middle there sprang up a tall stout stem. Some of the leaves of the plant were so old that they curled up in the air no longer; they turned back, they were split and broken; some of them lay flat and withered on the ground. Whatever could it be? She had never seen anything like it before. She stood and stared. And then she saw her mother coming down the path. (p. 34)

A few lines further down we find Linda's perception, quite different from Kezia's:

> Linda looked up at the fat swelling plant with its cruel leaves and fleshy stem. High above them, as though becalmed in the air, and yet holding so fast to the earth it grew from, it might have had claws instead of roots. The curving leaves seemed to be hiding something; the blind stem cut into the air as if no wind could ever shake it.
> 'That is an aloe, Kezia,' said her mother.
> 'Does it ever have any flowers?'
> 'Yes, Kezia,' and Linda smiled down at her, and half shut her eyes. 'Once every hundred years.' (p. 34)

To the naive and innocent Kezia the aloe is thick, grey-green, thorny, or 'tall stout, 'old' and 'curled up', 'split and broken'. To the experienced and afflicted Linda, - in a cinematic close up - the same aloe is 'a fat swelling plant', another image reinforcing her swelling syndrome. Linda's distorted perception of the aloe is contrasted here with Kezia's because it underscores all her emotional problems. It epitomises the paradox of life, but only for Linda. The antithesis, supported by other strains of images in previous fragments, is linked with Linda's visual sensations. The description is visually sharp and is recorded in precise imagistic details linked with imagistic patterns in Linda's dreams and day-dream. It anticipates a later imagistic pattern in the following fragment: the swelling syndrome with the swelling birds, the fat bud and the fleshy stem with the poppy. These are all related sexual images and psychologically they all spring from Linda's sex-ridden imagination. The paradox of nature is conveyed. The tree is calm and steadfast (but has claws), the wind cannot even shake this tree and nature is hiding something from Linda (like the birds in her day-dream). The untouchable, unshakable aloe, with its strength, and its brute force, paradoxically attracts Linda. ('I like that aloe. I like it more than anything here and I am sure I shall remember it long after I've forgotten all the other things.' p. 53)

Looking at it from below she could see the long sharp thorns that edged the aloe leaves, and at the sight of them her heart grew hard (...) she particularly liked the long sharp thorns (...) Nobody would dare to come near the ship or to follow after. 'Not even my Newfoundland dog', thought she. (p. 53)

Linda always transforms objects and scenes in her imaginary perception.[54] Paradoxically she sees the fearful aloe as a sanctuary, changing the animate tree into an inanimate ship, that she herself can steer away. Linda's dilemma provides her with no catharsis. She cannot be reconciled to life, and only wishes to escape in her many dreams:

As they stood on the steps, the high grassy bank on which the aloe rested rose up like a wave, and the aloe seemed to ride upon it like a ship with the oars lifted. Bright moonlight hung upon the lifted oars like water, and on the green wave glittered the dew.
'Do you feel it, too,' said Linda, and she spoke to her mother with the special voice that women use at night to each other as though they spoke in their sleep or from some hollow cave - 'Don't you feel that it is coming towards us?'
She dreamed that she was caught up out of the cold water into the ship with the lifted oars and the budding mast. Now the oars fell striking quickly, quickly. They rowed far away over the top of the garden trees, the paddocks and the dark bush beyond. Ah, she heard herself cry: 'Faster! Faster!' to those who were rowing. (pp. 52, 53)

Linda wishes to sail to nowhere. In her escapism, ironically, in her very desire to escape, lies her frustration. Her affliction at the same time leads towards her fulfilment; Stanley, her Newfoundland dog. This antithesis in Linda, all supported by previous strains of imagery, is now revealed in the dog image. Linda's subconscious mind as revealed in the poppy and the aloe, and her conscious mind as revealed here, share the same paradoxical attitude. She now turns toward her husband, who arouses Linda's emotions in another imagistic correlative. Stanley's love for Linda has been expressed in an image of offering (the cherries), 'as though he had brought her back all the harvest of the earth' (p. 37), and now Mansfield uses the contrasting image of the little packets and the surprise packet, another more direct and concrete image to characterise Linda. She loves him and she hates him. The two opposite feelings exist side by side. She hates her 'Newfoundland dog' who rushes at her, 'he's too strong for her' (p. 53), but she loves him for his childish devotion. When Linda's reflection upon the aloe tree comes to an end, Linda's fanciful mind is contrasted with her mother's practical one. Linda, seeing fertility in imaginary buds ('Are those buds, or is it only an effect of light?') (p. 52) starts thinking of escape, while her mother's mind turns to making currant jam.

It is true, that one of the key images in "Prelude" is Linda's perception of the aloe tree in fragment VI. As we have seen, it cannot be separated from the images which portray Linda's dreamlike escape on the aloe in fragment XI, from its link with Stanley, and from the other contrasting, linking or associative strains of images. All the imagistic correlatives underscore Linda's paradox. The ultimate meaning of the image of the aloe tree, one of the disputed figures in Mansfieldian criticism, must be found within the narrative surroundings and not outside the text, not in symbolist or mythological structures.[55]

Critics, such as Clare Hanson & Andrew Gurr, in their thematic interpretation, argue that Symbolism is the key to Mansfield's short stories.[56] Hanson, being more specific in an article, 'Katherine Mansfield and Symbolism: The Artist's Method in "Prelude", contends that, the aloe 'is the central symbol in "Prelude", that 'in the symbolic patterning of "Prelude" the aloe emerges as an image of the fundamental life force itself, which includes sexual force in human life. It represents the essential will or energy behind all things, endlessly, inalienable present, the fundamental donnée (...)'. Hanson's interpretation seems highly unconvincing, and is contradictory on a number of levels. Firstly, it seems to be generated by an *a priori* Symbolist assumption. Hanson departs from an initial supposition that the aloe, come what may, must function as a symbol. She writes that 'the relationship between Symbolism and Katherine Mansfield's short story method has not been sufficiently recognized'. The reason why the early critics never discovered the Symbolist link, according to Hanson, is because John M. Murry omitted to publish the annotation, which she herself has found in an early notebook:

179

The role of Symbolism in the formation of this aesthetic has been obscured largely because of John M. Murry's highly selective editing of her notebooks, which he published as successive editions of her *Journal* (1927, 1954) and *Scrapbook* (1939). He omitted a good deal of the early material especially. (pp. 25, 26)

In a 1908 notebook[57] Hanson has found a forgotten annotation, scribbled down by the twenty-year-old Mansfield, and on this Hanson bases her *a priori* Symbolist interpretation of the aloe. The annotation, copied by Mansfield from Arthur Symons is here, quoted directly from Symon's *Studies in Prose and Verse*:

> The partisans of analysis describe the state of the soul; the secret motive of every action as being of far greater importance than the action itself. The partisans of objectivity - give us the result of this evolution *sans* describing the secret process. They describe the state of the soul through the slightest gesture - i.e. realize flesh covered bones - which is the artist's method for me - in as much as art seems to me pure vision - I am indeed a partisan of objectivity. (ATL notebook, 2, p. 58) (Italics KM)

The annotation quoted, however, endorses only Mansfield's indirect method of oblique presentation within a plotless story and does nothing to reveal her Symbolist aesthetics. Mansfield's annotation may best be paralleled by a quotation from her own letters, written to explain her indirect method of presentation.[58] Inner emotions may best be illustrated by small gestures, they should not be analysed.

Mansfield, as is shown by an investigation of her aesthetics as recorded in her secondary writing, may have borrowed and copied some ideas from Symons or Wilde, but those authors clearly did not influence her writing permanently. Certainly not in the manner Hanson & Gurr suggest. Besides, Hanson's methodological short-cut enforces a Symbolist reading of Mansfield's total work, and this must be rejected.

Secondly, a Symbolist interpretation cannot be endorsed by a reading of her stories. Let us return to the interpretation of the aloe tree in "Prelude", which, as Hanson argues, 'is the central symbol of the story.' Hanson attempts to give extra weight to her Symbolist assumption by adding that the aloe must be the central symbol, because it provided the original title for the story. There appears, however, to be no ground to support this view. The aloe did indeed provide the original title of earlier draughts of "Prelude", but it appears from biographical information that Mansfield at this point intended to write a novel. The first part, "Prelude", was to be followed by "At the Bay", which is a parallel piece of fiction to "Prelude". In "Prelude" we find some of the same characters, and Linda is expecting the baby which has been born in "At the Bay". In Mansfield's secondary writing there is evidence found that her general practice of choosing titles and subsequently changing them, does not corroborate a Symbolist interpretation. Mansfield often made provisional notes for stories, with provisional titles. She did so, for example, when illustrating characterisation and theme in 'The Exile', which was later changed into "The Man Without a Temperament", for 'The Washerwoman's Children' which became "The Doll's House", and in a special note of Else's final utterance: 'I seen the little lamp'.[59] Nor do the other titles of Mansfield's stories support a Symbolist interpretation. A setting frequently leads to the final choice of a title[60], or the name of the main character is used as a title.[61] Equally an ironic twist in a main character's perception of reality may serve as a title, hinting at the instigation for a possible change of character.[62]

There is also a third reason to reject Hanson's or indeed any Symbolist interpretation of the aloe tree in "Prelude". If the aloe is considered to be 'the controlling symbol' for this particular story, it appears that the particular tree is approached and perceived only by Linda, Kezia and Mrs Fairfield. All three characters perceive and react differently to it. As we have seen, it arouses conflicting feelings only in Linda. The other main characters, Beryl and Stanley and the minor ones remain uninvolved. Although Hanson claims that 'the unity of "Prelude" is sustained through its technique of repeated and interwoven imagery', she narrows down her argument by writing that 'there is space here only to look briefly at some of the more important images' and excludes the image of the aloe as Linda's final means of escape.[63]

Finally, Mansfield's own comments on her stories, recorded in her letters, do little to support a Symbolist interpretation of her images. In her letters she rarely indicated that she was consciously aiming at an imagistic device. Her critical remarks on "Mr and Mrs Dove" are the only ones extant, which reveal clearly her rejection of a too overt, direct, imagistic pattern.[64]

Any Symbolist interpretation of the aloe as a possible central symbol must be rejected. There is no one central symbol. Let us agree that Symbolism for Mansfield was an early influence soon shaken off. Mansfield, as a Literary Impressionist interpretation shows, needed a structuring imagistic pattern to characterise her protagonists. The chain of images is stressed by other contrasting and enforcing images, for Kezia and Mrs Fairfield, and is fused into a new pattern which presents Stanley's character. The aloe in "Prelude" does not refer to any external value for its significance. That must be found within the narrative itself. Mansfield's imagistic patterns are multi-layered and require more elaborate exegesis than any Symbolist interpretation provides.

In conclusion, it may be argued that Mansfield's indirect, concatenated, broken or fused chains of images, producing vivid sensory evocations and psychological revelations, represent another dimension of her Literary Impressionist aesthetic. Her use of patterns of images as an oblique means of characterisation reveals a decided and fundamental relationship to the central tenets of Literary Impressionism. In common with the Realists of the late nineteenth century, Mansfield avoided figures that would draw on spiritual and supernatural planes for their meaning. No outward systems of mythology, or supernatural or Symbolist planes[65] are referred to. Mansfield's images momentarily refer inward to meanings established by a fragmentary context, to a 'Stimmung' evoked by nature, colour, and objects, to the personal values underlying the thoughts and feelings of the major characters.

In essence, the nature of Mansfield's imagery is often determined by her selection of narrative methods, and the expressive narrator's device of a momentary identification with the consciousness of a central character. Striking sensory images may be evoked in blurring outlines and with clusters of imagistic correlatives. These imagistic correlatives constitute the most subtle of her dramatic methods of revealing psychological insights, in a manner consonant with her aesthetic methodology of obliqueness. Other devices of imagery, ironic concatenation and contrasting imagistic juxtapositions indicate the range of Mansfield's experimentation. What a consideration of Mansfield's images as manifestations of Literary Impressionism ultimately reveals, over and above the standard critical approaches, is that her figures are closer to objective correlatives than to traditional symbols. For Mansfield, one of the ways of expressing emotion was to find a set of objects, a situation or a chain of events which conveyed the formula of the particular emotion.

It is this aim that L. Thon sums up in her characterisation of Literary Impressionism as 'die Kunst des Treffens', the art of getting at the most strikingly adequate rendering of an impression of reality.[66] The personal impression of any experience is of greater importance to the Impressionist than any accurate description of reality. These impressions, when perceived, may be surrounded by intuitive and strikingly particular associations. Mansfield often attempts to arrest the reader's attention through an unexpected, rare or even bizarre image, so that the impression will strike home. The image may create an illusion of objectivity, but the reader is nevertheless aware of the particular manner in which the illusion is created.

Mansfield's images are evocative and suggestive. Their primary function is to throw light on a character, on atmosphere, or on an object or action described. In order to catch the impression in its origin, Mansfield, the Literary Impressionist, prefers to produce a sense of spontaneity through the associations evoked by a scene, rather than analyse it more deeply and arrive at a more accurate description. Sometimes the comparisons are purely atmospheric in their effect, but there are also images that qualify the Impressionist's personal impression of what is perceived, reminding us of the Impressionist's subjective attitude towards reality. The effect of Mansfield's imagery is to allow the reader to participate in the cognitive and sensational life, illusion, dream or fantasy of her characters. The Impressionist's images tend to be particular and momentary. They are striking, rather than general and universal. No deep revelations are professed or hidden universal truths revealed which will be valid for all time. An interpretative stance sensitive to Literary Impressionist methods is essential to an understanding of Mansfield's method and the meaning of her rich and varied chains of images.

Chapter 5 CONCLUSION

Viewed in their totality, and with regard to both technique and meaning, Mansfield's short stories must be described and interpreted as being essentially Impressionistic. The Literary Impressionist tendencies in her short stories are evident from the first of her artistic efforts to the last, with indications of a growing dominance in her mature work. In the early story "A Woman at the Store" (1912), in "The Little Governess" (1915) and in her fragmented, last one, "The Canary" (1922) reality is made up of confused, fragmented, changing sense impressions.

The stress is on the process of an apperceptive consciousness perceiving reality. The episodic scenes are composed of fragmentary moments of experience, enclosed and highlighted by sensory imagistic chains and clusters and pictorial atmospheric descriptions of nature. The rendering of atmosphere and mood, the restricted perceptive consciousness and the phenomenological relationship of subject and object are inextricably woven into Mansfield's Impressionist tapestry, depicting a fragmentary relativistic world.

Mansfield employs the characteristic Literary Impressionist devices: episodic scenes, sensory clusters of images and a shifting and restricted narrative stance, by which she stresses the relativity of perspective and the irony of illusionary perception. Perceptual distortions are brought about by uncertainty, fear, limited knowledge, immaturity or innocence and solipsism. Throughout, the preference for a sensory experience over an information of restricted data reveals a reality that must be tentative, qualified by the perspective of the viewer. Reality in Mansfield's stories remains disordered. It inserts itself into a momentary subjective reality of values. Each experience, isolated in time and space, becomes its own subjective momentary reality.

In an attempt to create order where there is none, the narrator intuitively selects and interprets. The rendering of apperception is presented like a fluid, poetic, enigmatic substance, fusing form and meaning in the portrayal of the human condition in a concentrated, momentary impression. The central character often moves towards a progressively more restricted view of circumstances.

Mansfield's characters may experience a 'glimpse' into the fragments of their existence. In a stretch of time the disparate elements of objective and subjective time are fused in a moment of coming together, in an epiphany, so that a character is suddenly diminished and the absurdity of a situation is revealed.

The tone of her stories is one of apprehension, irony and cynicism, born of isolation and uncertainty, in which the characters seem to be

184

stranded on isolated stumps in an environment which they cannot comprehend. This is an emblem of the generic human condition in all Mansfield's fiction. Many of the mature works, those written after 1911, represent a significant advance upon the earlier satirical sketches, though even they already share the thematic and artistic traits that link Mansfield to Literary Impressionism. The stress is on perception, on mental blindness and self-serving delusion. In her later work this point is established more subtly.

It is Mansfield's Literary Impressionist tendencies which constitute her most significant influence on short story writing in the twentieth century and evoke the Modernist tone in her fiction. The stress is on sensory data, those observable details of scene and action that a person could perceive as the action took place. There is no background, no expression of sympathy by the narrator, no moral opinion on offer. No conclusions are drawn. Her work is sparse, crisp, sensory, with virtually no overt authorial presence, little unobserved description, little judgement, and few wasted words. There is no Symbolist reference.

Her line of influence may lead to the economy of Imagist poetry. The relativist realities of Mansfield's Literary Impressionism play a key role in the development of what came to be known as Modernism, an influence often overlooked by the critics. The recognition of Mansfield's role as a Literary Impressionist is a significant determinant of her place in literary history. The significance of her achievement has not been ignored, though her short stories have been widely interpreted in terms of biographical relationships. The enthusiastic interest in her fiction in the nineteen seventies and eighties attests to the continuing value of her contribution, which is fundamentally part of the development of Literary Impressionism. In the history of literature, therefore, Literary Impressionism should be given a place side by side with Realism, Naturalism, Symbolism, Expressionism, Modernism and Post-Modernism.

Footnotes to PREFACE

1. Virginia Woolf, in *A Writer's Diary*, 16/1/1923, quoted in Leonard Woolf, *Beginning Again*, 1964, pp. 202-207. Katherine Mansfield died at Fontainebleau on 9/1/1923. A week later, on hearing the news, Virginia Woolf wrote in her diary a lengthy analysis of her feelings about the other writer, both personal and literary: 'one feels - what? a shock or relief? - a rival the less? (...) When I began to write, it seemed to me that there was no point in writing. Katherine won't read it. Katherine's my rival no longer'.

2. It was J.M.Murry who distorted the picture and in the process managed to direct attention away from Mansfield's critical writings. See C. Hanson & A. Gurr, p. 3.

3. C.S. Beachcroft, *The Modest Art: A Survey of the Short Story in English*, 1968, pp. 162-176.

4. C. Hanson, *Short Stories & Short Fictions 1880-1980*, 1985, p. 63; Charles Palliser, *The Early Fiction of Virginia Woolf and her Literary Relations with Katherine Mansfield*, 1975, pp. 88-132.

5. Hanson & Gurr, pp. 21-23. See Chapter 4.5 of this thesis on 'Images or Symbols?'

6. Kate Fullbrook, *Katherine Mansfield*, 1986, Chapter I, pp. 11-31.

7. Martin S. Day, *History of English Literature - 1837 to the Present*, 1964, p. 403.

8. Margaret Drabble, 'The New Woman of the Twenties: Fifty Years On', *Harpers and Queen*, June 1973, p. 135.

- - -

Abbreviations will be used to refer to the most frequently used Mansfield sources in this way:

IGP   *In a German Pension*, 1911.
B   *Bliss and other Stories*, 1920.
GP   *The Garden Party and other Stories*, 1923.
DN   *The Doves' Nest and other Stories*, 1923.
SCH   *Something Childish and other Stories*, 1924.
J   *The Journal of Katherine Mansfield*, ed. J.M. Murry, 1927.
LI   *The Letters of Katherine Mansfield*, Vol. I, ed. J.M. Murry, 1928.
LII   *The Letters of Katherine Mansfield*, Vol. II, ed. J.M. Murry, 1928.
NN   *Novels and Novelists*, ed. J.M. Murry, 1930.
SC   *The Scrapbook of Katherine Mansfield*, ed. J.M. Murry, 1939.

CS   *Collected Short Stories*, 1945.
DefJ   *The Journal of Katherine Mansfield*, Definitive Edition, ed. J.M. Murry, 1954.
CLI   *The Collected Letters of Katherine Mansfield*, Vol. I, 1903-1917, ed. Vincent O'Sullivan and Margaret Scott, 1984.
CLII   *The Collected Letters of Katherine Mansfield*, Vol. II, 1918-1919, ed. Vincent O'Sullivan and Margaret Scott, 1987.

Chapter 1 Footnotes: INTRODUCTION

1. C. Hanson & A. Gurr, *Katherine Mansfield*, 1982, pp. 21-23; C. Hanson, 'Katherine Mansfield and Symbolism: The Artist's Method in 'Prelude', *Journal of Commomwealth Literature*, 1981, pp. 25-39.
2. K. Fullbrook, *Katherine Mansfield*, 1986. E.M. Braekkan, *From Feminist to Feminine: A Comparative Study of Katherine Mansfield's Short Stories*, 1981; C. Hanson & A.Gurr, 1982, pp. 10-14.
3. Cf. *The Pelican Guide to English Literature: The Modern Age*, 1961, ed. Boris Ford; *The Penguin Companion to Literature-British and Commonwealth Literature*, 1971, ed. D. Daiches; *Sphere History of Literature in the English Language*, vol. 7: *The Twentieth Century*, 1970, ed. B. Bergonzi; Malcolm Bradbury in *The Social Context of Modern English Literature*, 1971, Chapter IV (p. 73) in 'The Coming of the Modern' groups Impressionism as part of (vaguely defined) Modernism: 'perhaps we should employ modernism to mean this oscillation, though that is not generally how we use the word. In fact it is very vaguely defined,though what we *usually* mean to suggest by it is a whole cluster of international movements and tendencies (impressionism, post-impressionism, realism, symbolism, imagism, dadaism, surrealism and so on) which are actually often at great variance one with another'; In *Modernism*, ed. Malcolm Bradbury and James McFarlane, 1976, one essay is included on 'Symbolism, Decadence and Impressionism' by Clive Scott. Though the term is mentioned in the title and the introductory passage, Scott focuses mainly on French symbolism and some decadent poetry. As a kind of afterthought (section 4, p. 218) he vaguely compares painting with poetry (Monet, Degas, Rilke, Verlaine), recruits Oscar Wilde into Impressionism, but also contends that (p. 224, 225): 'literary Impressionism not only runs parallel with Naturalism, not only opens up into Expressionism and Futurism, but also may be regarded as the early manifestation of the peculiarly modern plight of an exploded consciousness caught in a fragmented universe.'; Fokkema & Ibsch in *Modernist Conjectures*, 1987, in their first chapter 'What is

Modernism?', pp. 1-41, do not mention the term.

4. Cf. L. Thon, 1928. See Chapter 2.2 'A Chronological Survey of the Term Literary Impressionism.'

5. Cf. Ulrich Weisstein, 'Comparing Literature and Art: Current Trends and Prospects in Critical Theory and Methodology' in *Interrelations of Literature*, ed. J.P. Barricelli & J. Gibaldi, Modern Language Association, 1982, p. 20.

6. Ibid, p. 23.

7. An author who is emphasised by one critic will frequently be excluded by another. Virginia Woolf, for example, represents to some the 'quintessential Impressionist' (Paulk, Kronegger), while others have argued that she must be considered a Modernist (Fokkema & Ibsch), and still others have contended that she must be considered an Expressionist (Weidner).

8. Mario Praz, *Mnemosyne*, 1970, p. 20.

9. René Huyghe, 'Shifts in Thought during the Impressionist Era: Painting, Science, Literature, History and Philosophy' in *Impressionism : A Centenary Exhibition*, p. 15, 1974.

10. LII, p. 160.

11. For a longer list see the many biographical works on Katherine Mansfield in Bibliography B.

12. *Mnemosyne*, p. 25.

13. In 'The Parallel of the Arts: Some Misgivings and a Faint Affirmation' in *JAAC*, 31 (1972/73), pp. 154-164 and 309-321.

14. See S.F. Paulk, *The Aesthetics of Impressionism: Studies in Art and Literature*, 1979, Chapter IV.

15. In *Yearbook of Comparative and General Literature*, 1978, 78, p. 13.

16. Ibid, p. 13.

17. In 'Butterfly Wings without a Framework of Steel: The Paradigmatic Impressionism of Katherine Mansfield's Short Story "Her First Ball", *Os Estudos Literários entre Ciência E Hermenêutica*, I, Proceedings of the first Congress of PCLA, 1990, pp. 57-77.

18. Ibid, p 61.

19. See footnote 35, p. 77.

20. J. Rewald, cf. footnote no. 29, p. 589, quoting Monet's letter to Geffroy, Oct. 1890, in Geffroy, II, Chapter X.

21. Paul Ilie, *Symposium*, p. 51. See Bibliography C.

22. R. Rogers, 'Stephen Crane and Impressionism', *Nineteenth Century Fiction*, 24 Dec, 1969, pp. 292-304.

23. Todd K. Bender, 'Hanging Stephen Crane in the Impressionist Museum', *Journal of Aesthetic and Art Criticism*, 35, 1976, pp. 47-56.

24. Ford is quoted in S.L. Weingart, *The Form and Meaning of the Impressionist Novel*, 1964, p. 16.

25. Besides, if Monet's 'trick' of painting a series were related to Impressionist literature in the sense that Weisstein proposes, then Mansfield would have written, perhaps, seven different short stories, all with a similar theme and setting, in which the main character, Leila, might encouter the old, bald man at different moments, in dreams and fantasies, and above all (cf. Monet's concern) with differing atmospheric effects of light.

26. See Chapter 4.2 for a detailed discussion of Mansfield's major themes.

27. See in Chapter 3 the section 'Epiphany'.

28. Cf. Jean Seznec, 'Art and Literature: A Plea for Humility', in *NLH*, 3 (1972), 569-574, as quoted in Weisstein, 1982, pp. 24-25.

29. Ulrich Weisstein, 'Verbal Paintings, Fugal Poems, Literary Collages and the Metamorphic Comparatist' in *Yearbook of Comparative Literature*, 27, 1978, pp. 7-19. The quotation appears on p. 8.

30. Rewald does not include Vincent van Gogh.

31. I shall use the term *impressionism* in the broad sense, in its original historical meaning,of an aesthetic movement that mainly found expression in painting from around 1874. See Chapter 2.1.

32. Cf. H. Overland, 241; Kronegger, p. 25. Cf. also Mansfield's comments on Th. Hardy: 'I read *the well beloved* by Thomas Hardy. It really is *appallingly bad, simply rotten* - withered, boring and pretentious. This is very distressing (...) The style is so *preposterous* too. I've noticed that before in Hardy occasionally - a pretentious, snobbish, schoolmaster vein (Lawrence echoes it) an 'all about Berkeley Square-ishness', too, and then to think as he does that it is the study of a temperament.' (Italics KM) in *The Collected Letters of Katherine Mansfield*, vol. II, 1918-1919, eds. Vincent O'Sullivan and Margaret Scott, 1987, p. 219.

33. In C. Hanson & A. Gurr, 1981, p. 24. As a kind of afterthought, Mansfield is related to Cézanne: 'Her writing is most often described as though it were a kind of verbal equivalent of an Impressionist painting, and stress is laid on the physical 'surface' of her work - its tone, colour and texture. She is commonly praised for her acuteness of ear, her visual memory, her exquisite rendering of impressions of the natural world. There is a string of verbal nouns - flash, colour, sparkle, glow - by means of which her critics have tried to convey the effect that her work has had on them (...) we need more emphasis on the solidity of the structure of her stories and on their weight of implication. In this Cézanne, whom she admired, is a better parallel than Renoir, whom she did not.'

34. As quoted in H. Müller, 'Impressionism in Fiction: Prism vs. Mirror', *The American Scholar*, 7, 1939, p. 356.

35. See Nochlin, 1966, p. 96.

36. Garland, *Crumbling Idols*, 1960, pp. 97-98.

37. Ibid, p. 109; Cecelia Waern, 'Some Notes on French Impressionism,' *Atlantic*, 69, 1892, p. 535, 537.

38. Ford Madox Ford, 'Techniques', *Southern Review*, I, 1935, p. 31.

39. Müller, 1938, pp. 357-58.

40. Michel Benamou, 'Symposium', p. 51.

41. Kenneth E. Bidle, *Impressionism in American Literature to the Year 1900*, 1969.

42. The use of the term 'parallax' is derived from Carol P. Knowle, 'Impressionism and Arnold Bennett', p. 45 in Todd K. Bender, *Literary Impressionism in Ford Madox Ford, Jospeh Conrad and Related Writers*, (Madison: Text Development Program, 1975), from J.T. Johnson in an unpublished paper entitled 'Towards a Definition of Literary Impressionism' delivered at the Midwest Modern Language Association meeting in 1970 (See also Johnson, 1973). For an explanation of the term 'parallax' see footnotes: Chapter 4.1 footnote 34; Chapter 4.2 footnote 1.

43. Rodney O. Rogers, 1969, pp. 292-304.

44. Stowell, 1980, pp. 24-33.

45. Overland, 1966, pp. 275-276.

46. Ruth Moser, *L'Impressionisme Francais, Peinture, Littérature, Musique*, 1952.

47. See Bibliography B. for the debate on "The Fly".

48. See Michel Décaudin, 'Poesie Impressioniste et Poesie Symboliste', *Cahiers de l'Association Internationale des Études Francaises*, XII, 1960, pp. 132-142.

49. Ibid. Cf. also Leo Spitzer, *Stilstudien*, II, p. 296; Beverley Gibbs, 'Impressionism as a literary Movement', *Modern Language Journal*, 36, 1952, pp. 175-183.

50. For a detailed discussion see in Chapter 4.5 the section 'Image or Symbols?'

51. LI pp. 234, 236, 237.

52. Cf. Kurylo, *Checkhov and Katherine Mansfield*, 1974, Chapter III and IV, pp. 44-45; Stowell, 1980.

53. CLII, p. 353.

54. See Chapter 4.5 on Images.

55. Cf. Madden, p. 134.

56. CS, p. 96.

57. See Lionelle Venturi, 'The Aesthetic Idea of Impressionism', *The Journal of Aesthetics and Art Criticism*, The Philosophic Library, no. 1, Spring, 1941, p. 44.

58. Cf. Kurylo, p. 45.

59. Cf. Yuan She Yen, *Katherine Mansfield's Point of View*, 1967, p. 425.

60. Cf. F.S. Madden, *The Development of a Consistent Structural Pattern in Katherine Mansfield's Short Stories*, 1978, p. 330.

61. Ibid, p. 331.

62. Ibid, p. 3: 'In Mansfield's fiction the central theme of a great number of her stories is the disparity between illusion and reality, or between falsehood and truth. The tone of her handling of this theme is most often ironic. Usually a character is steeped in illusion and falsehood. Then, for a moment, the veil drops, and the character or reader *or both* see truthfully. This moment of revelation may ironically produce anguish or a sense of entrapment (a thematic motif).

63. For example, in "Millie", "The Man without a Temperament", "The Little Governess", "Bliss", and "The Garden Party".

64. In "Sun and Moon", for example, Sun appears too priggish, serious and jealous to realise that a nut on an ice pudding is meant to be eaten, but Sun observes appearances, he dreams and does not perceive 'reality'. In "Her First Ball", Leila appears too ignorant to understand that the dazzling appearance of the ball is simply an illusion that cannot last forever. In "Bliss" Bertha cannot perceive 'her reality' and the world around her, because she envelops it with false illusions, that will be shattered.

65. Cf. Overland, p. 241.

66. As, for example, Kezia, Linda, Beryl, Mrs Fairfield in "Prelude" and "At the Bay" it is their normality, in Kezia's childlike apprehensions, Linda's love-hate relationship with Stanley, Beryl's romantic longings and Mrs Fairfield's domesticity.

67. Cf. Ulrich Weisstein, 'Expressionism: Style or *weltanschauung?*, reprinted in *Expressionismus as an International Phenomenon*, ed. Ulrich Weisstein, 1973, pp. 42-62; 'Vorticism: Expressionism English Style', in *Yearbook of Comparative and General Literature*, XIII, 1964, 28-40; reprinted in *Expressionism as an International Phenomenon*, 1973, pp. 167- 180.

68. A. Friis, 1946, p. 132.

69. P. Halter, 1972, pp. 178-185; B. Haferkamp, 1969, pp. 221-39.

70. Stowell, pp. 4, 13, 244; Nagel, pp. 174, 175: 'The relativistic realities of Crane's Impressionism play a key role in the development of what came to be known as Modernism, especially in its sense of an indifferent and undefinable universe and a lack of individual significance.' Paulk and Kirschke blend the two phenomena in their analyses of James, Conrad, Ford, Richardson, Woolf and Joyce.

71. Stowell, p. 244.

72. Ibid, p. 4.

73. Fokkema/Ibsch, pp. 34, 35, 318.

74. Ibid, p. 29.

75. Stowell, p. 13.

76. Fokkema/Ibsch, p. 122.
77. Ibid, p. 23.
78. Ibid, p. 318.

2.1 Footnotes: IMPRESSIONISM IN PAINTING

1. Müller, 356.
2. Cf. Todd Bender, *Literary Impressionism in Ford Madox Ford, Joseph Conrad and RFelated Writers*, 1975, p. 179. Bender provides a useful overview of the philosophical backgrounds of Impressionism.
3. Cf. Linda Nochlin, *Impressionism and Post-Impressionism, 1874-1904, Sources and Documents*, p. 25.
4. In a defence of the Impressionists' *Sketches and Abbreviated Summaries*, 1876, we read: 'Impressionism is not only a revolution in the field of thought, but it is also a physiological revolution of the human eyes. It is a new theory that depends on a difference of perceiving the sensations of light and of expressing the impressions. Nor do the Impressionists fabricate their theories first and then adapt the paintings to them, but on the contrary, as always happens with discoveries, the pictures were born of the unconscious visual phenomenon of men of art, who, having studied, afterward produced the reasoning of the philosophers.' As quoted from Nochlin, p. 25.
5. As quoted from Stowell, p. 46.
6. Cf. Müller, p. 356.
7. Characteristics were summarised from Stowell, pp. 46-59; Dürer, reprinted, 1922; E.H. Gombrich, 1963; Rewald, 1961, Ph. Pool, 1967. For more information on the importance of rendering what the eye sees in the work of the Impressionist, cf. Th. Duret, *Histoire des Peintres Impressionistes*, 3rd ed. Paris, 1922.
8. Duret, p. 175.
9. Cf. W. Harms, p. 43.
10. From William Gaunt, *Impressionism*, 1970, p. 11
11. De Maupassant, as cited in Gaunt, p. 24.
12. Cf. Hauser, 1951, Vol IV, p. 179.
13. Bergon's philosophic recognition (1892) of the important distinction between 'time' and 'duration' had preceded Einstein's theory of relativity by thirteen years. It was not until the French Impressionist movement was already history that Bergson systematised what the French painters had discovered in their art. In delineating his theory of time - which takes into account the fact that human time seems to pass more rapidly on some occasions and more slowly on others - Bergson formulated and made accessible a development in the

arts that had first been fully realised with Impressionism in painting. Cf. also Stowell, Chapter I.

14. Cf. Rewald, p. 196, p. 239, for studies done by Sisley and Monet, on the changes in aspects on colour and form which seasonal change brings about in the same subject. See Rewald, too, for the Impressionists' painter's observations on a subject in multiple views. Monet painted the same lake forty times and he did many versions of *The Garden at Giverny*.

15. Cf. Todd Bender, 1975, p. 2.

16. Quoted from Stowell, p. 32.

17. As cited in Huyghe, 1963, p. 172.

18. Chevreul, 1864, as cited in Courthion, p. 184.

19. As cited from Denis Thomas, *The Age of the Impressionists*, 1987, p. 47.

20. Hauser, p. 171.

21. Cf. Gombrich, p. 436.

22. Cf. Rewald, p. 196.

23. Stowell, p. 54.

24. As cited by Nochlin, p. 34.

2.2 Footnotes: A CHRONOLOGICAL SURVEY OF the use OF THE TERM 'LITERARY IMPRESSIONISM'.

1. Only the most outstanding, innovative and controversial studies on the issue will be summarised here. For a more detailed chronology with reference to German literary history see R.M. Werner, *Impressionismus als Literärhistorischer Begriff - Untersuchung am Beispiel Arthur Schnitzlers*, 1981, Chapter 2.2.2, pp. 16-61. Biased though he is towards a stylistic analysis in isolation, Werner provides computer-aided analyses and concludes that a purely stylistic investigation based on L. Thon's indexes does not work. (p. 250) For my survey of German studies I am greatly indebted to Werner's study. Cf. L'Impressionisme dans le Roman', in *Revue des deux Mondes*, 15/11/1879, which article was slightly altered for the publication of Brunétière's volume *Le Roman Naturaliste*, 1883. Subsequent references will be abbreviated and will follow the text in parentheses.

2. L. Desprez, *L'Evolution Naturaliste*, especially the chapter 'Les Goncourts', 1884, pp. 67-117.

3. E.g. F. Brunétière, *Le Roman Naturaliste*, 1879, p. 94.

4. L. Petit de Julleville, *Histoire de la Langue et de la Littérature Francaise*, 1896, vol. 8, p. 183; M. Spronk, *Les Artistes Littéraires: Études sur le XIX Siecle*, 1889.

5. G. Loesch, 1891, in *Theoretische Schriften 1887-1904*, re-edited by Gotthart Wünberg, 1968, pp. 33-102.

6. C. Grottewitz, 'Wie kann sich die moderne Literaturrichtung weiter entwicklen?' as quoted from *Die Literärische Moderne*, re-edited by Gotthart Wünberg, 1971, p. 59.

7. M.G. Conrad, 'Die Sozialdemokratie und die Moderne' in *Die Literärische Moderne*, re-edited by Gotthart Wünberg, 1968, pp. 94-123.

8. K. Lamprecht, 'Deutsche Geschichte der jüngsten Vergangenheit und Gegenwart', 1912, überarbeitete Ausgabe der Originalausgabe von 1902, p. 308; K. Lamprecht, 'Liliencron und die Lyriker des psychologischen Impressionismus: Stefan George, Hugo von Hofmannsthal', in 'Porträtgalerie aus Deutscher Geschichte', pp. 167-198.

9. *Die Hauptrichtungen im Deutschen Geistesleben der Letzten Jarhzehnte und ihr Spiegelbild in der Dichtung*, 1914.

10. In *Dialog vom Tragischen*, in Hermann Bahr, *Zur Überwindung des Naturalismus. Theoretische Schriften*, re-edited by Gerhart Wünberg, pp. 181-198.

11. *The Analysis of Sensations and the Relation of the Physical to the Psychical* (transl. from the 1st German ed. by C.M. Williams, rev. and suppl. from the 5th German ed. by S. Waterlow, 1914, p. 12.

12. Herman Bahr, p. 198.

13. E. Friedell, *Kulturgeschichte der Neuzeit*, 1976, vol. 2, p. 1388.

14. 1907. (2nd ed. of 1923 is used here).

15. *Das Ende des Impressionismus*, 1916, cf. Fritz Bürger, *Der Impressionismus in der Strausz-Hofmannsthalschen Elektra*, in 'Die Tat, Jg. 1, 1909, quoted here from *Literärische Manifeste*, re-edited by Rupprecht/Baensch, pp. 218-224.

16. G. Frübrodt, *Der Impressionismus in der Lyrik der Annette von Droste-Hülshoff*, 1930; R.V. Charlowitz, 'das Impressionistische bei Goethe' (Sprachliche Streifzüge durch Goethes Lyrik, *Jahrbuch der Goethe Gesellschaft III*, 1916, pp. 41-99.

17. Cf. O. Walzel, 'Die Wesenzüge des deutschen Impressionismus', *Zeitschrift für Deutsche Bildung*, 6, 1930. pp. 169-182, here p. 174.

18. 'Edmond und Jules de Goncourt, die Begründer des Impressionismus', 1912 e.g. Eugen Lerch's *La Fontaines Impressionismus*, in *Ärchiv für das Studium der neueren Sprachen*, Jg. 139, 1919, p. 247.

19. 1919.

20. Daniel Wenzel, *Der Literärische Impressionismus dargestellt an der Prosa Alphonse Daudets*, 1928; Hans Hoppe, *Impressionismus und Expressionismus bei Emile Zola*, 1933.

21. *Flaubert als Begründer des Literärischen Impressionismus in Frankreich*, 1933.

22. In *Impressionismus und Expressionismus bei Emile Zola*, 1933.

23. A. Wegener, *Impressionismus und Klassizismus im Werk Marcel Prousts*, 1930; H. Schneider, 'Maupassant as Impressionist in "Une Vie", "La Maison Tellier", "Au Soleil", *Arbeiten zur Romanischen Philologie*, 1933, vol. 9; H. Wiemann, 'Impressionismus im Sprachgebrauch La Fontaines', *ARP*, vol. 8, 1934; K. Rost, 'Der Impressionistische Stil Verlaines', 1936, in *ARP*, vol. 29, 1936.

24. E.g. Irene Betz, *Tod der Deutschen DIchtung des Impressionismus*, 1936; U. Lauterbach, 'Herman Bang. Studien zum dänischen Impressionismus', 1937.

25. E.g. G. Loesch, *Die Impressionistische Syntax der Goncourt*, 1919; K. Brösel, *Veranschaulichung im Realismus, Impressionismus und Frühexpressionismus*, 1928; L. Thon, *Die Sprache des Deutschen Impressionismus*. Ein Beitrag zur Erfassung ihrer Wesenszüge, 1928.

26. G. Loesch, p. 24.

27. Cf. M. Werner, pp. 36-43.

28. E.g. Chapter Bally, 'Impressionisme et Grammaire' in *Mélanges D'Histoire Litteraire et de la Philologie Offerts a M.B. Bouvier*, 1920; E. Richter, 'Studien über das neueste Französisch', in *Archiv für das Studium der Neuen Sprache und Literatur*, 1917.

29. Joseph Warren Beach, *The Twentieth Century Novel: Studies in Technique*, 1932.

30. Henry James, 'The Art of Fiction', in *Theory of Fiction: Henry James*, ed. J.E. Miller, 1956.

31. In 'El Impressionismo en al Lenguaje', 1956, 3rd ed. as quoted from Paul Ilie, *Symposium*, 1968, p. 46.

32. Cf. *Investigaciones Linguisticas*, V, 1938, pp. 273-278.

33. H. Hatzfeld, *Literature Through Art - A New Approach to French Literature*, 1952, reprinted 1969; Ibid, 'Literary Criticism through Art and Art Criticism through Literature', in *The Journal of Aesthetics and Art Criticism (JAAC)*, Sept., pp. 1-20, 1947.

34. In *The English Institute Annal*, 1942, pp. 29-63.

35. Wolfgang Iskra, *Die Darstellung des Sichtbaren in der Dichterischen Prosa um 1900*, 1967, p. 2.

36. Ibid, p. 19.

37. A. Schmidt, *Literaturgeschichte, Wege und Wandlungen Moderner Dichtung*, 1957, 3rd vol.; Ibid, *Die Geistigen Grundlagen des 'Wiener Impressionismus'* in *Jahrbuch des Wiener Goethe-Vereins, Neue Folge der Chronik*, Jg. 78, 1974, pp. 90-108, esp. p. 92.

38. *Geschichte der Deutschen Literatur von Goethes Tod bis zur Gegenwart*, in 2 volumes, 1950., e.g. p. 233.

39. Hauser, 1958, pp. 166-225.

40. Cf. on this issue e.g. C. Kurylo, *Checkhov and Katherine Mansfield*, 1974, p. 43.

41. Cf. also W. Falk, *Impressionismus und Expressionismus als Literatur*, re-edited by W. Rothe, 1969, who analyses German literature from 1890; W. Nehring, who discusses Hofmannsthal's contribution to Austrian Impressionism in *Hofmannsthal und der Österreichische Impressionismus*, in *Hofmannsthal - Forschungen II*, 1974, pp. 57-72.

42. H.Sommerhalder, *Zum Begriff des Literärischen Impressionismus*, 1961.

43. R.Hamann/J.Hermand, 'Impressionismus', Band 3, Epochen deutscher Kultur von 1870 bis zur Gegenwart, 1977.

44. Mandfred Diersch, *Empiriokritizismus und Impressionismus, über Beziehungen zwischen Philosophie, Aesthetik und Literatur um 1900 in Wien*, 1977.

45. Cf. B.J. Gibbs on Spanish Impressionism in 'Impressionism as a literary movement', in *Modern Language Journal*, 36, 1952, pp. 175-183: 'I have tried to demonstrate that Impressionism originated in realism and naturalism as a pure secondary movement; that in the writing of E. and J. de Goncourt and Daudet this latent force broke forth and acquired characteristics of its own and finally that in the writing of G. Miro, it reached its culmination and became a literary movement in its own right.' (p. 182); Cf. J.Th. Johnson (jr)' Literary Impressionism in France: a survey of criticism', in *L'Esprit Createur*, 13, 1973, Chapter 4, pp. 271-297.

46. 'The Impressionism of Stephen Crane: a study in style and technique', in *Americana Norwegica*, vol. 1, 1966, pp. 239-285.

47. Rodney O. Rogers, 'Stephen Crane and Impressionism' in *Nineteen Century Fiction*, 24, 1969, 292-304. Kenneth E. Bidle, *Impressionism in American Literature to the Year 1900*, 1969; James Nagel, 'Impressionism in 'The Open Boat' and 'A Man and Some Others', in *Research Studies*, 43, 1975, pp. 27-37.
For the discussion on Literary Impressionism I am greatly indebted to these works. I am also indebted to Müller (1938), Nagel (1975 and 1980), Stowell (1972 and 1980), H. Sommerhalder (1961) and Overland (1966). For every word taken from them I cannot give page references instead I prefer to acknowledge here a debt greater than footnotes can express.

48. M.E. Kronegger, *Literary Impressionism*, New Haven, 1973; Ibid, 'The Multiplication of the Self from Flaubert to Sartre' in *L'Esprit Createur*, 13, 1973, Chapter 4, pp. 310-319; Ibid, 'Authors and Their Centuries' republished by Ph. Crant, 1974, pp. 155-166.

49. She gives examples by Balzac and others, p. 30.

50. R.M. Werner, 1981.

51. P. Bürger, 'Naturalismus-Aesthetizismus und das Problem des Subjektivität', *Naturalismus / Aesthetizismus*, 1979, p. 18-55.

52. Sarah Paulk, 1979.

53. P. Stowell, *The Prismatic Sensibility: Henry James and Anton Cexov as Impressionists*, 1972; P. Stowell, *Literary Impressionism: James ans Chekhov*, 1980, Esp. Chapter 5, 6, 7 on James and Chapter 2, 3, 4 on Chekhov.

54. Stowell links Mach's 'philosophy of Impressionism' with Gestalt thinking. (p. 36): 'Gestalt thinking is at the heart of the way impressionist characters learn to deal with their world.'

55. See L. Thon, pp. 5-6 and Eva Weidner, *Impressionismus und Expressionismus in den Romanen Virginia Woolfs*, 1934, pp. 20-21.

56. In translations from German into English, for example, certain phrases have to be turned from active into passive constructions. French impersonal clauses with 'on' may outnumber certain equivalent German constructions, while there is no real counterpart in English, but a variety of possibilities with 'one', 'people', 'you', 'they' or the passive voice. See also Busch, p. 61.

57. One convenient example here is the use of the possessive pronoun, which in German has a notable Impressionist effect, and which is obligatory in English. Cf. L. Thon, pp. 16-17.

58. See R. Moser, 1952.

59. Cf. P.R. Albères, 1962; Todd K. Bender, 1976.

60. Literary Impressionism is indeed something more than a series of separate fleeting impressions, as Calvin Brown has suggested: 'Literary Impressionism's aim is to catch and reproduce the shifting, fleeting, intangible impressions by which the outside world impinges on our senses - or as some more philosophically minded critics like to put it: Literary Impressionism attempts 'to break down the distinction between the subject and the object.' In this pursuit the Impressionist abandons causality, formal logic, and any attempt or desire to fit his impressions into such predetermined forms as the sonnet and the sonata', in Calvin Brown, 'Symposium in Literary Impressionism, *Yearbook*, p. 80.

61. Cf. Stowell, p. 9.

2.3 Footnotes: SOME BASIC AESTHETICS OF LITERARY IMPRESSIONISM

THE PERCEPTION OF REALITY

1. Cf. William Harms, p. 10: 'Impressionistic painting is an art of reproducing instantaneous sense-perception, a point of view which is rooted in the sheer delight of visual effects', in *Impressionism as a*

Literary Style, 1971, p. 10.

2. As cited from Kronegger, p. 35.

3. Cf. Kronegger, p. 36.

4. Cf. Overland, p. 246.

5. J. Conrad, as cited from Müller, p. 357.

6. Cf. Overland, p. 252.

7. Cf. Kronegger, p. 38.

8. Cf. Overland, p. 242.

9. Overland, p. 241.

10. Overland, p. 242.

11. Müller, p. 356.

12. Stowell, p. 25.

13. Kronegger, 1969, p. 531; Hauser, p. 170; Stowell, p. 43.

14. Stowell, p. 43.

15. Cf. Kronegger, p. 60.

16. Cf. Stowell's analysis of Tsjechov's and James's characters, p. 44.

17. Cf. Stowell, pp. 33-35.

18. Cf. Overland, p. 242.

19. Cf. Stowell, p. 49.

20. Chiaroscuro= in French 'clair obscur'.

21. From Jules Laforgue, *Mélanges Posthumes*, 'Critiques d'Art'-l'Impressionisme', Paris, 1903, pp. 137, p. 144.

22. R.M. Albères, 1962, pp. 184-86.

23. Kronegger, p. 40.

24. Kronegger, p. 41.

25. Kronegger mentions Proust and Cl. Simon, p. 41.

26. Kronegger (p. 41) mentions Proust, Joyce, V. Woolf, N. Sarraute, and Cl. Simon.

27. From Gustave Geffroy, *La Vie Artistique*, Salon de 1894, 1895.

28. Impressionism is also called *Simultansehen*, 'simultaneous vision' or *Farbigwerden der luft*, 'the air is becoming (pure) colour' by Georg Marzynski in 'Die Impressionistische Methode' in *Zeitschrift für Ästhetik und Algemeine Kunstwissenschaft*, XIV, 1920, pp. 90, 84. The critic Leo Spitzer, in his article on 'Spreizstellung bei präpositionalen Ausdrücken im Französischen' discusses the phenomenon of simultaneous vision in language, referring to Proust, Musil, Kafka, possibly Joyce and V. Woolf, and later in M. Butor and Alain Robbe-Grillet.

29. Cf. René Huyghe, 'L'Impressionisme et la Pensée de son Temps', in *Promothée*, Nouvelle Serie, 1, 1939.

30. Laforgue, 1966 edition, pp. 176-177.

LIGHT AND ATMOSPHERE

1. Kronegger, p. 43.
2. Cf. Kronegger, p.42, states 'to their own soul'. Light is the soul of Impressionist painting and the soul of Impressionist literature.
3. Sommerhalter, p. 16.
4. E. Zola in his *Salon de 1880* (p. 241) recognised that the exhaustive analysis of the properties of colour and light is the essence of Impressionism in painting: 'their discovery properly consists of having recognized that intense light fades colours, that the sun reflected by objects tends, by sheer brightness, to bring them to this luminous unity that blends its seven prismatic colours into a single tone of dim brilliance, of light. Colours dissolve into the light, in the brilliant clarity of full sunshine. This study of light in its thousands of decompositions and recompositions is what we called, more or less accurately, Impressionistic, because from then on, a painting becomes the impression of a moment experienced in the presence of nature'. (*Salons*, récueillis, annotés et presentés par F.W.J. Hemmings, et R.J. Niess, 1959, p. 194).
5. Kronegger, p. 43.
6. Cf. Kronegger, p.46.
7. Cf. B. Haferkamp's analysis of Mansfield's imagery of nature.
8. Kronegger, p. 47.

CHANGE

1. Laforgue, as quoted from Stowell's thesis, 1972, p. 26.
2. Stowell, 1980, p. 2.
3. Ibid, p. 53.
4. Cf. the concept of 'memory' in grown-up characters.

SPACE AND TIME

1. As cited from Herman Bahr, 1968, pp. 197-198: 'Alle Trennungen sind hier aufgehoben, das Physikalische und das Psychologische rinnt Zusammen, Element und Empfindung sind eins, dasz Ich löst sich auf und alles ist nur eine ewige Flut, die hier zu stocken scheint, dort eiliger fliesze, alles ist nur Bewegung von Farben, Tönen, Wärmen, Drücken, Räumen und Zeiten, die auf die audere seite, bei uns herüben, als Stimmungen, Gefühle (...) es dauert vielleicht gar nicht lange und mann nennt die weltanschauung Machs einfach die 'Philosophie des Impressionismus'.

THE ACT OF BECOMING IN A MOMENTARY FRAGMENT

1. Cf. L. Thon, pp. 5-6; Eva Weidner, 1934, pp. 20-21; Stowell, p. 32.

2. Cf. Herman Bahr, p. 197.

3. It has been argued that the concept of time and its major paradoxes has become the actual subject of modern literature. Cf. Robert Humphrey, *Stream of Consciousness and the Modern Novel*, 1959; Shiv Kumar, *Bergson and the Stream of Consciousness Novel*, 1963; A.A. Mednilov, *Time and the Novel*, 1952; Hans Meyerhoff, *Time and Literature*, 1960.

4. Cf. Stowell's psychological discussion of 'Space and Time' p. 35; Müller's vague term of 'the centrifugal tendencies in modern fiction', p. 361.

5. Stowell, p. 35.

6. Cf. Max Wertheim's 1912 paper, in Stowell's *Introduction*, p. 36.

7. Cf. Stowell, p. 37.

8. Ibid, p. 37.

9. Ibid, p. 38.

10. Ibid, p. 39.

11. Ibid, p. 24.

12. Stowell, p. 13.

13. Ibid, p. 13.

14. Müller, p. 335.

15. Stowell, pp. 14-15.

16. Cf. Stowell, pp. 18-19 and see the discussion of Mansfield's 'glimpses' in chapter 3.3 on 'Epiphany'. Cf. M. Albères, 1962, 'un moment de la durée'.

17. All characteristics are collected from the major works on Literary Impressionism, (See Bibliography) and summarised in a concise survey.

18. Cf. Overland, p. 241.

19. Cf. Müller, p. 357.

20. Ibid, p. 353.

3 Footnotes: MANSFIELD'S LITERARY IMPRESSIONISM in her SCRAPBOOKS, JOURNALS, LETTERS and REVIEWS

LIFE AND ART

1. For example, her difficult relationship with John M. Murry and her now well-known quarrels with D.H. Lawrence.

2. Cf. C.K. Stead (1977), pp. 16, 17; Ida Baker (1985), p. 233: 'She was like a lantern with many sides, not octagonal, but centagonal'.

3. Comparing Mansfield's journals, and notebooks in the A.T. Library, Wellington with the definitive *journal*, published by John M. Murry in 1954, more omissions may be found, for example from a notebook, donated by Clara Wood, on 14 July, 1906, in which additional quotations drawn from her reading were noted from Oscar Wilde, John Stuart Mill, George Eliot, La Rochefoucault and Merryman. Murry only selects a few fragments drawn from the great mass of her unpublished writing.

4. LJMM, p. 476 (11/2/1920).

5. LII, p. 225.

6. LJMM, p. 435 (8/12/1919).

7. LII, p. 225.

8. LJMM, p. 697 (26/12/1922).

9. NN, pp. 196, 7.

10. NN, p. 53.

11. Cf. 'Art and Philosophy', *Rhythm*, I, printed in *The Critical Writings of Katherine Mansfield*, edited and introduced by Clare Hanson, 1987, pp. 21-23.

12. J, p. 237.

13. Cf. also LJMM, p. 267 (6/11/1918).

14. LII, p. 9 (31/1/1920).

15. LII, p. 416.

16. NN, p. 235.

17. LII, p. 92.

18. LII, p. 79.

19. J, p. 321.

20. LII, p. 268.

ART AND HISTORY

21. LII, p. 365 (29/2/1921).

22. LII, p. 387 (29/6/1921).

23. J, p. 80; Cf. also p. 203.

24. LJMM, pp. 380-1 (10/11/1919).

25. LJMM, p. 388 (10/11/1919).

26. LJMM, p. 392-3 (16/11/1919).

27. LII, p. 208 (1/5/1922).

28. LII, p. 94 (Febr. 1921).

29. LJMM, p. 544 (25/9/1920).

31. NN, p. 157.

32. Madden, p. 3; Berkman, p. 196; Daly, p. 126,127; Hanson & Gurr, p. 77.

33. Sc, p. 205. For everybody perceives and imagines things differently, each in his own way. (All translations in this study are my own, JvG)

34. Sc, p. 26.

35. J, p. 273 (Nov. 1921).

DEFEAT OF THE PERSONAL

36. LII, p. 93.

37. LII, pp. 91-2.

38. J, p. 195.

39. J, p. 72.

40. J, p. 72.

41. Cf. E.A. Stauffer, *The Problem of the Personal in the Art of Katherine Mansfield*, 1973, Chapter I, pp. 1-30.

42. J, p. 271.

43. J, p. 331.

INTUITION

44. *Rhythm*, 'The Meaning of Rhythm', I, 1911, as quoted from *The Critical Writings of Katherine Mansfield*, edited and introduced by Clare Hanson, 1987, p. 23.

45. Cf. Muller, 357.

46. NN, p. 222.

47. NN, p. 222.

48. NN, p. 224.

49. NN, p. 213.

50. NN, p. 213.

51. NN, p. 305.

52. NN, p. 306.

EMOTION

53. NN, p. 236.

54. NN, p. 200.

55. NN, p. 31.

56. See also H.E.P. Theimer, *Conrad and Impressionism*, 1962; S. Weingart, *The Form and Meaning of the Impressionist Novel*, 1964, Chapter 2, pp. 36-71; S.F. Paulk, *The Aesthetics of Impressionism - Studies in Art and Literature*, 1979, on Conrad's *Heart of Darkness*, pp. 126-138.

57. NN, p. 214.

58. NN, p. 264.

59. NN, p. 236.

60. NN, p. 301, and p. 107.
61. NN, p. 255.
62. J, p. 121.
63. NN, pp. 237-238.
64. NN, p. 269.
65. NN, p. 271.
66. NN, p. 271.
67. NN, p. 64.
68. NN, p. 94.
69. NN, p. 95.
70. NN, p. 108.
71. NN, p. 108-109.

EMPATHY

72. Cf. E. Baldeswhiler, 'Katherine Mansfield's Theory of Fiction', *Studies in Short Fiction*, vol. 7, 1970, p. 421.
73. LJMM, p. 584 (3/11/1920).
74. LII, p. 63 (27/10/1920).
75. LJMM, pp. 278-279 (10/11/1919).
76. NN, p. 107-111.
77. LJMM, p. 447.
78. LJMM, p. 544.
79. J, p. 110-111 (1916).
80. LI, p. 82 (11/10/1917).
81. J, p. 203.

EPIPHANY

82. NN, p. 151.
83. NN, p. 206. Cf. also NN. p. 12: 'For though her desire for expression was imperative and throughout the book there are signs of the writer's longing to register the moment, the glimpse, the scene, it is evident that she had no wish to let her reserved fastidious personality show through. NN, p. 300: 'The novel fails to convey that moment (...), that moment when the light breaks along the edge of the curtain and the music sinks down, lower, lower'.
84. NN, p. 32.
85. LII, p. 182 (1918). Mansfield describes the (blocked) epiphany in 'The Daughters of the Late Colonel': 'All was meant, of course, to lead up to that last paragraph, when my two flowerless ones turned with that timid gesture to the sun, it seemed to me, they died as surely as Father was dead'. Cf. also LII, p. 120 (23/6/1921).
86. J, p. 203.
87. J. Joyce, *Stephen Hero*, p. 18.

88. As quoted from Morris Beja, *Epiphany in the Modern Novel*, 1971, p. 18. The Joycean definition has a very definite focus, which increases its usefulness in a wider literary context.

89. J, p. 273 (Nov. 1921).

ATMOSPHERE

90. Cf. B. Haferkamp, 'Zur Bildersprache Katherine Mansfields', *Neueren Sprachen*, vol. 18, 1969, p. 223.
91. Cf. Müller, 357; Stowell (1972), pp. 1-34.
92. LJMM, p. 18 (20/3/1915).
93. LJMM, p. 26 (25/3/1915).
94. LJMM, pp. 33-34 (8/5/1915).
95. J, p. 92.
96. J, p. 94.
97. J, p. 174.
98. LI, p.447; NN. p. 168.
99. LII, pp. 188-189.
100. J, p. 280.
101. J, p. 287.
102. J, p. 144.
103. LJMM, p. 544.
104. NN, p. 192.
105. NN, p. 237 (8/8/1920).
106. NN, p. 417-418 (Nov. 1920).
107. LII, p. 417-418 (26/2/1922).
108. LII, p. 33.
109. LJMM, p. 657.
110. NN, p. 50-51.

OBLIQUE

111. J, p. 236.
112. LJMM, p. 46.
113. LJMM, pp. 392-393 (16/11/1918).
114. J, p. 73.
115. NN, p. 193.
116. NN, p. 176.
117. LII, p. 152.
118. NN, p. 176.

STRUCTURE

119. Cf. NN, p. 40, 92, 95, 107, 188, 262.
120. NN, p. 227.

121. NN, p. 4.

122. Sc, pp. 219-221.

123. Cf. Hanson & Gurr, p. 22.

124. Cf. Sc, pp. 220, 221.

125. NN, pp. 125-126.

126. NN, p. 140.

127. LII, p. 89.

128. LII, p. 89; LJMM, p.6.

129. LII, p. 88.

130. NN, p. 297.

131. NN, p. 301.

132. NN, p. 301, 305.

133. LII, p. 92.

134. NN, p. 182.

135. NN, pp. 50-53.

136. NN, p. 50.

137. NN, pp. 261, 154, 158.

138. NN, pp. 154, 158.

139. Ibid.

140. See 'Introduction' to *Scrapbook*, ed. John M. Murry, 1939, p. VI, VII.

141. Sc, p. VI, VII.

142. NN, p. 206.

143. NN, p. 252.

144. NN, p. 297.

145. NN, p. 28.

146. NN, p. 140.

147. NN, p. 148, 149.

FRAGMENTS

148. NN, p. 211.

149. NN, p. 211.

150. Sc, p. 162.

151. Ibid.

152. J, p. 226.

153. *The Letters of Katherine Mansfield*, ed. J.M. Murry, 1941, p. 389. This is the American edition.

154. NN, p. 18, 19.

155. NN, p. 28.

156. Cf. Bibliography on Literary Impressionism.

157. CLII, p. 353 (Letter to S.S. Kotelianski, 21/8/1919).

158. NN. p. 101, p. 188; Sc. p. 162.

4.1 Footnotes: NARRATIVE METHODS

1. Cf. G. Genette, 1972, p. 206. A person is capable of both seeing and speaking at the same time and he is also capable of narrating what another person sees, hears, feels or has seen etc. Thus seeing and speaking, focalisation and narration, may, but need not be attributed to the same person. In principle, focalisation and narration are two distinct activities. If a narrator records not what he sees himself, but what is perceived by the character (focaliser), the effect is a distancing, a supposed objectivity, which makes the illusion of a sensory activity more difficult. The 'limitation' of narrative data into the narrator's projection of the mind of a character is essential to the concept of Literary Impressionism. It ultimately reveals that reality cannot be fully comprehended by a single mind.

2. Müller, p. 363; Overland, p. 241; Kronegger, p. 60; Stowell, p. 22, 23.

3. Booth, 1961, p. 164.

4. Cf. Stanzel's theory of 'mediacy' (Mittelbarkeit), when choosing between two contrary manifestations of presentation: the 'overt' and the 'covert' one.

5. McHale, 1978, p. 262.

6. Graham Hough, 1970, p. 204.

7. In 'auctorial FID' the character's evocation in FID remains the instrument of the narrator. It presents the shorthand of a character's thought or speech, but is subordinate in status to the narrator's judgement and his insertion into the other narrative means.

8. Todorov's effaced narrator hypothesis influenced Bansfield's in relation to 'speechless sentences' and has influenced some narratologists, who now devise 'narratorless' narratives. S. Chatman, e.g., when attempting to articulate Booth's views on narration within a semiotic model of communication, sometimes subsumes the narrator's functions among the implied author's concept. According to Chatman every text has an implied author but a narrator is optional. When the latter is absent, communication is confined to the implied author (and the implied reader). However, in some cases, Chatman's semiotic interpretation of the implied author prevents the implied author (+ optional narrator) from communication altogether. Here is Chatman's interpretation: 'unlike the narrator, the implied author can tell us nothing. He, or better, it, has no voice, no direct means of communication; it instructs us silently, through the design of the whole, with all the voices, by all the means it has chosen to let us learn. (S. Chatman, 1978, p. 148). Another option would be to include the narrator and make the implied author optional, since there must always be some agent responsible for an utterance, even without communication. As Rimmon writes: 'there is always a teller in the

tale. Even when a narrative text presents passages of pure dialogue, manuscripts found in a bottle or forgotten letters or diaries, there is - in addition to the speaker or writer of this discourse - a 'higher narratorial authority' responsible for 'quoting the dialogue or transcribing the written records.' (Rimmon, 1983, p. 88).

9. M. Bal, 1985, p. 120.

10. A 'higher' narrational authority is responsible for 'the transcription' of selection and combination of the written record into the text. When analysing a narrator's text we cannot only study the narrator's selection and combination of available possibilities. There is also the sheer, idiosyncratic handling of the material. As we all know, there are many different tools, instruments. There are witty, ironic narrators, dry, objective reporters, lively mimicking tellers. There are anecdotalists, yarners, describers, relaters, fablers, biographers, diarists, relaters etc. In short, there is a great variety of 'tellers behind a tale'.

11. Rimmon, 1983, p. 94.

12. Chatman, pp. 220-252.

13. Ibid, p. 223. In any discourse there is someone responsible for the discourse, when ordering the linguistic signs in a process of selection and combination (Jakobson, 1960). These are the two fundamental ordering principles in verbal behaviour. First, a choice is made out of the available possibilities and second, the chosen possibilities are combined into a new linguistic utterance, based on equivalence, similarity and dissimilarity, synonyms and antonyms.

14. Cf. Genette, 1980, p. 164.

15. Ibid, pp. 171-186:

1. *Reported Speech*-(DD): dramatic in type (imitated speech). The most mimetic of the three, the reproduction of dialogue, monologue by the narrator. Though the narrator effaces himself and lets the character's words stand on their own.

2a. *Transposed Speech*-(ID): a little more mimetic than narratized speech. This form never gives the reader any guarantee or any feeling of literal fidelity to the words really uttered in DD, because the narrator's presence is perceptible in the syntax.

2b. *Free Indirect Speech*-(FID): not entirely the same as 'transposed speech'. The absence of a declarative verb can involve a double confusion.

3. *Narratized or Narrated Speech*-(ID): the most distant and generally the most reduced in a summary or dialogue by the narrator.

16. Brian McHale, 1978, pp. 249-87. See also Page, 1973, pp. 31-5. Since TG Grammar has failed to derive the patterns between ID, DD, or FID (Banfield, pp. 4-10,13-33) demonstrating the implausibility of any account claiming to derive ID from DD or DD

from ID, or FID from either, we presume, broadly speaking, that the three main types of reported ID are not outputs at different levels of one and the same transformational route, but that each discourse has a separate route of its own. (Cf. McHale, 257). But how else than in a traditional derivational manner might a systematic account be given of the interrelations among the types of represented and reported discourse? The alternative would be to bring the question of representation and illusionism to the forefront again, as suggested by McHale. This was precisely Hernadi's approach when reviving the Platonic typology of modes of poetic discourse. (Hernadi, 1972). Hernadi's invention was to posit a third category midway between 'authorial' presentation (diegesis) and representation/mimesis, i.e. 'substitutionary narration' (in broad terms McHale's fourth category: ID, mimetic to some degree). Hernadi inverts the traditional priority of syntactical categories over to representational ones. Therefore, one is now free to take his three traditional categories as points on a continuum, along which other types of represented discourse may be located.

NB In the analysis of the text of 'The Fly' the original order of the two frameworks has been reversed. First DD was located in the text, after which FID was selected within ID, and finally the different modes of telling in ID were selected.

17. Cf. Jakobson, who distributed the functions of language. In order to avoid a new set of confusing names the most functional of Bühler/Jakobson and Genette's framework were selected and regrouped into a division, which far from being exhaustive, is meant as a convenient survey, in order to describe the different roles of the narrator within one text. Jakobson (1960, pp. 350-377) defines six possible functions: 1. the referential (denotative, cognitive), 2. the expressive (emotive), 3. the conative. These three were borrowed from Bühler's traditional linguistic model. (1933, pp. 19-90). Jakobson adds another three functions: 4. the phatic 5. the metalingual and 6. the poetic.

In addition to a typology of narrators, Genette (1980, pp. 255-259) also defines some narrative functions, being related to the different narrative aspects: 1. narrative, 2. directing, 3. communication, 4. testimonial and 5. ideological function.

18. See also Banfield (1978b, pp. 437-8), who defines the two functions of the first person narrator: the communicative and the expressive. Halliday (1971) describes three socio-linguistic functions: 1. the ideational function, which has to convey a message, e.g. about reality, from the speaker to the hearer; 2. the interpersonal function, which must fit appropriately into a speech situation, fulfilling the particular social designs that the speaker has upon the hearer; 3. the textual function, which must be well constructed as an utterance or

text, so as to serve the decoding needs of the hearer.

Frans Stanzel (1981) opts for a distinction between 'teller' and 'reflector' character's discourse, a distinction which is compared to the older distinction between first and third-person narrative or between external and internal perspective for narrative discourse.

Booth (1961) also provides a systematic account on the question of 'types' of narrators: 'dramatized' and 'undramatized' narrators (pp. 151-3), roughly corresponding with Stanzel's 'teller- and reflector-characters' theory.

Friedman (1955) distinguishes between a 'non-personal narrative' (summary) which is 'a generalised account or report' and a personal narrative (immediate scene), or 'showing', which focuses on the successive details of time, place, action, character and dialogue. (1169).

19. Cf. Jakobson (1956) and Wellek and Warren (1948): metaphor because of the possibilities of comparison, of joining a plurality of worlds and metonymy because of the possibilities it offers for association and its principle of contiguity, of movement within a single mode of discourse.

20. Genette, 1980, p. 256.

21. Jakobson, 1960.

22. Cf. S. Ullmann, 1957, p. 214.

23. The *directing* function is a function difficult to qualify and quantify. Selection and combination of modes of discourse, e.g. of focalisation will be difficult to record without an analysis of a rough copy of an earlier draft, or a comparison with another 'similar' text. The *communication* function is also difficult to illustrate, since not all narrative texts contain indexes which may illustrate this function. In "The Fly" there is one example which might be listed. On p. 417 we read in the narrator's discourse: 'But behold', which might be considered to be conative (in the communication function), if directed at contact with the reader. Another interpretation, however, when focusing on the narrator's involved, lively attitude towards the contents of the message, might read it as 'expressive', introduced here as a possible expression of the narrator's identification with the fight for life put up by both the boss and the fly.

24. For example:
p. 412 - So there sat (...) Woodifield, (...) in his office chair (...), five years older than he. On Tuesday he was dressed (...)
p. 423 - It had been there for over six years.
p. 424 - (...) two tumblers that stood on the table with the water-bottle.

25. Cf. the relationship with the ubiquitous, near-omniscient 'spirit' of the story.

209

26. For example:

p. 413 - His hands began to tremble (...) He took a key off his watchchain, unlocked a cupboard below his desk and drew forth a dark squat bottle (...).

27. Cf. the directing function. For example:

p. 415 - He came round by his desk, (...) and saw the (...) fellow out. Woodifield was gone (...) the door shut.

p. 416 - At that moment the boss noticed that a fly had fallen into his (...) inkpot.

p. 418 - The fly was dead.

28. The graphological words with an expressive and a poetic function may be coloured first, in different colours, after which the referential function may be selected. The 'purely' poetical ones may be selected from these blocks. Finally, the blocks may be counted separately. In the text of "The Fly" referential narration (66%) is contrasting with the considerable amount of expressive (27%) and poetic (7%) narration.

29. For example:

p. 412 - It did one good to see him. (Old W., as 'a messenger of death' will disturb the boss's peace).

30. Expressive adjectives and adverbs, for example:

p. 412 - old (17 x), greedily, rosy, wistfully, admiringly;

p. 413 - deep, solid, in full view, frail, how many?, bright, red, exultantly, transparent, pearly, kindly, jokingly;

p. 414 - feebly, lovingly, wonderingly, generous, hastily, faintly, various, nice broad;

p. 416 - violent, over and done with, feebly, desperately;

p. 417 - small sodden, immense, over and under (2 x), lightly, joyfully, horrible, great heavy, cowed, stunned, laborious, fair and square, tenderly, brilliant;

p. 418 - timid and weak, deep, draggled - in vain, dead grinding, positively frightened, sternly.

Expressive and ironic verbs, for example:

p. 412 - piped (3 x), peered (2 x), boxed up, dressed and brushed;

p. 413 - flipped, planted;

p. 414 - swooping across, tossed off, cocked an eye, heaving himself, quavered;

p. 415 - brightened, dodged in, plumped down, sprang, groaned;

p. 416 - (weeping), crashing, clamber;

p. 427 - struggling, waved, oozed round, dragged, (behold);

p. 418 - seized, padded away.

31. Presented acoustically, when read aloud, and grammatically. (cf. the large amount of inversion).

210

32. For example:

p. 422 - All the same, we cling to our last pleasures as the tree clings to its last leaves.

33. For example:

p. 413 - the legs of the boss's table are like twisted treacle, and his electric fire looks like 'five transparent pearly sausages'.

p. 413 - The son is photographed with a background of 'spectral photographer's parks' with 'photographer's storm clouds'.

p. 415 - the boss's son is in his grave . This is how the boss feels: 'as though the earth had opened and he had seen the boy lying there with Woodifield's girls staring down at him'.

pp. 415, 418 - Old Macey is portrayed as 'a dog that expects to be taken for a run' and is presented as 'the old dog'.

Metaphors and similes:

p. 412 - as a baby peers out of its pram, as the tree clings to its last leaves;

p. 413 - like twisted treacle;

p. 415 - like a dog that (...) as though the earth had opened (...)

p. 417 - as the stone goes over and under the scythe.

Metonymy and synechdoche:

p. 412 - the boss, boxed up, still at the helm;

p. 413- the five transparent, pearly sausages, spectral photographer's parks with photographer's storm-clouds;

p. 416- Learning the ropes, the whole place crashing about his head, a broken man.

34. As Peter Sloat Hoff described the Impressionistic narrator: 'The reader is placed at the same epistemological level as the confused characters, who serve as centers of consciousness. The reader becomes to some degree, a receiver of temporally fragmented sense impressions rather than organized narration. The information which reaches the reader of an Impressionistic novel is potentially incorrect, for it often comes through an observer who may be mistaken, and it is information often broken and distorted.' P. Sloat Hoff, in an unpublished paper, delivered at the Literary Impressionism session of the 1975 Modern Language Convention. Cf. also Chapter I, footnote 42.

35. Cf. Linda's unreliable information on the aloe's flowering period.

36. In McHale's study the term *Free Indirect Discourse* (FID) was favoured, since it is *free*, i.e. free of conjunctions, free of an introductory verb, not being dominated by a 'higher' clause, which means that its range of formal possibilities is extremely large. (250, 253). It is *indirect* because it implies that both narrator and character are involved. It is *discourse*, i.e. it is a mode, like direct and indirect discourse. Then it is FID, and I hope to be excused for using the

abbreviation FID.

In general, English literary critics have been less responsive to the phenomenon of FID, than e.g. German or French ones. It appeared that many of them lacked a generally recognized term for the device. It is understandable, therefore, that practical criticism of Katherine Mansfield over the world has only hinted at the phenomenon of FID, constantly inventing new, usually undefined terms. The few critics that have recognised the phenomenon in Mansfield's work will be listed here chronologically:

In 1946 Anne Friis hints at FID for the first time. She gives some examples (p. 125), although she cannot define the phenomenon. She does not grasp the narrator's function and mixes up DD, ID and FID. On p. 124 she writes: 'She (KM) has found her method (...) She eliminates everything which may remind the reader of the writer's personality. All description is rendered as an impression of one of the characters, or in the form of direct speech'. On p. 125: 'Peculiar to Katherine Mansfield's method is her way of letting her characters talk and think in their own characteristic language, in this way revealing their personalities.'

In 1954 Sylvia Berkman focuses mainly on themes and images in her critical study, but is the only critical biographer to hint at the difference between FID in general and the expressive and poetic narrator in Mansfield. On p. 179 she explains: 'Miss Mansfield, like Virginia Woolf, sustains throughout a story one persisting note. Mrs Woolf, focusing always on inner consciousness, rapidly transcribes in stylized language the sensations she wishes to depict (...) Miss Mansfield frequently reverses Mrs Woolf's method. Instead of transmitting thought or feeling through a formalized literary medium, she casts the whole narrative into the informal tone she employs for the expression of interior consciousness.' Berkman also hints at the 'contamination' of Mansfield's use of FID and the expressive narrator's mode. Commenting on a particular character (Rosemary in "A Cup of Tea") she writes: 'It is the author who is speaking, in the very cadence for Rosemary's interior monologues' (which were, however, presented in DD.)

Another critic, Yuan She Yen, basing his 1967 point-of-view study on Friedman's analysis, misinterprets the function of the expressive narrator, focalisation and FID. Yuan's new term is 'experienced speech' ('Erlebte Rede' in German), which he defines as follows: 'In experienced speech the consciousness of the character, and the author is imposed upon the consciousness of the character, and the author makes her opinion or attitude clear while expressing simultaneously the point-of-view of the character.' Yuan quotes the same example from "The Garden Party" which Franz Stanzel chose when testing his newly developed theory of 'teller and reflector-characters' (1981) from "The Garden Party" ('That was really extravagant ...'). Sometimes Yuan introduces a new term for the same phenomenon. Discussing "The Garden Party", for instance, he also uses the term 'articulated thinking'.

In 1968, T.Q. Beachcroft in *The Modest Art: A Survey of the Short Story in ENglish* (p. 171) hints at the phenomenon of FID: 'We see the vision, the technique, and the prayer combined. It is in this mood that she becomes the most intense practitioner of the technique by which the story reveals itself - the mime form. But a mime form in which the characters are suffused with light from within. All the information, the narrative flow, is contained in the words spoken and the scene, as it appears in the eyes of the characters. The use of interior vision is brilliantly externalized in imagery, so that when we enter into somebody's thoughts and feelings we do not leave the world of sensation. In this way she accomplishes what Virginia Woolf accomplished later, but she does it in far less space. If Virginia Woolf had written "At the Bay" it might well have the length of *To the Lighthouse*.

Mary Rohrberger, discussing point-of-view, in 1977 (p. 85), seems another disciple of the 'exit-narrator' assumption. She claims the technique to be Mansfieldian, when she writes: 'Most of the stories either focus through the consciousness of the central character or characters or employ the peculiar shifting view-point, called multipersonal by Berkman, which in Mansfield's hands can be considered innovative, to the point of standing as a Mansfield signature'.

Finally, in 1981, Clare Hanson, one of the most energetic Mansfield critics in the Anglo-Saxon world, still supports the 'exit-narrator assumption' in her description of the opening lines of "Bliss". Together with A. Gurr, in *Katherine Mansfield* (p. 59), she writes: 'The story is cast in indirect free form, the narrator's voice merging with the thoughts, the vocabulary, the very mode of perception of the central character.' Here is the text, quoted from "Bliss" (p. 91): 'Although Bertha Young was thirty she still had moments like this when she wanted to run instead of walk, to take dancing steps on and off the pavement, to bowl a hoop, to throw something in the air and catch it again, or to stand still and laugh at - nothing - at nothing, simply.' Hanson & Gurr's view presents a narratological misinterpretation of FID, focalisation and narrative mode.

Here is another inaccuracy by Hanson, committed in *Short Stories and Short Fictions (1985)*, when she presents Joyce, Virginia Woolf and Mansfield as 'the first authors to develop initially in their short fiction, the 'indirect free style of narration' (p. 56). She was clearly unaware of Roy Pascal's excellent 1977 survey of FID: *The Dual*

Voice: Free Indirect Speech and its Functioning in the 19th Century European Novel, published in the UK, in which Pascal identifies FID in e.g. Goethe, Austen, Dickens and claims that FID 'cropped up here and there, since the Middle Ages' (p. 34).

36. Katherine Mansfield, *The Collected Short Stories*, Penguin edition, 1981, pp. 412-418.

Section I runs from p. 412, l. 1: 'Y're very snug in here' - p. 415, l. 15: Woodifield was gone.

Section II runs from p. 415, l. 16: For a long moment the boss stayed, (...) - p. 416, l. 33: The boy had never looked like that.

Section III runs from p. 416, l. 34: At that moment the boss noticed that a fly had fallen into his broad inkpot, (...) - p. 418, l. 9: The fly was dead.

Section IV runs from p. 418, l. 10: The boss lifted the corpse on the end of the paper-knife (...) - p. 418, l. 19: For the life of him he could not remember.

In general, Mansfield reserves FID for the main character(s) only. Although the information on Mr Woodifield, a minor character, might be read as FID: It was time for him to be off; since ... his stroke; the wife and the girls kept him boxed up. With Graham Hough (1970) I prefer to label these utterances 'coloured narrative' which Hernadi (1971) calls 'substitutionary narration'. I subsume this mode of discourse under category no. 4 in McHale's scale (1978, pp. 259, 260): 'indirect discourse, mimetic to some degree.'

37. Here is FID in a mirror text:

In A- The rejection of the boss's possible survival after his son's death.

In B - The Boss's reverie, an 'in memoriam' of his son.

In C - The Boss's present puzzlement.

In D - The Boss's lively interest in the fighting fly.

In E - The Boss's positive identification with the fly's instinctive fight for survival. In F - The Boss's final puzzlement and the answer to the main question in the possible subtitle: 'How the Boss fights the loss of his Son'. He has forgotten the death of his son, for the life of him has killed his sorrow.

38. There are to my knowledge three ways of describing the topography of this hazy region, where inner and outer fictional realities are intertwined in the narrator's and character's mind. R.J. Lethcoe, a critic who has studied this territory, suggests the term 'narrated perception' which he defines as 'the report of a character's conscious perceptions (...) presented in such a manner that they resemble objective report, but on careful consideration can be shown to be transcriptions of consciousness rather than reality' (in 'Narrated Speech and Consciousness', p. 205). Similar terms have been suggested by other critics: 'style indirect libre de perception' (Lips); cf. 'erlebte

214

Eindruck (W. Bühler); cf. 'substitutionary description' (Hernadi). The many terms point to the difficulty of deciding whether a specific passage should be understood as FID, a 'narrated perception' or a narrator's discourse.

Another way to describe this overlap between FID and narrator's discourse is provided by Dolozel's concept of a 'diffuse' type of FID, which, in contrast to the 'compact' type, does not contain a sufficient number of discriminating features to distinguish it clearly from a narrator's discourse, or to assign it to character's discourse, even if the passage as a whole cannot be convincingly transposed into an 'interior monologue' by shifting its pronouns and tenses. This way of looking at the region between inner reflection and outer reality in no sense invalidates the concept of FID itself, but - though limiting it to the 'compact' type of represented discourse' in FID allows for traces of this technique for rendering a character's mind to pervade the surrounding narrator's discourse.

Finally, a third manner was selected, in this study, since Mansfield shuns FID for extended mediation and the 'contaminated' passages are often inserted into narrator's discourse, first of all Mansfield's employment of different functions of narrators was accounted for. When analysing the diffuse passages, the initial distinction between FID and the referential, poetic and expressive narrator appeared to be a most exact and distinctive procedure. When going down the scale from diegesis to mimesis McHale's scale was preferred to D. Cohn's system (1978) of 'authorial narration' leading to 'figural language', in which she grouped her analysis of 'psycho-narration', 'quoted monologue' and 'narrated monologue in third person context'. Cohn is concerned with fragments, isolated passages in fictional representation only.

39. Nagel, p. 25; For an explanation of the terms 'extra- diegetic' and 'homo-diegetic' see Genette (1972), pp. 238-51 and Bal, 1981a, pp. 41-59. Bal uses the terms 'external narrator' (EN) when the narrator never refers to itself as a character and the 'character-bound narrator' (CN) when the I of the story is to be identified with a character.

40. Cf. Yuan She Yen, p. 292.

41. Weingart, 1964, p. 25.

42. Cf. Mansfield on "Bliss": 'What I MEANT (I hope I didn't sound high falutin') was Bertha, not being an artist, was yet artist manquée enough to realise that these words and expressions were not and could not be hers. They were, as it were, *quoted* by her, borrowed with ... an eyebrow ... yet, she'd none of her own.' (LJMM, p. 211) (Suspension-points KM)

43. So far Bertha's faulty mental perception has been tested, and this, in its naivety and immaturity, may be convincing for the reader.

However, when Bertha's purely visionary faculties are at stake, the narrator suddenly has Bertha 'see with her own eyes', (...), she saw' Harry with Miss Fulton:

> 'His lips said: 'I adore you' and Miss Fulton laid her moonbeam fingers on his cheecks, and smiled her sheepy smile. Harry's nostrils quivered; his lips curled back in a hideous grin while he whispered: 'Tomorrow' and with her eyelids Miss Fulton said: 'Yes'. (p. 105)

The main trouble with this passage is, that a different manner of perception is required. Bertha is suddenly able to see with clear eyes. One critic interpreted this as 'overwriting' because the narrator is here presenting observations (Yuan She Yen, p. 312). Apart from the practical question, whether from the distance at which one stands Bertha could actually 'read' Harry's lips and distinguish the words he apparently utters, whether she could see Harry's nostrils quiver and whether she could read the word 'yes' in the fluttering of Miss Fulton's eyelids, the reversal of her fate and mood comes too suddenly. Too soon and too fast the narrator makes Bertha read her own feelings from what she has seen, forcing Bertha to face the reversal and recognise it immediately.

44. Cf. James W. Gargano, 'Mansfield's Miss Brill', *Explicator*, XIX, 1960, 10, who argued that 'Brill' is the name of a European fish, actually a flatfish, 'commonly thought of as creatures with unique, but extremely limited visual power'.

45. Cf. also Yuan She Yen's interpretation, p. 328.

46. Cf. Mansfield's comment on the narrative technique: 'I've written a long story of a rather new kind. It's the outcome of the "Prelude" method - it just unfolds and opens - But I hope it's an advance on "Prelude". In fact, I know it is because the technique is stronger.' (LII, p. 87).

47. The term 'parallax' is derived from Knowle, Johnson and Hoff. See Chapter 1, footnote 42, Chapter 4.1 footnote 34 and Chapter 4.2 footnote 1.

48. Cf. M. Rohrberger, p. 96: 'The structure creates a metaphor, the metaphor reveals the meaning.' Cf. Overland, pp. 251, 254, 263, 273-80; Nagel, p. 25.

49. This method is named 'the contrapuntal' method by Yuan She Yen, p. 421, 425. See the examples in "Prelude", "At the Bay" and "The Daughters of the Late Colonel".

50. Cf. Yuan She Yen on "Prelude" and "At the Bay" (p. 421): 'The reason for this technique lies in the fact that the two stories are primarily the inner drama of two characters and that the dramatic conflict exists between the two characters on the one hand, and the human situation on the other.'

51. Cf. Müller, p. 356; Nagel, p. 25.

52. Ibid, p. 109.

53. Cf. Nagel, p. 122.

54. See Chapter 4.3. on Characterisation. The narrator dissolves into powdery, hazy, dissected fragments himself.

4.2 Footnotes: THEMES

1. To my knowledge, 'parallax' was first used to describe the Impressionistic device of seemingly variable and changing multiple perspectives by J.T. Johnson, in a paper entitled 'Towards a definition of Literary Impressionism' delivered at the Midwest Modern Language Association meeting in 1970. Yuan She Yen uses the term 'contrapuntal point-of-view' for the same phenomenon.

2. H.E. Bates, *The Modern Short Story*, London, 1941, p. 129.

3. Berkman, p. 178: 'But Mr. Bates seems to have given Miss Mansfield's work only superficial consideration.' Cf. also Daly, p. 112; Friis, p. 154; Hanson & Gurr, p. 25.

4. Berkman, p. 159.

5. Daly, p. 23.

6. Except for a flurry during the war, when her patriotic hatred for the calloused attitude of many civilians made her write such stories as "Stay-laces" or "Two Tuppenny Ones, please", Mansfield's attack on suburbia and the bourgeoisie grow more infrequent after 1913. Before that date one finds an occasional story (the vignette) "Along the Gray's Inn Road", "The Woman at the Store", "The Swing of the Pendulum", ("A Blaze") in which either directly or indirectly, she defines the odd blow at the bourgeoisie. After that date Mansfield's sarcasm was tied in with her slow turning away from the satiric method and her release from Wildean influence.

7. The British are on the whole dealt with lightly on this point. The early story "Sunday Lunch" attacks gossip, more than it does gluttony. In 1917, however, in "A Suburban Fairy Tale", the British family show themselves almost monomaniacal on the subject of food.

8. In Mansfield's earlier work there are quite a few predatory women: Fraulein Godowska in the "The Modern Soul", "The Advanced Lady" and "A Marriage of Passion". Here they are combined with the theme of artistic affectation. Frau Fischer seems to consider babies a necessary trap into which to ensnare the husband.

9. In "A Birthday", "New Dresses" and "The Little Girl", too, the family circle is not pleasant.

10. Cf. the hilarity of the guests at the wedding party Frau Brechenmacher attends. Other examples are given in "At Lehman's", "Frau Fischer" and "A Birthday", and Edna in "Something Childish but very Natural". After 1913 this theme grows less shrill.

11. A few stories, like "The Little Governess" or "The Common Round" ("Pictures") have seduction as part of the theme.

12. For example, in "The Baron", "The Sister of the Baroness". As for chauvinism, "Germans at Meat", "The Baron", "The Sister of the Baroness", "Frau Fischer", "The Modern Soul", and "The Advanced Lady" all contain passages in which at least one character sneers at the British or their institutions, or shows a misplaced admiration for something German.

13. "At Lehman's", and "Frau Brechenmacher Attends a Wedding", both from 1910, present a marriage which the women would be well out of. "A Fairy Story" presents the recurrent theme of the conflict between a girl's love for a boy and her search for identity. "Something Childish but very Natural" (1913) deals with the coarsening effect of the physical on young love.

14. The same theme is dealt with more subtly and indirectly in "The Man Without a Temperament", "The Escape", "The Stranger", "Honeymoon" and "Psychology".

15. E.g. Linda in "Prelude", the main character of "A Dill Pickle", the narrator in "A Married Man's Story", Virginia in "Late at Night", the narrator in "The Canary"; these and others are essentially alone in observing the fragmentary world around them.

16. LJMM, p. 149.

17. In "Picnic", Miranda's initial conversation is interrupted by her little son, who has been 'gathering snails in a tin pail'. Mansfield's poem about the snail in her scrapbook (p. 111) is entitled 'Caution'. In THE ALOE, in a passage expunged from 'Prelude", the Josephs' children bait Kezia by discussing their way of getting pocket-money by collecting a hundred 'tiny blue and grey snails'. (pp. 10-11) Mansfield uses the figure of 'the snail under the leaf', both in her secondary writing (LJMM, p. 344, p. 423; LII, p. 229) and in her stories. In the pastiche "At the Club", the women who are satirised are compared to 'a company of garish snails'. (p. 447) Similarly in "A Married Man's Story", the narrator soliloquizes: 'But one could go on with such a catalogue for ever - on and on - until one lifted the single arum lily leaf and discovered the tiny snails clinging, until one counted ... and what then?' (CS, p. 433).

18. Mr Reginald Peacock, Raoul Duquette, and Beatrice in "Poison".

19. In "In Confidence", it is the theme of betrayal between women. Throughout her writing Mansfield dealt with the betrayal theme. The stories "The Modern Soul", "The Mating of Gwendolen", "This Flower" and "A Cup of Tea" may serve as examples.

20. In "The Tiredness of Rosabel", "The Child who was Tired", "The Common Round", and particularly the later stories "Life of Ma Parker", "The Fly", and "The Canary".

21. "The Child who was tired", "A Fairy Story", "The Woman at the Store", "Ole Underwood", and "Millie", in which death is usually introduced for reasons of plot.

22. For example, "The Wrong House", "Anguish", "Revelations", "The Stranger", "Poison", "The Daughters of the Late Colonel", "Life of Ma Parker", "At the Bay", "The Garden Party"; "The Fly", the fragmentary "Widowed", "Weak Heart" and "Six Years After" are all concerned with the memory of the dead.

23. After 1914 a few stories deal with nostalgia and with New Zealand: "New Dresses", "The Woman at the Store", "Ole Underwood", "A Birthday", "A Little Girl" and "Millie".

24. For example, *The Aloe*, "Prelude", "A Picnic", "The Stranger". From 1921 onwards there are many stories or fragments, all of them revealing nostalgia and 'the flight of time' theme, in "An Ideal Family", "Her First Ball", "Sixpence", "The Voyage", "At the Bay", "The Garden Party", "The Doll's House", "Weak Heart", "Taking the Veil", "The Fly", "The New Baby", "The Sheridans'", "The Dressmaker", "At Putnams's Pier", "A Man and his Dog", "Susannah" and "Six Years after". The relentless movement from past to future is also implicit in non-New Zealand stories. E.g. the vignette "Along the Gray's Inn Road", "Spring Pictures" and most impressionistically in "Bank Holiday".

25. For example, in the early stories, "The Tiredness of Rosabel", "The Child Who Was Tired", and in Mansfield's description of the characters Miss Ada Moss, Ma Parker, the Kelvey-girls, the little governess, the daughters of the colonel, Ole Underwood, Mouse, Ian French, and the old lady in 'The Canary'.

26. LII, p. 156.

27. Kezia in "Prelude" is running down the stairs, fleeing from 'IT' that 'was just behind her, waiting at the door, at the head of the stairs, at the bottom of the stairs, hiding in the passage, ready to dart out at the back door.' She is fleeing not from real external danger but because 'she was frightened'; 'with wide open eyes and knees pressed together' she imagined 'IT' was after her. (CS, p. 202).

28. Cf. Magalaner, pp. 31, 34.

29. CS, p. 18.

30. As Madden contends (p. 3) 'The central theme of a great number of her stories is the disparity between illusion and reality or between falsehood and truth.'

31. For example in "The Little Governess", "Miss Brill", "The Stranger","Poison", and "An Ideal Family", to grand distortions of self-perception, or in "Bliss", "The Escape", "Miss Brill", "The Daughters", and "A Cup of Tea".

32. See B. Haferkamp, 1969, p. 223.

33. For example, Frau Brechenmacher's illusion of a finer life and her expectation of a pleasant time are shattered by the brutality and grossness of life, by the imagistic correlative of the bride and Herr Brechenmacher's presentation of the wedding-present. In "Millie", there is the disparity between the illusion of mother-love and the reality of her betrayal, atavistic bestiality and blood-lust glorification of the chase. In "The Little Governess", the illusion of finding much-needed security and protection in the old German "Grandfather" and the betrayal implied in his lust for her. In "Pictures", Ada Moss's bravery, her hopefulness in her search for a job, the hopelessness of the situation and its reality at the end, when Ada goes home with the "Stout Gentleman". In "This Flower", the woman's bravery in facing her illegitimate pregnancy and the reality of her lover's cowardice. Miss Brill's enjoyment of her life and the cruelty of the girl overheard in the park; in "Poison", the narrator's love for Beatrice and the reality of her corruption; in "Bliss" Bertha's illusion of a blissful existence in her home, with her flowers, her husband, her baby, and her friends versus the reality of the betrayal by Miss Fulton and her husband; in "The Doll's House" the illusion of a bourgeois 'caste' system and being invited to join in, 'our Else' seeing the false lamp versus the reality of being chased away by Beryl; in "The Stranger", the illusion of an idyllic relationship in marriage and Hammond's realisation that as a couple they will never be alone together again. In "A Cup of Tea", the illusion of Rosemary's wish to help someone in trouble versus the reality of her vanity and her selfishness that brings about her betrayal.

34. The ice pudding has become the epitome of Sun's illusion and dreams. Sun doesn't understand that ice puddings, though made in the shape of a house, are meant to be eaten.

35. As Kronegger argues (pp. 66, 67): 'Impressionist protagonists often feel helpless, hopeless, they feel a crippling of the will power and a fruitlessness of all effort.'

36. Cf. P. Halter, p. 111.

37. Cf. Kronegger, p. 66.

38. In "Her First Ball", Leila's 'joie de vivre' is contrasted with age and its sorrows. Leila enbodies the former, the old bald man with the patch, the latter. The old man is introduced fleetingly when he signs her dance-programme, but Leila spends more time on the positive picture of the ball. When she returns 'to find the fat man waiting for her by the door' the epiphanic moment is built up: 'It gave her quite a shock to see how old he was; he ought to have been on the stage with the fathers and mothers'. (CS, pp. 341, 342) But he is not, and has been dancing at the same ball every year, for thirty years. He functions as a harbinger of life's transitoriness to Leila. The old man shatters Leila's dreamlike, youthful illusion of life, so that Leila

thinks: 'Was it - could it all be true?' Leila's epiphanic awareness does not last long. Youth's triumphant forgetfulness makes her go on, and when she bumps into the old fat man, ironically 'she smiled at him more radiantly than ever'. She knows, but prefers to forget. The experience of the husband in "The Escape" is presented in a similar pattern. Cf. Clare Hanson's interpretation of the same story in *Short Stories and Short Fictions*, 1880-1980, (1985), p. 81: 'After his epiphany he subsequently goes on to a more aware existence. (He) comes to full consciousness of his position, of the exhaustion of his spirit(...) the beauty of the tree and of the woman's voice make their way into his heart (...) and are accepted not as passing distractions, but as having as much validity as his suffering.' He feels even more insignificant than before his wife's hysterical outbursts, but the epiphanic moment has set him free, because he has perceived a wider perspective for his own insignificant existence, which he now accepts as it is. Here we have a subtle modification of the theme of shock effect and relative insignificance.'

39. As in "Ole Underwood", "Millie" and "The Woman at the Store", "The Child Who Was Tired", "The Little Governess", "Something Childish but very Natural", "A Dill Pickle", and "The Lady's Maid".

40. For example, in "Miss Brill", "An Album Leaf", "The Daughters of the Late Colonel", "The Canary", "An Indiscreet Journey", and "Je ne Parle pas Francais".

41. "Ole Underwood", one of the early studies of insanity, is a story in which a former convict, who murdered his unfaithful wife thirty years ago, is wandering around aimlessly, but is unnaturally sensitive to his surroundings. Children scatter at his approach, and adults at the bar avoid him, heightening his feeling of agitation. The blood pounds in Ole's head and he loses control of his mind again. His isolation is increased by the evidence that no one wishes to understand his condition. A similar situation is developed in 'The Woman at the Store', in which the woman's isolation has contributed to her imbalance. The anguish and hopelessness in Mansfield's 'cry against corruption' is presented obliquely.

4.3 Footnotes: STRUCTURE

1. Cf. the studies by H.E. Bates, 1941; Sean O'Faolain, 1951 and Frank O'Connor, 1963.

2. Cf. also V. Propp, 'The Morphology of the Folktale', 1929; V. Shlovski, 'Theory of Prose', 1929; T. Todorov, *Poétique de la Prose*, 'The Structural Analysis of Literature: The Tales of Henry James', 1971, pp. 73-103.

3. Cf. Terence Hawkes, *Structuralism and Semiotics*, 1977, p. 101.

4. Clare Hanson, 1985, p. 13.

5. For example Propp's study.

6. Cf. Cl. Hanson & A. Gurr, p. 18.

7. Ibid, p. 13.

8. Ibid, p. 15.

9. Ibid, p. 13.

10. Ibid, p. 15.

11. Ibid, p. 17.

12. Introduction to *The Aloe*, 1985, ed. V. O'Sullivan, p. XVI.

13. Ibid, p. XVII.

14. Gillian Boddy, *Katherine Mansfield: The Woman and The Writer*, 1988, p. 162.

15. Cf. Beverley Gibbs, pp. 175-183.

16. Cf. Berkman on "The Fly", p. 195 and Magalaner's final chapter, pp. 120-133.

17. CS, p. 426. Counterposed are a nursery scene, where the two children Sun and Moon feel protected; a party scene, where they are exposed to adult roles; and a post-party scene, where Moon accepts initiation into the woman's role while Sun rejects his initiation into the man's role. The nursery is an archetypal nursery, full of light and sweetness. The party room is initially the scene of busy preparations. When the room has been decorated it has acquired a stale perfection for Sun, while in the post-party scene the room is a shambles. It has played its part in the entertainment by being used so well that it is no longer Sun's perfect room. It is a wreck. Sun's wail is a protest against such use of his perfect room, as well as an expression of his refusal to accept initiation into a man's illusionary role.

18. CS, pp. 563, 564; Miss Meadows is upset at being jilted by her fiancé, Basil. In her distraught state of mind she forgets to go through the usual morning ritual. Even the trees outside the windows reflect Miss Meadow's despair. The willow trees, outside the high narrow windows, wave in the wind. They have lost half their leaves. The tiny ones that cling wriggle like fishes caught on a line. Big rain drops fall from overcast skies. Put besides this set of moods and setting is the abrupt change that occurs in Miss Meadow when Basil telegrams his intention to marry her. She flies up the hall to the classroom, changes the song the girls are practising to a joyful one, snatches up a chrysanthemum, and beams at the girls who instinctively catch the same mood. The room has become a scene of joyful instruction.

19. In "Prelude", for example, only Mrs Fairfield and Linda descend to examine the aloe.

20. E.g. "A Truthful Adventure", "See-Saw", "Spring Pictures", or "An Indiscreet Journey". The games the children play in "Prelude" and "At the Bay" are juxtaposed with the adult games.

21. The innocent Katie in "Carnation" is counterposed to the knowing Eve; the excited and searching Bertha is set next to the calm and contained Pearl Fulton in "Bliss"; Sabina in "At Lehman's" against the pregnant woman; Kezia is set next to Linda, Beryl and her grandmother, Mrs Fairfield, in "Prelude" and "At the Bay". The characters' attitudes or moods are juxtaposed to give structural unity to a story.

22. In "The Wind Blows", the wind is the concrete embodiment of Matilda's trepidations. Similarly in "A Birthday", the storm parallels Binzer's inner turmoil as well as his wife's labour pains and delivery.

23. Cf. P. Halter, p. 178.

24. LII, p. 120.

25. Cf. Don Kleine, 'Mansfield and the Orphans of Time, *Modern Fiction Studies*, vol. 24, 1978, p. 425. Kleine hints at Mansfield's structural design by using the term 'envelope': 'Sections one to five are an enveloped memory of the preceding week'.

26. Other examples are "Bliss" with the flowering pear tree, "A Dill Pickle" with the glove, "The Young Girl" with the blue dress, "Miss Brill" with the furs, and "The Doll's House" with the little lamp.

27. The story begins with a characteristic passage of sensory Impressionistic description: 'It is raining' (p. 644). This scene is juxtaposed with the next one which also opens with 'Here are Lilies! Here are roses! Here are pretty violets!' Meanwhile a Literary Impressionist technique of concatenation is employed to create a depressive atmosphere with the 'faded cauliflowers' (p. 644), 'A tattered frill of soiled lace and dirty ribbon' (p. 645), and the mackintoshes ironically in the wrong order: 'Blue ones for girls and pink ones for boys.' (p. 645) There are no buyers, and there is no movement. Again the old hag repeats her phrase: 'Here are roses! Here are lilies! Who will buy my violets?' (p. 646) and the depressing atmosphere leads up to section II and III, in which a lonely woman finds herself crying. The large warm drops of the rain melt with the tears of the woman. Finally the lonely woman herself fuses into the surroundings and vanishes.

28. In "The Escape", for example, the narrator, structuring the story towards the husband's epiphany, he first introduces the sensory image of a tree and a woman's voice. We are never informed of the idenitity of this significant voice, that comes 'floating, falling' (p. 202). These sounds seem to exist independently, giving only a vague, though sweeping impression of an epiphanic scene, in which contours are blurred.

29. For example, in "The Modern Soul": 'Good-evening, said the Herr Professor, (p. 725); or in "The Wrong House": 'Two purl - two plain - woolinfrontoftheneedle - and knit two together.' (p. 675).

30. For example, in "Daughters of the Late Colonel",'The week after was one of the busiest weeks of their lives' (p. 262); or in "Pictures": 'Eight o'clock in the morning. Miss Ada Moss lay in a black iron bedstead (...)' (p. 119); in "See Saw": "Spring" (p. 667); and in "The Lady's Maid": 'Eleven o'clock, a knock at the door.' (p. 375).

31. For example, in "Mr and Mrs Dove": 'Of course he knew - no man better - that he hadn't a ghost of a chance, he hadn't an earthly (...)' (p. 285).

32. Cf. F. Busch, p. 62. For example, in "The Garden Party": 'And after all the weather was ideal' (p. 245); or in 'Honeymoon': 'And when they came out of the lace shop (...)' (p. 401).

33. For example in "Prelude" (p. 60); "The Lady's Maid" (p. 380); "A Married Man's Story" (p. 447); "The Doves Nest" (p. 465); "Six Years After" (p. 470); "Daphne" (p. 476); "Father and the Girls" (p. 482); "All Serene" (p. 487); "A Bad Idea" (p. 490); "A Man and His Dog" (p. 494);"Such a Sweet Old Lady" (p. 496); "Honesty"(p. 501);"Susannah" (p. 503); "Second Violin" (p. 507); "Mr and Mrs Williams" (p. 511); "Widowed" (p. 519);"Two Tupenny Ones, Please" (p. 654); and "The Wrong House" (p. 678).

34. See A. Alpers, 1982, p. 216.

4.4 Footnotes: CHARACTERISATION

1. V.S. Pritchett, 1946, p. 86.
2. Ibid, p. 87.
3. S. Berkman, 1951, p. 164.
4. Ibid, p. 200.
5. S. Magalaner, 1971, pp. 125, 126.
6. Cf. Overland, p. 258.
7. As quoted from S. Rimmon-Kenan, 1983, p. 31, who quotes M. Mudrick, 1961, 'Character and Event in Fiction', *Yale Review*, 50, pp. 202-218.
8. Cf. Kronegger, 1973, pp. 57-68.
9. P. 18: when he 'felt an extraordinary pride; felt the wind and the cyclamen and the violets for he was walking with a beautiful woman for the first time in his life.'
10. P. 19.
11. P. 35: 'he saw (...) divinely innocent and occupied with little trifles at their feet and somehow entirely defenceless against a doom which he perceived, his wife and son, together, in the window.'
12. P. 60.
13. In fact, the aloe plant ('the century plant') usually bears flowers every 8-10 years. Though an irregular bloomer it does not have flowers only 'Once every hundred years.'On p. 34 Linda subconsciously multiplies by ten.

14. Cf. V. Woolf, DIARY I, p. 173.

15. Ibid, pp. 153-155.

16. Fokkema & Ibsch, p. 44.

17. Cf. F. Busch, p. 76.

18. For example in "Psychology", "Spring Pictures" and the anonymous minor characters in other stories.

19. For example, the Baron, the sister of the Baroness, The Boss, The Lady's Maid, and the General.

20. Others appear as Germans, or as the American Woman.

21. For example The Two Topknots, The Man without a Temperament, The Advanced Lady, The Modern Soul, A Married Man, Father and the Girls, The Young Girl, A Man and his Dog, The Woman at the Store, The Honeymoon Couple.

22. Cf. Kronegger, pp. 61-67.

23. CS, p. 413.

24. The term D.H. Lawrence referred to, when he protested against the 'old-fashioned human element 'in the old-stable ego'- concept of character. See A. Huxley, ed. *The Letters of D.H. Lawrence*, p. 198.

25. Cf. Kronegger, 1973, pp. 46, 47.

26. Ibid, p. 63.

27. Cf. E.M. Forster's (1927) important distinction between 'flat' and 'round' characters. Not being 'flat' involves having more than one quality and 'developing' in the course of action.

28. M. Drabble, 1978, p. 135.

4.5 Footnotes: IMAGES

1. Cf. H.E. Bates, in *The Modern Short Story*, London, 1941, p. 24: 'It's no longer necessary to describe, it is enough to suggest.'

2. As in "Something Childish but very Natural" the images of the good life of Eden and the betrayal that ends Henry's Eden, the images of the knowledge of good and evil, of Adam and Eve, the snake and the apple, and other images which are less quickly identified, such as Edna's cape of hair as a covering of innocence. The charm bracelet hints at incantation rituals that may ward off evil spirits which all indicate the tie that Edna has to childlike innocence.

3. J.A. Cuddon, *A Dictionary of Literary Terms*, 1977, pp. 316-319.

4. Bertha Haferkamp, Zur Bildersprache Katherine Mansfield's, *Neueren Sprachen*, vol. 18, pp. 221-39, 1969.

5. C.F.E. Spurgeon, *Shakespeare's Iterative Imagery*, 1935, p. 18.

6. See Mansfield's letter to John M. Murry (LJMM, p. 467) on 4/2/1920; 'I cannot have the *German Pension* republished under any circumstances. It is far too immature and I don't even acknowledge it

today. I mean I don't hold by it. I can't go on foisting that kind of stuff on the public - *it's not good enough* (...) It's positively juvenile, and besides it's not what I mean: it's a lie.'

7. All possible forms of comparison are used and oblique images are produced, with: 'to seem', 'as though','as if', 'somehow', 'almost', 'as it were', 'a kind of', 'sort of', 'in some way', 'rather like', 'like someone', 'something', 'might have been', 'as one might say (imagine)', 'it reminds of', 'makes you think of', 'something between', 'if you know what I mean'. See Haferkamp, p. 230.

8. The narrator also reveals a reverse tendency when the intensity, the striking force of the image must be enforced either by means of words like 'yes,'exactly','marvellously'. By stressing the ingenuity of the comparison the convincing power may be lost.

9. Cf. Busch, p. 64.

10. Cf. Busch, p. 62; Weingart, 1964, p. 25.

11. See CS, pp. 442, 573, 677.

12. Ibid, p. 47, 129, 191, 311, 330, 495, 543.

13. See Busch, p. 63.

14. The choice of image seems improvised, unintentional, when the first word is named. Cf. B. Haferkamp, p. 235.

15. In the often used expression 'to be part of' the identification may be slightly restricted. See CS, p. 80, 112, 210, 361, 672.

16. Cf. also CS, p. 232: (...) She (Isabel) looked like a rooster, and on p. 233 we read: said the rooster. Cf. also CS, p. 128 - the little yacht image, p. 425 the old, old dog image, p. 442, 447 the plant in the cupboard image.

17. Cf. B. Haferkamp, pp. 224, 225.

18. CS, p. 237, 437; p. 190, 440; p. 334, 370, 372, 665.

19. CS, p. 58.

20. For example, Old Woodifield in "The Fly". See also CS, p. 25, 213, 353, 331, 332, 408.

21. For example, Mrs. Kember in "At the Bay". See also CS, p. 562, 570, 660.

22. See CS, p. 235, 538.

23. See CS, p. 116, 156, 162, 192, 218, 220, 261, 406, 630, 632.

24. Cf. F. Busch, p. 68: 'With Katherine Mansfield the synechdoche is more than a mannerism' and B. Haferkamp on PARS PRO TOTO, p. 225.

25. For example, 'adjectival': CS, p. 26: the silly voice went baa-bashing; Lottie's stolid, compact little voice, p. 88: the cold, salty little voice, p. 208: velvety bass voice, p. 372: She laughed her hard, bright laugh, p. 407: except a thin faint voice; Cf. also p. 88, 208, 372, 407, 82, 238, 246, 249, 371, 645, 646.

'Verbal': p. 102: Eddie Warren drank his coffee and set down the cup with a face of anguish as though he had drunk and seen the spider. p. 164: and suddenly, as if in answer to his gaze, two wings of windows opened, p. 176; and her anger, far stronger than she, ran before her and snatched the bag out of the wretch's hand. p. 372: She laughed her hard, bright laugh ... she had a soft hesitating voice ... it rang out as though she were on the stage. p. 645: as the harsh voices float out into the warm rainy air. Cf. also p. 238, 340, 421, 434.

26. Cf. 'human face': CS, p. 12, 40, 167, 449, 576, 585, 588, 592, 636; 'eye': p. 132, 185, 186, 331, 439, 573. Cf.'smile': CS, p. 63, 69, 77, 99, 105, 215, 218, 334, 335, 397, 453, 629, 666.

27. CS, p. 86; One of those kisses that not only puts one's grief to bed, but nurses it and warms it and tucks it up and keeps it fast enfolded until it is sleeping sound. p. 91: - absolute bliss - as though you'd suddenly swalled a bright piece of that late afternoon sun and it burned in your bossom, sending out a little shower of sparks into every particle, into every finger and toe ... p. 170: she felt the strange beast that slumbered so long within her bosom stir, stretch itself, yawn, prick up its ears, and suddenly bound to its feet, and fix its longing, hungry stare upon those far-away places. p. 173: the strange beast in her bosom began to purr ... p. 237: The new fire blazed in Jonathan; you almost heard it roaring softly as he explained, described and dilated on the new thing; but a moment later it had fallen in and there was nothing but ashes, and Jonathan went about with a look like hunger in his black eyes. Cf. also CS, p. 64, 99, 148, 176, 343, 361, 362, 573, 649.

In the animal-comparisons it is man that is more indicated than animals. The personified animal, however, is introduced to arouse the reader's agreement, when disagreeable characteristics in human beings must be revealed. In "The Fly" the fly is 'a regular little actor', or 'a little beggar'. In "The Canary" the little bird is' a professional singer' and in 'At the Bay' the old sheep-dog is absent-minded and ashamed, and perceives an enormous giant, which appears to be 'a big gum tree'. (p. 206)

Animals are also compared with other animals. Their movements are similar to human behaviour: a fly behaves like a cat, a cat like a camel, horses are jumping like mosquitoes. Animals are often compared with moving objects. The movement may express a visual or acoustic impression, in which a different sensation is mixed and a kinetic reality is created. When a character is in emotional turmoil the narrator often introduces highly unexpected comparisons: sheep are not patient, dogs are not loyal, but they are compared in sensory apperceptionary impressions. For example, p. 207: it was the Burnell's cat Florrie, sitting on the gate-post, far too early as usual, looking for their milk-girl. When she saw the old sheep-dog she sprang up quickly, arched her back, drew in her tabby head, and seemed to give a little fastidious shiver. 'Ugh! What a coarse, revolting creature!' said

227

Florrie. But the old sheep-dog, not looking up, waggled past, flinging out his legs from side to side. Only one of his ears twitched his legs from side to side. Only one of his ears twitched to prove that he saw, and thought her a silly young female. P. 288: Biddy lay down with her tongue poked out; she was so fat and glossy she looked like a lump of half-melted toffee. But Chinny's porcelain eyes gloomed at Reginald and he sniffed faintly, as though the whole world were one unpleasant smell. P. 353: The gulls rose; they fluttered away like bits of white paper. P. 427: the fly, seeming to stand on the tips of its toes, tried to expand first one wing and then the other ... it began, like a minute little cat, to clean its face. P. 433: while the house-dog, like a soaking doormat, springs, shakes himself over me. Cf. also p. 205, 206, 235, 258, 311, 334, 353, 427, 433, 468, 561, 582.

28. Cf. B. Haferkamp, p. 277.

29. For example, CS, p. 135: Every leaf, every flower in the garden lay open, motionless, as it exhausted, and a sweet, rich rank smell filled the quivering air. Out of the thick, fleshy leaves of a cactus there rose an aloe stem loaded with pale flowers that looked as though they had been cut out of butter; light flashes upon the lifted spears of the palms; over a bed of scarlet waxen flowers some big black insects 'zoomed-zoomed'; a great gaudy creeper, orange splashed with jet, sprawled against a wall. P. 242: We are dumb trees, reaching up in the night, imploring we know not what', said the sorrowful bush. P. 245: ... the green bushes bowed down as though they had been visited by archangels.

But also the urge to create an atmosphere of overwhelming joy, apart from the feeling of loneliness, sadness, is apparent. P. 245: As for the roses, you could not help feeling they understood that roses are the only flowers to impress people at garden-parties; p. 249: Nothing but lilies - canna lilies, big pink flowers, wide open radiant, almost frighteningly alive on bright crimson stems. P. 439: ... some slender silky daisies ... one of the daisies and the flower leaned over, swayed, shook ... the petals fluttered as if joyfully. Cf. also CS, p. 245, p. 247, p. 328, p. 374, p. 628. For more examples, see p. 205: And from the bush there came the sound of little streams flowing, quickly, lightly, slipping between the smooth stones, gushing into ferny basins and out again; and there was the splashing of big drops on large leaves, and something else - what was it? - a faint stirring and shaking, the snapping of a twig and then such silence that it seemed someone was listening. p. 221: Pretty - yes, if you held one of those flowers on the palm of your hand and looked at it closely, it was an exquisite small thing. Each pale yellow petal shone as if each was the careful work of a loving hand. The tiny tongue in the centre gave it the shape of a bell. And when you turned it over the outside was a deep bronze colour. But as soon as they flowered, they fell and were

228

scattered. p. 622: the new leaves quivered like fountains of green water steeped in sunlight. Cf. also CS, p. 238, p. 370, p. 592. For more examples of nature comparisons with animals + movement, see CS, p. 242, 347, 496.

30. 'Velvet' is one of Mansfield's favourite fabrics. She is also carried away by toilet-tables, perfume-bottles and its fragrances, flacons and powder-compacts, and feels attached to them, so that she reserves a place for them in man's emotions and her comparisons.

Garments and hats of all sorts often personify the social stratum of a character. In "Bank Holiday" the guitarist wears a 'hat much too small for hem, perched at the back of his head' (p. 364), an old fat woman wears ' a quivering bonnet', Roddie in "Weak Heart" wears a straw hat with a broad black band. Cf. also CS, p. 80, 109, 231, 337, 396, 537.

31. In "A Married Man's Story" the room changes too. 'It relaxes like an old actor' (p. 248).

32. For example, CS, p. 179: The train seemed glad to have left the station. With a long leap it sprang into the dark. Cf. also p. 107, 112, 113, 152, 322, 328, 329, 368, 393, 408, 455, 470, 476, 479, 481, 491, 545, 588, 595, 636, 637.

33. Its rays may define pieces of furniture or a photograph, one of Mansfield's favourite motifs. There is a sense of pity or understanding. For example, p. 249: and there were the two tiny spots of sun, one on the inkpot, one on a silver photograph frame, playing too. Darling little spots. Especially the one on the inkpot lid. P. 282: The sunlight pressed through the windows, thieved its way in, flashed its light over the furnitureand the photographs (...) when it came to mother's photograph, the enlargements over the piano, it lingered as though puzzled to find so little remained of mother, except the ear-rings shaped like tiny little pagodas and a black feather boa.

34. In Mansfield's sensory imagistic patterns man may be linked with the stars and often the moon may enchant. The ocean may breathe, moan, be asleep, or love and devour the land. For example, CS, p. 205, 217, 239, 403, 577.

35. For example, CS, p. 59: She saw the real Beryl - a shadow ... a shadow. Faint and unsubstantial she shone. Wat was there of her except the radiance? P. 184: The sun came out, the pink clouds in the sky, the strawberry clouds were eaten by the blue. P. 206: The sun was rising. It was marvellous how quickly the mist thinned, sped away, dissolved from the shallow plain, rolled up from the bush and was gone as if in a hurry to escape; big twists and curls josled and shouldered each other as the silvery beams broadened. The far-away sky - a bright, pure blue - was reflected in the puddles, and the drops, swimming along the telegraph poles, flashes into points of light.

36. See CS, p. 19, 224, 242, 433, 503, 565.

37. See CS, p. 115, 187, 234, 244, 259, 352, 410, 530, 538, 586, 627.

38. See CS, p. 37, 334, 468, 530, 628, 670.

39. Cf. Jules Laforgue, who maintained that an Impressionist is a 'modernist painter endowed with an uncommon sensibility of the eye': 'the Impressionist sees and renders nature as it is-that is, wholly in the vibration of colour. No line, light, relief, perspective or chiaroscuro, none of those childish classifications: all these are in reality converted into the vibration of colour and must be obtained on canvas solely by the vibration of colour.' (Quoted from Nochlin, pp. 15, 17).

40. When Laura begs her mother to stop the party for the sake of the dead carter, her mother puts a hat on Laura's head to divert her attention. Then Laura forgets about the dead man, when she is bewitched by her own image in the mirror. When the party has started, everybody praises her for her hat. Finally she takes her hat off, when she presents herself before the body of the dead carter: the hat as an image of status of the Sheridans. The way of life of the leisured rich and their false visions are satirically reflected in Laura's awareness of the hat in front of the dead man.

41. Much of the controversy over "The Fly" arose from critical attempts to find too many symbols in the story. The Boss stood for mastery over everything and everyman. All men are flies to him. (R. Stallman, 1945). Even Shakespeare's famous King lear - quotation was introduced into the discussion; 'As flies to wanton boys are we to th'gods, They will kill us for their sport.' (Th. Bledsoe, 1947). The Boss was interpreted as a tyrannical god, who enslaves everybody. Or the Boss stood for Mansfield's father and the fly was Mansfield herself. Or the Boss was Mansfield's tuberculosis. As the Boss kills the fly, so does tuberculosis kill Mansfield. (W. Jacobs, 1947). Sylvia Berkman was influenced by Shakespeare's line. She dismissed the story as a failure, as 'the central symbolism is confused.'

42. Cf. Greenwood, 1962.

43. In the next paragraphs in "Bank Holiday": A stout man with a pink face wears dingy white flannel trousers, a blue coat with a pink handkerchief showing, and a straw hat much too small for him, perched at the back of his head. He plays the guitar. A little chap in white canvas shoes, his face hidden under a felt hat like a broken wing, breathes into a flute. A tall thin fellow, with bursting over-ripe button boots, draws ribbons, long, twisted, streaming ones, of tune out of a fiddle. They stand, unsmiling, but not serious, in the broad sunlight opposite the fruit-shop. The pink spider of a hand beats the guitar, the little squat hand, with a brass-and-turkoise ring, forces the reluctant flute, and the fiddler's arm tries to saw the fiddle in two.

230

The light 'in the broad sunlight' transfers to the perception of all these auditory images a sense of blurring Impressionist completeness, so that by the end of the passage it is difficult to decide if the phenomena described can be seen or heard. The cinematic technique of 'close up' has given the reader a sense of sharing the narrator's subjective and ironic vision at first hand. The focus is then moved to the crowd and we are presented with a picture of a young couple. One young girl has a basket of strawberries. She does not eat them. She stares at the tiny pointed fruits, as if she were afraid of them. The Australian soldier laughs. He likes to watch her little frightened face. He pushes out his chest and grins.

Not the characters words, but their gestures are revealed. Her puzzlement and his amused, self-conscious attitude of patronage is frozen in an act of timeless, perceptionary communication of gestures. Superimposed, as always in Mansfield's less complex perceptions, there is the impersonal force of the sun. The music, which partakes in the spectacle and draws it together ('in one big knot for a moment') is transforming it. All the separate observations in "Bank Holiday" are finally fused into one unifying image. (p. 365).

A forerunner to "Bank Holiday" can be found in an early sketch 'In the Botanical Gardens' (*Native Companion*, 2/12/1907, reprinted in *Katherine Mansfield: Publications in Australia 1907-1909*), in which the immediacy of observation in "Bank Holiday" is stressed by a rather self-conscious exercise in subjective appreciation by the first-person narrator. The people in the narrative are described as meaningless, as lacking in individuality, 'as the little figures in an Impressionist landscape' (p. 42). The narrative is concluded on a similar, though more subjective note of ambiguity. 'Here is laughter and movement and bright sunlight-but behind me- is it near- or miles and miles away?- The bush lies hidden in the shadow.' (p. 44). Mansfield's mixing of sensations, of merging characters and surroundings, when enforcing a dissolution of characters into an identification of the seperate selves with a larger reality, is visualized by synaesthesia in 'l'audition coloree' turned into an existential question frozen in a moment of suffusion.

44. Hanson & Gurr, p. 128.

45. Ezra Pound, *Literary Essays*, ed. 1964, p. 4.

46. For example, Ian French's hopeless infatuation in "Feuille d'Album" ('and a mouth pouting as though he were determined not to cry', p. 161). Fenella's awakening after her voyage ('a white cat that had been folded up like a camel, rose, stretched itself, yawned, and then sprang on to the tips of its toes', p. 330). Fanny's limitation of George's worldliness in contrasting images ('Fanny, trying to look as though she'd spent years of life threading her way through strangers ...' p. 404). The Boss's grief over his dead son in ' as though the earth

had opened and had seen the boy lying there with Woodifield's girls staring down at him' p. 425). The narrator's imaginary destruction of his father in "A Married Man's Story" (in 'as though his image, cut off at the waist by the counter, has remained solid in my memory'. p. 441). The narrator's frustration in "A Truthful Adventure" in ('one felt like a fish endeavouring to swim over an ice pond' p. 542). Ole Underwood's rhythmic urge for murderous revenge (in 'Something inside Ole Underwood's breast beat like a hammer: 'One, Two, One, Two, never stopping, never changing' p. 573). Violet's and the narrator's fused confessions in "Violet" ('and cried my name as though I had been given up for lost times without number; as though I had been drowned in foreign seas, and burnt in American hotel fires, and buried in a hundred lonely graves' p. 596). The ladies' vulgarity in "Bains Turcs"(in 'masses of gleaming orange hair like an over- ripe fungus bursting from a thick, black stem' p. 605) and the narrator's report in "An Indiscreet Journey" (in 'I jumped ... like an English lady in any French novel.' p. 628).

47. For more examples, see CS, p. 110 in "The Wind Blows": 'The Wind-the wind.'; p. 245 'At the Bay': 'A cloud, small, serene, floated across the moon. In that moment of darkness the sea sounded deep, troubled. Then the cloud sailed away, and the sound of the sea was a vague murmur, as though it waked out of a dark dream. All was still.'; p. 309 in "Life of Ma Parker": 'The icy wind blew out her apron into a balloon. And now it began to rain. There was nowhere.'

48. The now well known term used by T.S. Eliot in an essay on Hamlet (1919). The relevant passage reads: 'The only way of expressing emotion in the form of art is by finding an 'objective correlative' in other words, a set of objects, a situation, a chain of events, which shall be the formula of that *particular* emotion; such that when the external facts, which must terminate in sensory experience, are given, the emotion is immediately evoked.' (As quoted from Cuddon, p. 448).

49. Clare Hanson, 1981, p. 34: 'Through the controlling symbol of the aloe Katherine Mansfield expressed in "Prelude" the view of life which with different shading and emphasis underlies all her major stories.'

50. CS, p.15.

51. See CS, p. 16. The storeman is 'as big as a giant, and the new house is 'stretched upon the green garden like a sleeping beast.' (p. 18).

52. CS, p. 24. 'The stones' are 'hiding', 'the birds were members of a secret society and they smiled among themselves.' (p. 27).

53. Hanson here overemphasises a 'symbolist', thematic interpretation, by arguing: 'the garden is 'full of weeds. The image of the weed counterpoints that of the flower throughout Katherine

Mansfield's work. The weed symbolises the inevitable limitations of human nature, the rooted evil or bad habit, which we cannot overcome, though we may have the illusion that we may do so.' However, when reading the passage in 'Prelude' closely, no 'weeds' are mentioned in the text. Instead Mansfield reintroduced 'the tangle of big roots'. In Kezia's perception the geometrical shapes are linked with the feet of chicken. The path is 'wet', 'clayey' and obstructed by roots. Kezia finds it slippery and it is difficult to find her way. Here is the text:

(...) 'On one side they all led into a tangle of tall dark trees and strange bushes with flat velvet leaves and feathery cream flowers that buzzed with flies when you shook them-this was the frightening side, and no garden at all. The little paths here were wet and clayey with tree roots spanned across them like the marks of big fowls' feet.

But on the other side of the drive there was a high box border and the paths had box edges and all of them led into a deeper and deeper tangle of flowers. The camelias were in bloom, white and crimson and pink and white striped with flashing leaves. You could not see a leaf on the syringa bushes for the white clusters. The roses were in flower- in gentlemen's button-hole roses, little white ones, but far too full of insects to hold under anyone's nose, pink monthly roses on thick stalks, moss roses, always in bud, pink smooth beauties opening curl on curl, red ones so dark they seemed to turn back as they fell, and a certain exquisite cream kind with a slender red stem and bright scarlet leaves.

There were clumbs of fairy bells, and all kinds of geraniums, and there were little trees of verbena and bluish lavender bushes and a bed of pelargonium with velvet eyes and leaves like moth's wings. There was a bed of nothing but mignonette and another of nothing of pansies-borders of double and single daisies and all kinds of little tufty plants she had never seen before. The red-hot pokers were taller than she; the Japanese sun-flowers grew in a tiny jungle.' (CS, p. 32, 33).

54. Cf. also Linda's perception of Stanley and Beryl playing cribbage. CS, p. 51.

55. Its symbolist meaning has never been agreed on. Much of the controversy over the passage arose from the suggestion that the aloe is an image of female fertility, which is 'especially attractive to Linda because of its infrequency of bearing.' (Peter Alcock, 'An Aloe in the Garden: Something essentially New Zealand in Miss Mansfield', *Journal of Commonwealth Literature*, 7, pp. 58-64, 1977.)

Another suggestion was that the aloe was 'a phallic tree of knowledge'. Alcock has not checked Mansfield's letters. When, however, searching Mansfield's secondary writings, the critic may encounter the following, significant clue to sexual symbolism, which clearly illustrates that Mansfield rejected any kind of outward allusion to sex or symbols. On May 4, 1916, Mansfield wrote to her friend Beatrice Campbell some comments on conversations with D.H. Lawrence:

'And I shall *never* see sex in trees, sex in the running brooks, sex in stones and sex in everything. The number of things that are really phallic from fountain pen fillers onwards!' (*Letters*, I, 1903-1917, p. 262) (Italics KM)

56. Hanson & Gurr, 1981, pp. 21-23.

57. Hanson did not include Mansfield's *Scrapbook* in her research, as it is not mentioned nor included in the footnotes.

58. LJMM, p. 392-3, already quoted in Chapter 3.3.

59. Cf. Mansfield's *Scrapbook*, p. 192.

60. For example, in "At Lehman's", "Pension Seguin", "Bains Trucs", "The Singing Lesson", "At the Bay", "Her First Ball", "The Voyage".

61. For example, in "Frau Fisher", "The Sister of the Baroness", "The Tiredness of Rosabel", "Millie", "Mr. Reginal Peacock", "The Daughters of the Late Colonel", "Miss Brill", "The Canary", "The Lady's Maid".

62. For example, in "A Birthday", "Bliss", "The Lady's Maid, "The Doll's House", "Taking the Veil", "New Dresses", "Je ne Parle Pas Francais", "The Garden Party", "The Stranger", "The Young Girl", "Marriage a la Mode", "Pictures", "Revelations", "The Escape", "Psychology".

63. Hanson, 1981, pp. 33-37.

64. Mansfield on the too overt meaning of "Mr and Mrs Dove", J, p. 256: I finished "Mr and Mrs Dove" yesterday. I am not altogether pleased with it. It's a little bit made up. It's not inevitable. I mean to imply that those two may not be happy together - that is the kind of reason for which a young girl marries. But have I done so? I don't think so. Besides, it's not *strong* enough. I want to be nearer - far, far, nearer than that. I want to use all my force even when I am taking a fine line. And I have a sneaking notion that I have, at the end, used the Doves *unwarrantly*. *Tu sais ce que je veux dire*. I used them to round off something - didn't I. Is that quite my game? No, it's not. It's not quite the kind of truth I'm after.' (Italics KM).

65. See Haferkamp, Wagenknecht, Busch, Kurylo for concurrence on this point.

66. Cf. L. Thon, pp. 5-8.

PART IV

<u>BIBLIOGRAPHY</u>

A. WORKS BY KATHERINE MANSFIELD

(Unless otherwise indicated, the publisher is understood to be
Constable.)

In a German Pension, Stephen Swift, 1911.
Prelude, Hogarth Press, 1918.
Bliss and Other Stories, 1920.
The Garden-Party and Other Stories, 1922.
The Doves' Nest and Other Stories, ed. J.M. Murry, 1923.
Poems, ed. J.M. Murry, 1923.
Something Childish and Other Stories, ed. J.M. Murry, 1923.
The Journal of Katherine Mansfield, ed. J.M. Murry, 1927.
The Letters of Katherine Mansfield, ed. J.M. Murry, 2 vols, 1928.
Reminiscences of Leonid Andreyev by Maxim Gorki, trans.
Katherine Mansfield and S.S. Koteliansky, 1928.
The Aloe, ed. J.M. Murry, 1930.
Stories by Katherine Mansfield, ed. J.M. Murry, Knopf, 1930.
Novels and Novelists, ed. J.M. Murry, Knopf, 1930.
Reminiscences of Tolstoy, Chekhov and Andreyev by Maxim Gorki,
trans. Katherine Mansfield, S.S. Koteliansky and Leonard Woolf,
1934.
The Scrapbook of Katherine Mansfield, ed. J.M. Murry, 1937.
'To Stanislaw Wyspianski' (poem). Privately printed for Bertram
Rota, 1938, (reprinted in C.K. Stead, *The Letters and Journals of
Katherine Mansfield*, pp. 39-40, 1977).
Collected Stories of Katherine Mansfield, 1945. (rpt. 1972)
The Scrapbook of Katherine Mansfield, ed. J.M. Murry, Knopf,
1946.
Katherine Mansfield's Letters to John Middleton Murry, 1913-1922,
ed. J.M. Murry, 1951.
Journal of Katherine Mansfield, 'Definitive Edition', ed.
J.M. Murry, 1954.
The Collected Letters of Katherine Mansfield, Vol. I, 1903-1917, ed.
Vincent O'Sullivan and Margaret Scott, Clarendon Press (Oxford),
1984.
The Collected Letters of Katherine Mansfield, Vol. II, 1918-1919,
ed. Vincent O'Sullivan and Margaret Scott, Clarendon Press
(Oxford), 1987.

Other Collections

Selected Stories by Katherine Mansfield, ed. D.M. Davin, Oxford University Press, 1953, 1981.
Thirty Four Short Stories by Katherine Mansfield, selected and edited by Elizabeth Bowen, 1957.
Undiscovered Country: The New Zealand Stories of Katherine Mansfield, ed. Ian A. Gordon, 1974.
Katherine Mansfield - Short Stories, selected and introduced by Claire Tomalin, Everyman, 1983.
The Collected Short Stories by Katherine Mansfield, Penguin Modern Classics, 1981.
The Stories of Katherine Mansfield, ed. A. Alpers, Auckland, Oxford University Press, 1984.
The Critical Writings of Katherine Mansfield, ed. and introduced by Clare Hanson, MacMillan Press, 1987.

Translated into Dutch:
Gelukzalig en andere verhalen, vertaald door Jo Fiedeldij Dop, Querido, 1985.
Het Tuinfeest en andere verhalen, vertaald door Jo Fiedeldij Dop, Querido, 1986.

B. Works about Katherine Mansfield

Alcock, Peter. 'An Aloe in the Garden: Something Essentially New Zealand in Miss Mansfield', *Journal of Commonwealth Literature*, 11, April, 1977.

Alpers, Anthony. *The Life of Katherine Mansfield*, 1982.

Asaad, Thomas J. 'Mansfield's "The Fly"', *Explicator*, XIV, November, 10, 1955.

Auerbach, Frank. 'Einführung', *Letztes Abenteuer: Neuseeland in Erzählungen der Besten Zeitgenössischen Autoren*, pp. 13-41, 1972.

Baker, Ernest A. *The History of the English Novel*, Vol. X, pp. 239-240, 1939.

Baker, Ida Constance. *Katherine Mansfield: The Memories of LM*, 1971.

Baldeswhiler, Eileen. 'Katherine Mansfield's Theory of Fiction', *Studies in Short Fiction*, VII, pp. 421-432, 1970.

Bateson, F.W. and B. Shahevitch. 'Katherine Mansfield's "The Fly": A Critical Exercise', *Essays in Critisism*, 12, pp. 39-53, 1962.

Beachcroft, T. O. 'Katherine Mansfield', Chapter 14 of *The Modest Art: A Survey of the Short Story in English*, pp. 162-176, 1968.

--- 'Katherine Mansfield's Encounter with Theocritus', *English*, XXIII, Spring, pp. 13-19, 1974.

--- 'Katherine Mansfield 'Then and Now', *Modern Fiction Studies*, Vol. 24, 3, pp. 343-355, 1978.

Bell, Pauline P. 'Mansfield's "The Fly"', *Explicator*, XIX, December, item 10, 1968.

Berkman, Sylvia. *Katherine Mansfield: A Critical Study*, 1951.

Bledsoe, Thomas. 'Mansfield's "The Fly"', *Explicator*, V, May, 53, 1947.

Boddy, Gillian. *Katherine Mansfield: The Woman and the Writer*, 1988.

Bowen, Elizabeth. 'A Living Writer', *Cornhill Magazine*, 169, pp. 120-134, 1956.

Bowen, E. Introduction to *Thirty-Four Short Stories by Katherine Mansfield*, 1957.

Boyle, Ted E. 'The Death of the Boss: Another look at Katherine Mansfield's "The Fly"', *Modern Fiction Studies*, XI, pp. 183-185, 1965.

Braekkan, E.M. *From Feminist to 'Feminine': A Comparative Study of Katherine Mansfield's Short Stories*, Ph.D. Thesis, Univ. of Warwick, 1981.

Brophy, Brigid. 'Katherine Mansfield's Self-Deception', *Michigan Quarterly Review*, V, pp. 89-93, 1966.

Burgan, Mary. 'Childbirth Trauma in Katherine Mansfield's Early Stories', *Modern Fiction Studies*, Vol. 24, 3, 1978.

Busch, Frieder. 'Katherine Mansfield and Literary Impressionism in France and Germany', *Arcadia*, 5, pp. 58-76, 1970.

Calfin, Elizabeth. *Introducing Katherine Mansfield*, 1982.

Carswell, John. *Lives and Letters: A.R. Orage, Beatrice Hastings, Katherine Mansfield, John Middleton Murry, S.S. Koteliansky 1906-1957*, 1978.

Chatterjee, Atul Chandra. *The Art of Katherine Mansfield: An Enquiry into the Meaning and Technique of the Short Stories of Katherine Mansfield in the Background of the Modern Short Story in England and Elsewhere*, 1980.

Citari, Pietto. *Katherine Mansfield: Beschreibung eines Lebens*, transl. Dora Winkler, 1982.

Coles, Gladys Mary. 'Katherine Mansfield and William Gerhardi', *Contemporary Review*, p. 229, 1976.

Corin, F. 'Creation of Atmosphere in Katherine Mansfield's Stories', *Revue des Langues Vivantes*, I, pp. 65-78, 1956.

Conroy, G.L. 'Our Perhaps Uncommon Friendship': The Relationship between S.S. Kotelianski and Katherine Mansfield', *Modern Fiction Studies*, Vol. 24, 3, pp. 355-369, 1978.

Cox, Sidney. 'The Fastidiousness of Katherine Mansfield', *Sewanee Review*, 39, pp. 158-169, 1931.

Crone, Nora. *A Portrait of Katherine Mansfield*, 1985.

Daiches, David. *New Literary Values*, Chapter on Katherine Mansfield, 1936.

--- *The Novel and the Modern World*, pp. 83-108, 1963.

Daly, S.R. *Katherine Mansfield*, 1965.

Davin, D. 'Introduction to *New Zealand Short Stories*', In *Readings in Commonwealth Literature*, ed. William Walsh, 1973.

Davis, R.M. 'The Unity of "The Garden-Party"', *Studies in Short Fiction*, 2, 1964.

Delany, Paul. 'Short and Simple Annals of the Poor', *Mosaic*, Vol. 10, pp. 7-17, 1976.

Dowling, David. *Katherine Mansfield: Her Theory and Practice of Fiction*, Ph.D. Thesis, Univ. of Toronto, 1976.

--- 'Aunt Beryl's Doll's House', *Landfall 134*, 34, no. 2, June, pp. 148-158, 1980.

--- 'Something Childish But Very Natural', *Explicator*, 38, 1980.

Drabble, M. 'The New Woman of the Twenties: Fifty Years On', *Harpers and Queen*, June, 1973.

Eliot, T.S. *After Strange Gods* (a discussion of "Bliss"), 1934.

Fleisham, Avrom. *Revaluation and Continuity*, Chapter 4, pp. 44-70, 'Forms of the Woolfian Short Story,' 1980.

Friis, Anne. *Katherine Mansfield: Life and Stories*, 1946.

Fullbrook, Kate. *Katherine Mansfield*, 1986.

Garlington, J. 'Katherine Mansfield: The Critical Trend', *Twentieth Century Literature*, 2, 1956.

Glenavy, Lady Beatrice. *Today we will only Gossip*, 1964.

Gordon, Ian A. *Katherine Mansfield*, Writers and Their Work, 1954, revised 1971.

'The Editing of Katherine Mansfield's *Journal and Scrapbook*', *Landfall*, 13, 1959.

Greenfield, Stanley B. 'Mansfield's "The Fly"', *Explicator*, XVII, April, 1958.

Grindea, Miron, ed., *Adam*, 300, 1963-65. Contains an editorial on Katherine Mansfield and Beatrice Hastings, letters and the reminiscences of Dorothy Brett and Anne Estelle Rice.

--- *Adam*, special Mansfield issue, pp. 370-75, 1972-73. Editorial, letters and other contributions.

Haferkamp, Bertha. 'Zur Bildersprache Katherine Mansfields', *Neueren Sprachen*, Vol. 18, pp. 221-39, 1969.

Hagopian, John T. 'Capturing Mansfield's "The Fly"', *Modern Fiction Studies*, IX, 1963, pp. 38-390.

Hale, N. 'Through the Looking Glass', *Saturday Review*, Vol. 41, 8/Nov, 1958.

Halter, Peter. *Katherine Mansfield und die Kurzgeschichte*, 1972.

Hankin, Cherry. 'Fantasy and the Sense of an Ending in the Work of Katherine Mansfield', *Modern Fiction Studies*, Vol. 24, 3, pp. 465-475, 1978/79.

--- *Katherine Mansfield and her Confessional Stories*, 1983.

--- ed. *The Letters of John M. Murry to Katherine Mansfield*, 1983.

Hanson, Clare. 'Katherine Mansfield and Symbolism: The Artist's Method in "Prelude"', *Journal of Commonwealth Literature*, 16, no. 1, pp. 25-39, 1981.

Hanson, Clare and Andrew Gurr. *Katherine Mansfield*, 1981.

Harper, George McLean. 'Katherine Mansfield', *Quarterly Review*, 253, pp. 377-387, 1929.

Hartley, L.P. 'Katherine Mansfield', *Spectator*, September 6, pp. 328-330, 1924.

Hayman, Ronald. *Literature and Living: A Consideration of Katherine Mansfield and Virginia Woolf*, 1972.

Hoare, Dorothy M. *Some Studies in the Modern Novel*, pp. 148-154, 1938.

Hormasji, Nariman. *Katherine Mansfield: An Appraisal*, 1967.

Hudson, Stephan (S. Schiff). 'First Meetings with Katherine Mansfield', *Cornhill Magazine*, 170, pp. 202-212, 1958.

Hull, Robert T. 'Alienation in "Miss Brill"', *Studies in Short Fiction*, V, pp. 74-76, 1967-8.

Hubbell, George Shelton. 'Katherine Mansfield and Kezia', *Sewanee Review*, 35, pp. 325-35, 1927.

Huxley, A. 'The Traveller's Eye View', *Nation and Athenaeum*, 37, 1925.

Hynes, S. 'Katherine Mansfield: The Defeat of the Personal', *South Atlantic Quarterly*, 52, 1953.

Iverson, A. 'Life and Letters: Katherine Mansfield drawing on Kathleen Beauchamp', *English Studies*, 52, 1971.

--- 'A Reading of Katherine Mansfield's "The Garden Party"', *Orbus Litteratum*, pp. 5-33, 1968.

Jacobs, Willis D. 'Mansfield's "The Fly"', *Explicator*, February, Item 32, 1947.

Jones, L. 'The Road not Taken: Mansfield as Critical Realist', Lecture read at the Katherine Mansfield Centennial Conference, Wellington, 1988.

Justus, James H. 'Katherine Mansfield: The Triumph of Egoism', *Mosaic*, 6, 1973.

King, R.S. 'Francis Carco's *Les Innocents*' and Katherine Mansfield's "Je ne Parle Pas Francais", *Revue de la Littérature Comparée*, Vol. 47, pp. 427-441, 1972.

King, R.S. 'Katherine Mansfield as an Expatriate Writer', *Journal of Commonwealth Literature*, 13, 1973.

Kleine, D.W. *Method and Meaning in the Stories of Katherine Mansfield*, Ph.D. Thesis, Univ. of Michigan, 1961.

--- 'The Chekhovian Source of "Marriage a la Mode"', PQ, 42, 1963.

--- '"The Garden Party": A Portrait of the Artist', *Criticism*, Vol. 5, I, pp. 360-371, 1963.

--- 'Katherine Mansfield and the Prisoner of Love', *Critique*, 3, III, 21-33, 1965.

--- 'Eden for Insiders', *College English*, 27, pp. 201-209, 1965.

--- 'Mansfield and the Orphans of Time', *Modern Fiction Studies*, Vol. 24, 3, 1978.

Kobler, J.F. 'The Sexless Narrator of Mansfield's "The Young Girl", *Studies in Short Fiction*, Vol. 17, pp. 269-74, 1979.

Kominar, S.B. *Katherine Mansfield: The Way to Fontainebleau*, Ph.D. Thesis, Boston Univ, 1966.

Kurylo, C.C. *Chekhov and Katherine Mansfield: A Study in Literary Influence*, Ph.D. Thesis, Univ. of North Carolina, 1974.

Lea, F.A. 'Murry and Marriage', *D.H. Lawrence Review*, Vol. 2, 1969.

Lederman, M.J. 'Through the Looking-glass: Queens, Dreams, Fears in the fiction of Katherine Mansfield', *Women's Studies*, Vol. 5, pp. 35-49, 1976.

Madden, Fred Stanley. *The Development of a Consistent Structural Pattern in Katherine Mansfield's Short Stories*, Ph.D. Thesis, Univ. of Wisconsin-Madison, 1978.

Magalaner, Marvin. *The Fiction of Katherine Mansfield*, 1971.
--- 'Traces of Her 'Self' in Katherine Mansfield's "Bliss"', *Modern Fiction Studies*, Vol. 24, 3, 1978-9.
Mais, S.P.B. *Some Modern Authors*, pp. 108-114, 1923.
Mantz, Ruth Elvish. *The Critical Bibliography of Katherine Mansfield*, 1931.
Mantz, Ruth Elvish and J.M. Murry. *The Life of Katherine Mansfield*, 1933.
--- *Katherine Mansfield and other Literary Portraits*, 1949.
Mason, N.B. *Intimacy and Isolation: A Tension which Informs the Work of Katherine Mansfield*, Ph.D. Thesis, Purdue Univ., 1980.
Maurois, André. *Points of View: From Kipling to Graham Greene*, 1969.
McLaughlin, Ann L. 'The Same Job: Notes on the Relationship Between Virginia Woolf and Katherine Mansfield', *Virginia Woolf Miscellany*, 6, pp. 11-12, 1977.
--- 'The Same Job: The Shared Writing Aims of Katherine Mansfield and Virginia Woolf', *Modern Fictions Studies*, 24, no. 3, pp. 369-382, 1978.
Merlin, Roland. *Le Drame Secret de Katherine Mansfield*, 1950.
Meyers, J. 'Katherine Mansfield, Gurdjieff, and Lawrence's 'Mother and Daughter"', *Twentieth Century Literature*, 22, 1976.
--- 'D.H. Lawrence, Katherine Mansfield and *Women in Love*, *London Magazine*, 18, 2, 1978.
--- *Katherine Mansfield*, 1978.
--- 'The Two Katherine Mansfields', *Spectator*, 10 May, 1980.
--- 'To Stanislaw Wyspianski', *Modern Fiction Studies*, Vol. 24, 3, pp. 337-343, 1978.
Michel-Michot, Paulette. 'Katherine Mansfield's "The Fly": An Attempt to Capture the Boss', *Studies in Short Fiction*, IX, 1, Winter, pp. 85-92, 1974.
Morse, L.M. *Juxtaposition in the Short Stories of Katherine Mansfield*, Ph.D. Thesis, Oklahoma St. Univ, 1971.
Mortelier, C. 'Origines et Développement d'une Légende: Katherine Mansfield en France', *Etudes Anglaises*, 25, 1970.
Murry, J.M. *Son of Woman*, 1931.
--- *Between Two Worlds*, 1935.
--- *Katherine Mansfield, and other Literary Portraits*, 1949.
--- *Katherine Mansfield and other Literary Studies*, introd. by T.S. Eliot, 1959.
Nebeker, H.E. 'The Pear Tree: Sexual Implications in Katherine Mansfield's "Bliss"', *Modern Fiction Studies*, 18, 1972-73.
Nelson, Arthur. 'Katherine Mansfield: Artist in Miniature', *Yale Literary Magazine*, 106, pp. 95-97, 1941.

O'Connor, Frank. *The Lonely Voice: A Study of the Short Story*, pp. 128-142, 1963.

O'Faolain, Sean. Review of *The Garden Party and other Stories*, *New Statesman*, Vol. 35, 1711, pp. 54-55, 1948.

Orage, A.R. 'Talks with Katherine Mansfield', *Century Magazine*, 109, November, pp. 36-40, 1924.

O'Sullivan, Vincent. 'The Magnetic Chain: Notes and Approaches to Katherine Mansfield', *Landfall*, 114, 1975.

--- 'Introduction' to *The Aloe*, pp. V-XVIII, 1985.

Palliser, C. *The Early Fiction of Virginia Woolf and her Literary Relations with Katherine Mansfield*, 1975.

Peterson, R.F. 'The Circle of Truth: The Stories of Katherine Mansfield and Mary Lavin', *Modern Fiction Studies*, Vol. 24, 3, pp. 383-395, 1978.

Pritchett, V.S. 'Review of *Collected Stories*', *New Statesman*, 2 February, 1946.

Rohrberger, Mary H. *The Art of Katherine Mansfield*, 1977.

Schneider, Elizabeth. 'Katherine Mansfield and Chekhov', *Modern Language Notes*, 50, June, pp. 394-96, 1935.

Shanks, Edward. 'Katherine Mansfield', *London Mercury*, 17, pp. 286-293, 1928.

Smith, Angela. 'Katherine Mansfield and Virginia Woolf: "Prelude" and "To the Lighthouse"', *Journal of Commonwealth Literature*, 18, no. 1, pp. 105-119, 1983.

Sorkin, A.J. 'Katherine Mansfield's "The Garden Party": Style and Social Occasion', *Modern Fiction Studies*, Vol. 24, 3, 1978.

Stallman, Robert Wooster. 'Mansfield "The Fly"', *Explicator*, III, April, Item 49, 1945.

Stanzel, Franz. 'Teller-Characters and Reflector Characters in Narrative Theory', *Poetics Today*, 2, no. 2, pp. 5-15, 1981.

Stauffer Emily Ann. *The Problem of the Personal in the Art of Katherine Mansfield*, Ph.D. Thesis, Univ. of Conneticut, 1983.

Stead, C.K. 'Katherine Mansfield and the Art of Fiction', *New Review*, 4, No. 42, Sept, pp. 17-36, 1977.

Stone, J.E. 'New Light on Katherine Mansfield', *Quadrant*, August, 1978.

Sullivan, J.W.N. 'The Story-Writing Genius', *Athenaeum*, April 2, 1920.

Sutherland, R. 'Katherine Mansfield: Plagiarist, Disciple or Ardent Admirer?', *Critique 5*, 1962.

Tallentire, D.R. 'Confirming Intuitions about Style Using Concordances', *The Computer in Literary and Linguistic Studies. Papers from the Third International Symposium on the Use of the Computer in Linguistic Literary Research*, April 1974, pp. 309-328, 1976.

Taylor, D.S. and D.A. Weiss. 'Crashing "The Garden Party"', *Modern Fiction Studies*, 4, 1958.

Thomas, J.D. 'Symbol and Parallelism in "The Fly"', *College English*, 22, pp. 256-262, 1961.

Tomalin, Claire. *Katherine Mansfield: A Secret Life*, 1987.

Van Kranendonk, A.G. 'Katherine Mansfield', *English Studies*, XII, pp. 49-57, 1930.

Verzea, Ileana. 'Katherine Mansfield, an Innovator of the Short Story', *Revista de Istoria si Theorie Literara*, 23, pp. 79-85, 1974.

Virginia Woolf. 'A Terribly Sensitive Mind', Review of *The Journal of Katherine Mansfield* 1914-1922, *New York Herald Tribune*, no. 1819, 1927.

Wagenknecht, Edward. 'Katherine Mansfield', *English Journal*, 17, pp. 272-284, 1928.

--- 'Dickens and Katherine Mansfield', *Dickensian*, 26, 213, pp. 15-23, 1930.

Waldron, Philip. 'Katherine Mansfield's Journal', *Twentieth Century Literature*, XX, January, pp. 11-18, 1974.

Walker, Nancy. *Stages of Womanhood in Katherine Mansfield's "Prelude"*, 1976.

Walker, W. 'The Unresolved Conflict in "The Garden-Party"', *Modern Fiction Studies*, 3, 1957.

Walsh, William. *A Manifold Voice*, 1970.

Walt, J. 'Conrad and Katherine Mansfield', *Conradiana*, 4, 1972.

Wattie, Nelson. 'The Story Must be Told: Short Narrative Prose in the New English literatures', ed. P. Stummer, p. 23-34, 1985.

Whitridge, Arnold. 'Katherine Mansfield', *Sewanee Review*, 48, pp. 256-272, 1940.

Woolf, Virginia. *Collected Essays*, Vol. 1, pp. 356-358, 1966.

Wright, Celeste Turner. 'The Unresolved Conflict in "The Fly"', *Explicator*, XII, February, Item 27, 1954.

--- 'Darknes as a Symbol of Katherine Mansfield', *Modern Philology*, 51, pp. 204-207, 1954.

--- 'Katherine Mansfield's Boat Images', *Twentieth Century Literature*, I, 3, pp. 128-132, 1955.

--- 'Genesis of a Short Story', *Philological Quarterly*, 34, pp. 91-96, 1955.

Yuan-Shu Yen. *Katherine Mansfield's use of Point of View*, Ph.D. Thesis, Univ. of Wisconsin, 1976.

Zinman, Toby Silverman. 'The Snail Under the Leaf: Katherine Mansfield's Imagery', *Modern Fiction Studies*, 24, no. 3, Autumn, pp. 457-464, 1978.

Zorn, M. 'Visionary Flowers: Another Study of Katherine Mansfield's "Bliss"', *Studies in Short Fiction*, 17, no. 2, pp. 141-147, 1980.

Articles on "The Fly" in chronological order:

Robert W. Stallman. 'Mansfield's "The Fly"', *Explicator*, III, VI, April, Item 49, 1945.

Thomas Bledsoe. 'Mansfield's "The Fly"', *Explicator*, V, VII, May, Item 53, 1947.

W.D. Jacobs. 'Mansfield's "The Fly"', *Explicator*, V, IV, February, Item 32, 1947.

C.T. Wright. 'Mansfield's "The Fly"', *Explicator*, XII, IV, February, Item 27, 1954.

T.J. Asaad. 'Mansfield's "The Fly"', *Explicator*, XIV, II, November, Item 10, 1955.

S.B. Greenfield. 'Mansfield's "The Fly"', *Explicator*, XVII, I, April, Item 2, 1958.

P.B. Bell. 'Mansfield's "The Fly"', *Explicator*, XIX, III, December, Item 20, 1960.

J.D. Thomas. 'Symbol and Parellelism in "The Fly"', *College English*, XXII, pp. 256-262, 1961.

C.W. Oleson. "The Fly" Rescued, *College English*, XXII, pp. 585-596, 1961.

J.D. Thomas. Reply to Oleson's "The Fly" Rescued, *College English*, XXII, p. 586, 1961.

F.W. Bateson and B. Shahevitch. 'Katherine Mansfield's "The Fly": A Critical Exercise', *Essays in Criticism*, XII, pp. 39-53, 1962.

R.A. Jolly. 'Response to Bateson and Shahevitch's article', *Essays in Criticism*, XII, p. 336, 1962.

R.A. Copland. 'Response to Bateson and Shahevitch's article', *Essays in Criticism*, XII, p. 340, 1962.

E.B. Greenwood. 'Response to Bateson and Shahevitch's article', *Essays in Criticism*, XII, p. 340, 1962.

J.T. Hagopian. 'Capturing Mansfield's "The Fly"', *Modern Fiction Studies*, IX, pp. 385-390, 1964.

T. Boyle. 'The Death of the Boss': another look at Katherine Mansfield's "The Fly", *Modern Fiction Studies*, II, pp. 183-185, 1965.

P.P. Bel. 'Mansfields "The Fly"', *Explicator*, XIX, December, item 10, 1968.

P. Michel-Michon. 'Katherine Mansfield's "The Fly": An attempt to capture the Boss'. *Studies in Short Fiction*, IX, I, Winter, pp. 85-92, 1974.

C. Selected Bibliography on Impressionism

Adler, Kathleen & Garb, Tamar. *Berthe Morisot*, 1987.

Albérès, R.M. 'Aux sources du nouveau roman: L'Impressionisme Anglais', *Revue de Paris*, 69, pp. 74-86, 1962.

Albrecht, Hans. *Impressionismus* (Art.), *Musik in Geschichte und Gegenwart. Eine Allgemeine Enzyklopädie der Musik*, 1963.

Armstrong, Nancy. 'Character, Closure, and Impressionist Fiction', *Critisism: A Quarterly for Literature and the Arts*, 19-4, Fall, pp. 317-37, 1977.

Bahr, Hermann. *Zur Überwindung des Naturalismus, Theoretische Schriften 1887-1904*, 1968.

Bally, Charles. *'Impressionisme et Grammaire'*, *Mélanges d'Histoire Littéraire et de Philologie Offerts a M.B. Bouvier*, 1920.

Bazin, Germain. *French Impressionists in the Louvre*, 1958.

Bell, Clive. *The French Impressionists*, 1952.

Benamou, Michel. 'Symposium in Literary Impressionism', *Year-Book of Comparative and General Literature*, no. 17, pp. 91-94, 1968.

--- 'Wallace Stevens: Some Relations between Poetry and Painting', *Comparative Literature*, 2, pp. 47-60, 1959.

Bender, Bert. 'Hanging Stephen Crane in the Impressionist Museum', *Journal of Aesthetic and Art Criticism*, 35, pp. 47-56, 1976.

Bernard, Suzanne. 'Rimbaud, Proust et les Impressionnistes', *Revue des Science Humaines*, 78, pp. 257-262, 1955.

Bicilli, P.M. 'Impressionismus', *Anton P. Cechov: Das Werk und Sein Stil*, 1966.

Bidle, Kenneth E. *Impressionism in American Literature to the Year 1900*, Ph.D. Thesis, Northern Illinois Univ, 1969.

Bithell, Jethro. 'The Novel of Impressionism', *Modern German Literature 1880-1950*, pp. 279-321, 1959.

Blunden, Maria & Blunden, Godfrey. *Impressionist and Impressionism*, transl. by James Emmons, 1970.

Borréli, Guy, 'Littérature et Impressionisme en France de 1870 à 1900', *L'Information Littérature*, 28, Chapter 5, pp. 203-205, 1976.

Bowie, Theodore Robert. *The Painter in French Fiction*, 1950.

Bresky, Dushan, 'The Style of the Impressionistic Novel: A Study in Poetized Prose', *L'Esprit Créateur*, 13, Chapter 4, pp. 298-309, 1973.

Brösel, Kurt. *Veranschaulichung im Realismus, Impressionismus und Frühexpressionismus*, 1928.

Brown, Calvin S. 'Symposium in Literary Impressionism', *Year-Book of Comparative and General Literature*, 17, pp. 79-85, 1968.

Brunétière, Ferdinand. 'L'Impressionisme dans le Roman', *Revue des Deux Mondes*, 15 Nov., 1879.

--- *Le Roman Naturaliste*, 1879.

Champa, Kermit. *Studies in Early Impressionism*, 1973.

Chernovitz, Maurice E. *Proust and Painting*, 1945.

Cognist, Raymond. *The Century of the Impressionist*, transl. Gr. Snell, 1960.

Courthin, Pierre. *Impressionism*, transl. J. Shepley, 1972.

Davis, Harold E. 'Conrad's Revision of *The Secret Agent*: A Study in Literary Impressionism', *Modern Language Quarterly*, 19, pp. 244-54, 1958.

Diersch, Manfred. *Empiriokritizismus und Impressionismus. Uber Beziehungen zwischen Philosophie, Aesthetik und Literatur um 1900 in Wien*, 1977.

Durney, Ruth. *Impressionism and Naturalism in the Work of Stephen Crane*, Ph.D. Thesis, Univ. of Washington, 1936.

Desprez, L. *l'Evolution Naturaliste*, 1884.

Falk, Walter, *Impressionismus und Expressionismus, Expressionismus als Literatur. Gesammelte Studien*, ed. Wolfgang Rothe, pp. 69-86, 1969.

--- *Leid und Verwandlung. Rilke, Kafka, Trakl und der Epochenstil des Impressionismus und Expressionismus*, 1961.

Ford, Ford Madox. 'On Impressionism', *Poetry and Drama*, 2-6 June 1914, pp. 2-8 and 167-75, December, 1914.

Francastel, Pierre. 'La Fin de l'Impressionisme: Esthétique et Causalité', *Problems of 19th and 20th Century Studies in Eastern Art*, Vol. 4, 1963.

Frank, Joseph. 'Spatial Form in Modern Literature', *The Widening Gyre*, 1963.

Garland, Hamlin. *Crumbling Idols*, 1960.

Gaunt, William. *Impressionism: A Visual History*, 1970, rept. 1988.

Gibbs, Beverly Jean. 'Impressionism as a Literary Movement', *Modern Language Journal*, 36, pp. 175-83, 1952.

Hamann, Richard. *Der Impressionismus in Leben und Kunst*, 1923.

Hamann, Richard & Hermand, Jost. *Impressionismus*, Vol. 3, *Epochen Deutscher Kultur von 1870 bis zur Gegenwart*, 1977.

Hanson, Clare. *Short Stories and Short Fictions*, 1880-1980, 1985.

Harms, W. *Impressionism as a Literary Style*, Ph.D. Thesis, Indiana Univ, 1971.

Hartt, Frederick. *A History of Painting. Sculpture. Architecture*, pp. 839-882, 1985.

Hatzfeld, Helmut. *Literature Through Art*, 1952.

Hauser, Arnold. *The Social History of Art*, Vol. 4, *Naturalism, Impressionism, The Film Age*, 1951.

Hay, Eloise Knapp. 'Joseph Conrad and Impressionism', *Journal of Aesthetics and Art Criticism*, 34, Winter, pp. 37-44, 1975.

Hemmings, F.W.J. 'Zola, Manet, and the Impressionists', *PMLA*, 73, pp. 407-17, 1958.

Herbert, R.L. *Impressionism: Art, Leisures and Parisian Society*, 1988.

Hoff, P. Sloatt. 'The Impressionist Narrator', unpublished paper, Literary Impressionism session. *Modern Language Association*, 1975.

Hoppe, Hans. *Impressionismus und Expressionismus bei Emile Zola*, Ph.D. Thesis, Univ. of Münster, 1933.

Honour, Hugh & Fleming, John. *A World History of Art*, 1982.

Hourtique, L. 'Réalisme et Impressionisme', *L'Art et la Littérature*, 1946.

Howarth, Herbert. 'Symposium in Literary Impressionism', *Year-Book of Comparative and General Literature*, no. 17, pp. 66-71, 1968.

Huyghe, René. 'L'impressionisme et la Pensée de son Temps', *Promethée*, 1, pp. 7-16, 1939.

--- 'Shifts in Thought During the Impressionist Era: Painting, Science, Literature, History, and Philosophy', *Impressionism: A Centenary Exhibition*, 1974.

Ilie, Paul. 'Symposium in Literary Impresionism', *Year-Book of Comparative and General Literature*, no. 17, pp. 72-79, 1968.

Jacobs, Robert Glenn. *Psychology, Setting, and Impressionism in the Major Novels of Joseph Conrad*, Ph.D. Thesis, Univ. of Iowa, 1966.

Johnson, J. Theodore (jr.). 'Literary Impressionism in France: A Survey of Criticism', *L'Esprit Créateur*, 13, Chapter 4, pp. 271-297, 1973.

Johnston, William M. 'Prague as a center of Austrian Expressionism versus Vienna as a center of Impressionism', in *Modern Austrian Literature*, 6, Chapter 3/4, pp. 176-181, 1973.

Kirschke, J.J. *Henry James and Impressionism*, 1981.

Knowle, Carol P. 'Impressionism and Arnold Bennet' in Todd Bender, *Literary Impressionism in Ford Madox Ford, Joseph Conrad and Related writers*, (Madison: Text Development Program) 1975.

Kronegger, Maria Elizabeth. 'Impressionist Tendencies in Lyrical Prose', *Revue de Littérature Comparée*, 172, pp. 528-44, 1969.

--- *Literary Impressionism*, 1973.

--- 'The Multiplication of the Self from Flaubert to Sartre', *L'Esprit Créateur*, 13, Chapter 4, pp. 310-319, 1973.

--- 'Authors and Impressionist Reality', *Authors and Their Centuries*, pp. 155-166, 1974.

Laforgue, Jules. 'Impressionism', *Impressionism and Post-Impressionism 1874-1904: Sources and Documents*, ed. Linda Nochlin, 1966.

Lauterbach, Ulrich. *Herman Bang-Studien zum Dänischen Impressionismus*, 1937.

247

Lerch, Eugen. 'La Fontaines Impressionismus', *Archiv für das Studium der neueren Sprachen*, 139, p. 247, 1919.

Leymarie, Jean. *Impressionism*, 2 vols., translated by James Emmons, 1955.

Loesch, Georg. *Die Impressionistische Syntax der Goncourt. Eine Syntaktisch-Stilistische Untersuchung*, Ph.D. Thesis, Erlangen Univ, 1919.

Ivcie-Smith, Edward. *Impressionist Women*, 1989.

Lytle, A.N. 'Impressionism, the Ego, and the First person', *Daedalus*, 92, pp. 281-96, 1963.

Mathey, Francois. *The Impressionists*, transl. J. Steinberg, 1961.

Matson, Floyd. *The Broken Image*, 1964.

Melang, Walter. *Flaubert als Begründer des Literarischen Impressionismus in Frankreich*, Ph.D. Thesis, Univ. of Münster, 1933.

Mendilov, A.A. *Time and the Novel*, 1952.

Merleau-Ponty, Maurice. *Phenomenology of Perception*, transl. Colin Smith, 1962.

- - - 'The Primacy of Perception and its Philosophical Consequences', *Readings in Existential Phenomenology*, ed. by Nathaniel Lawrence and Daniel O'Connor, 1967.

Moser, Ruth. *L'Impressionisme Français, Peinture, Littérature, Musique*, 1952.

Müller, Herbert J. 'Impressionism in Fiction-Prism vs. Mirror', *The American Scholar*, 7, pp. 355-67, 1938.

Nagel, J. 'Impressionism in 'The Open Boat' and 'A Man and Some Others', *Research Studies*, 43, pp. 27-37, 1975.

- - - *Stephen Crane and Literary Impressionism*, 1980.

Nehring, Wolfgang. 'Schluck und Jau', 'Impressionismus bei Gerhard Hauptmann', *Zeitschrift für Deutsche Philologie*, 88, pp. 189-209, 1969.

- - - 'Hofmannsthal und der Österreichische Impressionismus', *Hofmannsthal-Forschungen II*, pp. 57-72, 1974.

Newton, Joy. 'Emile Zola and the French Impressionist novel', *L'Esprit Créateur*, 13, Chapter 2, pp. 320-328, 1973.

Nochlin, Linda. ed. *Impressionism and Post-Impressionism 1874-1904, Sources and Documents*, pp. 36-43, 1966.

O'Connor, W.V. 'Wallace Stevens: Impressionism in America', *Revue des Langues Vivantes 32*, pp. 66-77, 1966.

Overland, Orm. 'The Impressionism of Stephen Crane: A Study in Style and Technique', *Americana-Norwegica*, ed. by Sigmund Skard and Henry Wasser, pp. 239-285, 1966.

Pater, Walter. 'The Bases of Impressionism', *The Victorian Mind*, pp. 349-61, ed. by Gerald B. Kauver and Gerald C. Soresen, 1969.

Paulk, S.F. *The Aesthetics of Impressionism - Studies in Art and Literature*, Ph.D. Thesis, Florida Univ, 1979.

Picard, Max. *Das Ende des Impressionismus*, 1916.

Perosa, Sergio. 'Naturalism and Impressionism in Stephen Crane's Fiction', *Stephen Crane: A Collection of Critical Essays*, ed. by Maurice Bassan, 1967.

Pool, Phoebe. *Impressionism*, 1967.

Praz, Mario. *Mnemosyne*, 1970.

Reitz, Hellmuth. *Impressionistische und Expressionistische Stilmittel bei Arthur Rimbaud*, Ph.D. Thesis, Munich Univ, 1939.

Rewald, John. *The History of Impressionism*, 1946.

--- *Die Geschichte des Impressionismus. Schicksal und Werk der Maler einer Groszen Epoche der Kunst*, 1965.

--- *The Impressionist Brush*, 1974.

Rewald, John, & von Matt, Leonard, photographer. *The History of Impressionism*, 1973.

Rey, William H. 'War Schnitzler Impressionist? Eine analyse seines unveröffentlichten Jugendwerkes *'Aegidius'*, *Journal of the International A. Schnitzler Ass.*, Vol. 3, Chapter 2, pp. 16-31, 1964.

Rogers, Rodney O. 'Stephen Crane and Impressionism', *Nineteenth Century Fiction*, 24, December, pp. 292-304, 1969.

Rost, Karola. *Der Impressionistische Stil Verlaines*, Ph.D. Thesis, Univ. of Münster, 1936.

Saisselin, Rémy. 'Symposium in Literary Impressionism', *Year-Book of Comparative and General Literature*, No. 17, pp. 85-90, 1968.

Schmidt, A. *Die Geistigen Grundlagen des 'Wiener Impressionismus'*, *Jahrbuch des Wiener Goethevereins*, Neue Folge der Chronik, 78, pp. 90-108, 1974.

Servallaz, Maurice. *French Painting: The Impressionist Painters*, 1960.

Sommerhalder, Hugo. *Zum Begriff des Literischen Impressionismus*, 1961.

Stowell, Peter. *The Prismatic Sensibility-Henry James and Anton Chekhov as Impressionists*, 1972.

--- *Literary Impressionism: James and Chekhov*, 1980.

Stroka, Anna. 'Der Impressionismus der deutschen Literatur, ein Forschungsbericht', *Germanica Wratislaviensia*, 10, pp. 141-161, 1966.

--- 'Der Impressionismus in Arthur Schnitzlers 'Anatol' und seine gesellschaftlichen und ideologischen Voraussetzungen', *Germanica Wratislaviensia*, 12, pp. 97-111, 1967.

Stronkes, James. 'A Realist Experiments with Impressionism: Garland's Impressionism', *American Literature*, March, pp. 38-52, 1964.

Thomas, Denis. *The Age of the Impressionists*, 1987.

Thon, Luise. *Die Sprache des Deutschen Impressionismus. Ein Beitrag zur Erfassung Ihrer Wesenszüge*, 1928.

- - - 'Grundzüge Impressionistischer Sprachgestaltung', *Zeitschrift für Deutschkunde*, 43, pp. 385-400, 1929.

Venturi, Lionello. 'Impressionism', *Art in America*, 24, July, pp. 95-110, 1936.

- - - 'The Aesthetic Idea of Impressionism', *Journal of Aesthetics and Art Criticism*, no. 1, Spring, pp. 34-45, 1941.

- - - *Impressionists and Symbolists*, transl. Fr. Steegmuller, Modern Painters Series, Vol. 2, 1950.

Walzel, O. 'Die Wesenzüge des deutschen Impressionismus', *Zeitschrift für Deutsche Bildung*, 6, pp. 169-182, 1930.

Watt, Ian. 'Impressionism and Symbolism in *Heart of Darkness*', *Southern Review*, 13, Winter, pp. 96-113, 1977.

Weidner, Eva. *Impressionismus und Expressionismus in den Romanen Virginia Woolfs*, Ph.D. Thesis, Greifswald Univ, 1934.

Weingart, Seymour Leonard. *The Form and Meaning of the Impressionist Novel*, Ph.D. Thesis, Univ. of Münster, 1964.

Weisstein, Ulrich. 'A Bibliography of critical writings concerned with Literary Iimpressionism', *Year-Book of Comparative and General Literature*, 17, pp. 69-72, 1968.

- - - 'Butterfly Wings without a Framework of Steel: The Paradigmatic Impressionism of Katherine Mansfield's Short Story "Her First Ball", *Os Estudos Literários entre Ciência E Hermenêutica*, I, Proceedings of the first Congress of PCLA, 1990, pp. 57-77.

Wertheim, Stanley. 'Crane and Garland: The Education of an Impressionist', *North Dakota Quarterly*, Winter, pp. 23-28, 1967.

Wellek, René. 'The Parallelism between Literature and the Arts', *The English Institute Annal*, 1941, pp. 29-63, 1942.

Wenzel, Daniel. *Der Literarische Impressionismus, Dargestellt an der Prosa Alphonse Daudets*, 1928.

Werner, R.M. *Impressionismus als Literär-Historischer Begriff - Untersuchung am Beispiel Arthur Schnitzlers*, 1981.

D. Selected Bibliography

Allen, Walter. *The English Novel: A Short Critical History*,
   pp. 327-348, 1954.
- - - *Tradition and Dream: A Critical Survey of British and
   American Fiction from the Present Day*, 1964, rpt. 1965.
Auerbach, Erich. *Mimesis: The Representation of Reality in Western
   Literature*, transl. by W. Trask, pp. 272-273, 1957.
Balakian, Anna E. *The Symbolist Movement: A Critical Appraisal*,
   1967.
Bal, Mieke. *Narratologie. Essais sur la Signification Narrative dans
   Quatre Romans Modernes*, 1977.
- - - 'Mise en abyme et iconicité', *Littérature*, 29, pp. 116-23, 1978.
- - - 'Notes on narrative embedding', *Poetics Today*, 2,2,41-60.
   1981a.
- - - 'The laughing mice, or: On focalization', *Poetics Today*, 2, 2,
   pp. 202-10, 1981b.
- - - *Narratology* - Introduction to the Theory of Narrative, 1985.
Bally, Charles. 'Le Style Indirect Libre en Francais Moderne',
   Germanisch-Romanisch Monatsschrift, IV, pp. 549-556,
   pp. 597-606, 1912.
- - - 'Figures de Pensée et Formes Linguistiques' *GRM*, VI, 1914.
- - - 'Antiphrase et Style Indirect Libre' *A Grammatical Miscellany
   Offered to Otto Jespersen on his Seventeenth Birthday*, 1930.
Banfield, Ann. 'Narrative Style and the Grammer of Direct and
   Indirect Speech', *Foundations of Language*, 10, pp. 1-39, 1973.
- - - *Unspeakable Sentences: Narration and Representation in the
   Language of Fiction*, 1982.
Barthes, R. 'Introduction to the Structural Analysis of Narratives',
   Image - Music - Text, essays selected and transl. by Stephen
   Heath, 1977.
Bates, H.E. *The Modern Short Story*, 1941.
Baxtin, Mixail. 'L Énoncé dans le roman', *Languages 12*,
   pp. 126-132, 1968.
- - - *Rabelais and his World*, transl. Hélène Iswolsky, 1968.
- - - *Poetique de Dostoievski*, transl. Isabella Kolitcheff, 1970.
Bayley, J. *The Short Story: Henry James to Elizabeth Bowen*, 1988.
Beach, Joseph Warren. *The Twentieth Century Novel: Studies in
   Technique*, 1932.
Beachcroft, T.O. *The English Short Story*, 1964.
- - - *The Modest Art: A Survey of the Short Story in English*, 1968.
Beckson, Karl & Ganz, Arthur. *A Reader's Guide to Literary Terms*,
   1960.

Beebe, Maurice. 'Ulysses and the Age of Modernism', *James Joyce Quarterly*, X, 172-188, 1972.
- - - 'What Modernism Was', *Journal of Modern Literature*, Vol. 3,5, July 1974.
Beja, Morris. *The Epiphany in the Modern Novel*, 1971.
Bell, Quentin. *Bloomsbury*, 1968.
- - - *Virgiana Woolf: A Biography*, 2 vols., 1972.
Bell, Quentin. *Virginia Woolf*, 2 vols. 1972, 1973.
Bennett, Arnold. 'Is the Novel Decaying?', *Cassell's Weekly*, 28 March, 1923.
Bergson, Henri. *Time and Free Will: An Essay on the Immediate Data of Consciousness*, 1960.
- - - *Duration and Simultaneity: With Reference to Einstein's Theory*, transl. Leon Jacobson, Introduced by Herbert Dingle, 1965.
Bergonzi, Bernard 'Appendix on the Short Story', *The Situation of the Novel*, 1970.
- - - 'The Advent of Modernism: 1900-1920', Chapter 1 of *The Sphere History of Literature in the English Language*, Vol. 7: *The Twentieth Century*. Ed. B. Bergonzi, pp. 17-48, 1970.
- - - *The Turn of a Century*, 1973.
Bickerton, Derek. 'Modes of Interior Monologue: A Formal Definition', *Modern Language Quarterly*, 28, 2, pp. 229-239, 1967.
Bonheim, Helmut. *The Narrative Modes: Techniques of the Short Story*, 1982.
Booth, Wayne C. *The Rhetoric of Fiction*, 1961.
- - - *The Rhetoric of Irony*, 1974.
Bowie, T.R. *Relationships between French Literature and Painting in the Nineteenth Century. Exhibition Catalogue*, 1938.
Bowling, L.E. 'What is the Stream of Consciousness Technique?', *PMLA*, 65, June, pp. 333-45, 1950.
Bradbury, Malcolm. 'The Novel in the 1920's', Chapter 6 of *The Sphere History-The Twentieth Century*, pp. 180-221, 1970.
- - - *The Social Context of Modern English Literature*, 1971.
- - - 'Phrases of Modernism: The Novel and the 1920's', *Possibilities: Essays on the State of the Novel*, pp. 81-90, 1973.
Bradbury, M. & McFarlane, J. ed. *Modernism*, 1976.
Bronzwaer, W. *Tense in the Novel: An Investigation of some Potentialities of Linguistic-Criticism*, Chapter III and V, 1970.
- - - 'Mieke Bal's concept of focalization: a critical note', *Poetics Today*, 2, 2, pp. 193-201, 1981.
Bühler, Willi. *Die 'Erlebte Rede' im Englischen Roman: Ihre Vorstüfen und Ihre Ausbildung im Werke Jane Austens*, 'Schweizer Anglistische Arbeiten', 4, 1937.

Chatman, Seymour. 'New ways of analazing narrative structure, with an example from Joyce's' *Dubliner's, Language and Style*, 2, pp. 3-36, 1969.
--- *Story and Discourse*, 1978.
--- 'New Ways of Analysing Narrative', *Language and Style*, Vol. 2, pp. 3-36, 1968.
Chevreul, M.E. *The Principles of Harmony and Contrast of Colours and their Applications to the Arts*, rept., 1967.
Chiari, Joseph. *Symbolism from Poe to Mallarmé: The Growth of a Myth*, foreword by T.S. Eliot, 1956.
Cohn, Dorrit. 'Narrated Monologue: Definition of a Fictional Style', *Comparative Literature*, XVIII, 2, pp. 97-112, 1966.
--- *Transparent Minds: Narrative Modes for Presenting Consciousness in Fiction*, 1978.
--- 'The encirclement of narrative: on Franz Stanzel's *Theorie des Erzählens*', *Poetics Today*, 2, 12, pp. 157-82, 1981.
Cornell, Kenneth. *The Symbolist Movement*, 1921.
Cuddon, J.A. *A Dictionary of Literary Terms*, 1977.
Culler, J. *Flaubert: The Uses of Uncertainty*, 1975.
--- *Structuralist Poetics: Structuralism, Linguistics and the Study of Literature*, 1975.
Daiches, David. *The Novel and the Modern World*, 2nd. ed., 1960.
Davie, Donald, ed. *Russian Literature and Modern English Fiction: A Collection of Critical Essays*, 1965.
Day, M.S. *History of English Literature: 1837 to the Present Day*, 1964.
Dillon, George L. & Fred. Kirchoff. 'On the Form and Function of Free Indirect Style', *PTL*, 1, 3, pp. 431-440, 1976.
Dubrow, H. *Genre*, The Critical Idiom, 42, 1982.
Dujardin, Edouard. *Le Monologue Intérieur. Son Apparition, ses Origines, sa Place dans l'Oeuvre de James Joyce et dans le Roman Contemporain*, 1931.
Ewen, Joseph. 'The theory of character in narrative fiction', *Hasifrut*, 3, 1-3, English abstract, pp. I-II, 1973.
Faulkner, Peter. *Modernism*, 1977.
Fehr, Bernhard. 'Substitutionary Narration and Description: A Chapter in Stylistics', *English Studies XX*, pp. 3-97-107, 1938.
Fokkema, D.W. 'Nijhoff's Modernist Poetics in European Perspective', *Comparative Poetics: In Honour of J. Kamerbeek Jr.*, ed. D.W. Fokkema, Elrud Kunne-Ibsch and A.J.A. van Zoest, pp. 63-88, 1976.
Fokkema, Douwe & Ibsch, Elrud. *Het Modernisme in de Europese Letterkunde*, 1984.
--- *Modernist Conjectures: A Mainstream in European Literature 1910-1940*, 1987.

Forster, E.M. *Aspects of the Novel*, 1927.

Frank, Joseph. 'Spatial Form in the Modern Novel', *Critiques and Essays on Modern Fiction: 1920-1951*, ed. J.W. Aldridge, pp. 43-66, 1952.

Freeman, Ralph. *The Lyrical Novel: Studies in Hermann Hesse, André Gide, and Virginia Woolf*, 1963.

Friedman, Alan. *The Turn of the Novel: The Transition to Modern Fiction*, 1966; rpt. 1970.

Friedman, Melvin. *Stream of Consciousness: A Study in Literary Method*, 1955.

Friedman, Norman. 'What Makes a Short Story Short?', *Modern Fiction Studies*, 4, 1958.

--- 'Point of view in Fiction: The Development of a Critical Concept', *PMLA*, LXX December, 1160-84, 1955.

Funke, Otto. 'Zur Erlebten Rede' bei Galsworthy, *Englische Studien*, Vol. 64, 1929.

Furst, Lilian R. & Skrine, Peter N. *Naturalism*, 1971.

Genette, Gérard. *Figures III*, 1972.

--- In English: *Narrative Discourse*, 1980.

Glauser, Lisa. *Die Erlebte Rede im Englischen Roman des 19. Jahrhunderts*, 'Schweizer Anglistische Arbeiten', 20, 1948.

Gombrich, E.H.J. *The Story of Art*, 1950.

Guiraud, Pierre, 'A Modern Linguistics Look at Rhetoric: Free Indirect Style', *Patterns of Literary Style*, ed. Joseph Strelka, 1971.

Günther, Werner. Probleme der Rededarstellung: *Untersuchungen zur Direkten, Indirekten und 'Erlebten' Rede im Deutschen, Französischen und Italienischen*, 1928.

Hamburger, Käte. 'Zum Strukturproblem der epischen und dramatischen Dichtung', *DVLG*, XXV (1951), pp. 1-26, 1951.

--- *Die Logik der Dichtung*, pp. 72-114, 1957.

--- The Logic of Literature, transl. Marilynn J. Rose, 1973.

Hamilton, George Heard. *Nineteenth and Twentieth Century Art: Painting, Sculpture, Architecture*, 1970.

Harvey, W.J. *Character and the Novel*, 1965.

Hawkes, Terence. *Structuralism and Semiotics*, 1977.

--- *Metaphor*, 1972.

Hawthorn, J. *Unlocking the Text: Fundamental issues in Literary Theory*, 1987.

Hernadi, Paul. 'Verbal worlds between Action and Vision: a Theory of the Modes of Poetic Discourse', *College English*, 33, I, pp. 18-31, 1971.

--- 'Free Indirect Discourse and Related Techniques', Appendix to *Beyond Genre: New Directions in Literary Classification*, pp. 187-205, 1972.

Holroyd, Michael. *Lytton Strachey: A Critical Biography*, 2 vols., Vol. II, The Years of Achievement (1910-1932), 1968.
- - - *Lytton Strachey and the Bloomsbury Group: His Work, Their Influence*, 2nd. ed., 1971.
Hough, Graham. 'Narrative and Dialogue in Jane Austen', *Critical Quarterly*, 12, 3, pp. 201-229, 1970.
Humprey, Robert. *Stream of Consciousness in the Modern Novel*, 1954.
Ibsch, Elrud & Douwe Fokkema. *Het Modernisme in de Europese Letterkunde*, 1984.
- - - *Modernist Conjectures: A Mainstream in European Literature 1910-1940*, 1987.
Iser, Wolfgang. *The Implied Reader: Patterns of Communication in Prose Fiction from Bunyan to Beckett*, 1974.
- - - *The Act of Reading: A Theory of Aesthetic Response*, 1978.
Jakobson, Roman. 'Closing statement: Linguistics and Poetics', in Sebeok, Thomas A. (ed.), *Style in Language*, 350-77, 1960.
- - - 'Shifters, Verbal Categories and the Russian Verb', *Selected Writings II*, pp. 130-147, 1971.
- - - 'Two Aspects of Language: Metaphor and Metonymy' *European Literary Theory and Practice*, ed. V.W. Gras, 1973.
Jakobson, Roman & Morris Halle. 'Two Aspects of Language and Two types of Linguistic Disturbance', *Fundamentals of Language*, ed. Jakobson and Halle, 1956.
James, Henry. *The Art of Fiction and Other Essays*, ed. M. Roberts, 1948.
- - - 'The New Novel', Rpt. in *Henry James: Selected Literary Criticism*, Ed. Morris Shapira, pp. 358-91, 1968.
Janson, H.W. & Janson, Dora J. *History of Art: A Survey of the Major Visual Arts from the Dawn of History to the Present Day*, 1969.
Jespersen, Otto. *The Philosophy of Grammar*, pp. 290-292, 1924.
Johnstone, J.K. *The Bloomsbury Group: A Study of E.M. Forster, Lytton Stachey, Virginia Woolf, and their Circle*, 1954.
Jones, Charles. 'Varieties of Speech Presentation in Conrad's *The Secret Agent*', *Lingua 20*, pp. 162-176, 1968.
Josipovice, Gabriel. *The Lessons of Modernism*, pp. 109-124, 1977.
Kalepky, Theodor, 'Zur französischen Syntax, VII, Mischung indirekter und direkter Rede T, II, 7, *Zeitschrift für Roman, Philol XXIII*, 1899.
- - - Zum 'Style Indirect Libre' ('Verschleierte Rede'), in *GRM*, V, 1913.
- - - 'Verkleidete Rede', *Neophilologus*, 13, Jahrgang, 1928.

Kalik-Teljatnicova, A. 'De l'origine du prétendu 'Style Indirect Libre', *Le Francais Moderne*, XXXIII, 4, pp. 284-294: XXXIV, 2, pp. 123-136, 1965-66.

Karl, R. & Magalaner, M.V. *A Reader's Guide to Great Twentieth Century English Novels*, 1959.

Karpf, Fritz. Die Erlebte Rede im Englischen, *Anglia*, 57, 1933.

Kermode, Frank, *Continuities*, 1959.

--- *The Sense of an Ending: Studies in the Theory of Fiction*, 1967.

--- 'The English Novel-Twentieth Century Literature in Retrospect*, ed. Reuben A. Brower, pp. 45-64, 1971.

--- 'The Modern', *Modern Essays*, rpt., pp. 39-70, 1971.

Kettle, Arnold. *An Introduction to the English Novel*, Vol. 2, 'Henry James to the Present', 1953.

King, C.D. 'Edouard Dujardin, Inner Monologue and the Stream of Consciousness', *French Studies*, VII, 2, pp. 116-127, 1953.

Kruisinga, E. *A Handbook of Present-Day English*, I, II, 1925.

Kunne-Ibsch, Elrud. 'Erzählformen des Relativierens im Modernismus, dargestellt an Thomas Mann's *Joseph und seine Brüder* und Robert Musils *Der Mann ohne Eigenschaften*' in Alexander von Bormann e.a. ed. *Wissen aus Erfahrungen: Werkbegriff und Interpretationen Heute*, Festschrift für Hermann Meer, pp. 760-780, 1976.

--- 'Historical Changes in Spatial Description', *Poetics Today*, Vol. 3, no. 4, 1982.

Lanser, S.S. *The Narrative Act: Point of View in Prose Fiction*, 1981.

Lawler, James R. *The Language of French Symbolism*, 1969.

Lawrence, D.H. *Women in Love*, 1921.

--- *Selected Literary Criticism*, ed. Anthony Beal, 1956; rpt. 1964.

--- *The Collected Letters of D.H. Lawrence*, 2 vols., ed. and introd. Harry T. Moore, 1962.

Lea, F.A. *The Life of John Middleton Murry*, 1959.

Lehmann, Arthur G. *The Symbolist Aesthetic in France*, 1885-1895, 1968.

Leech, Geoffrey. *A Linguistic Guide to English Poetry*, 1919.

--- *Semantics*, 1974.

Leech, N. & Short, M.H. *Style in Fiction: A Linguistic Introduction to English Fictional Prose*, 1981.

Leisi, E. 'Der Erzählstandpunkt in der neueren englischen Prosa', *GRM*, NF, VI, pp. 40-51, 1956.

Lerch, E. 'Die Stilistische Bedeutung des Imperfektums der Rede', *GRM*, pp. 470-489, 1914.

--- 'Ursprung and Bedeutung der sog', 'Erlebten Rede' (Rede als Tatsache), *GRM*, XVI, 459-478, 1928.

Levin, Harry. 'What Was Modernism', *Refraction: Essays in Comparative Literature*, pp. 271-296, 1966.

Levine, George. 'Madame Bovary and the Disappearing Author', *Modern Fiction Studies*, IX, pp. 103-119, 1963.

Lips, Marguerite. *Le Style Indirect Libre*, 1926.

Lodge, David. *The Modes of Modern Writing: Metaphor, Metonymy and the Typology of Modern Literature*, 1977.

Loftmann, Emil. 'Stellvertretende Darstellung', *Neophilologus*, 14, 1929.

Lorck, E. *Die 'Erlebte Rede' - Eine Sprachliche Untersuchung*, 1921.

--- 'Noch Einiges zur Frage der 'erlebten Rede', *Die Neueren Sprachen*, 35, 1927.

Lubbock, Percy. *The Craft of Fiction*, 1921.

Lukacs, George. 'The Ideology of Modernism', *Twentieth Century Literary Criticism*, ed. David Lodge, pp. 474-488, 1972.

Lukacs, George. *The Theory of the Novel: A Historico-Philosophical Essay on the Forms of Great Epic Literature*, 1920, transl. Anna Bostock, 1971.

--- *The Meaning of Contemporary Realism*, 1958, transl. J. and N. Mander, 1962.

MacIntyre, Carlyl F. *French Symbolist Poetry*, 1958.

Markovic, Vida E. *The Changing Face: Disintegration of Personality in the Twentieth Century British Novel*, 1900- 1950, pp. 54-69, 1970.

McHale, Brian. 'Free Indirect Discourse: A Survey of Recent Accounts', *PTL*, Vol. 3. no. 2, April, pp. 235-249, 1978.

Meyer, Kurt Robert. *Zur 'Erlebte Rede' im Englischen Roman des Zwanzigsten Jahrhunderts*, 1957.

Meyerhoff, Hans. *Time in Literature*, 1960

Miller, J. Hillis. ed. *Aspects of Narrative*, 1971.

--- 'The Figure in the Carpet', *Poetics Today*, 1, 3, 107-18, 1980.

--- 'A Guest in the House', *Poetics Today*, 2, 1b, 189-91, 1980/81.

Miller, Norbert. 'Erlebte und Verschleierte Rede, Der Held des Romans und die Erzählform', *Akzente*, V, pp. 213-226, 1958.

Morgenstern, Barry. 'The Self-Conscious Narrator in *Jacob's Room*, *Modern Fiction Studies*, 18, Autumn, 351-61, 1972.

Muecke, D.C. *Irony and the Ironic*, 1970.

Murry, John Middleton. *Aspect of Literature*, 1920.

--- *The Evolution of an Intellectual*, 1920.

--- *The Problem of Style*, 1922.

--- *Countries of the Mind: Essays in Literary Criticism*, 1922.

--- *Son of Woman - D.H. Lawrence*, 1931.

--- *Between two Worlds, An Autobiography*, 1935.

Norris, Christopher. *Deconstruction: Theory and Practice*, 1982.

O'Connor, Frank. *The Lonely Voice: A Study of the Short Story*, 1936, rpt. 1962.

O'Faolain, Sean. *The Short Story*, 1951.

--- *The Vanishing Hero. Studies in Novelists of the Twenties*, 1956.
Page, Norman. *The Language of Jane Austen*, 1972.
--- *Speech in the English Novel*, 1973.
Pascal, Roy. 'Tense and the Novel', *Modern Language Review*, 57,
    1,pp. 1-11, 1962.
--- *The Dual Voice: Free Indirect Speech and its Functioning in the
    Nineteeth Century European Novel*, 1977.
. Preminger, Alex, ed. *Princeton Encyclopedia of Poetry and Poetics*,
    1965.
Prince, G. *Narratology: The Form and Functioning of Narrative*,
    1982.
--- *A Grammar of Stories*, 1973a.
Propp, Vladimir. *Morphology of the Folktale*, 1968. Orig. publ. in
    Russian, 1928.
Raban, Jonathan. *The Technique of Modern Fiction*, 1968.
Rahv, Philip. 'Mrs Woolf and Mrs Brown', *Image and Idea*,
    pp. 139-43, 1949.
Reid, Ian. *The Short Story*, 1977.
Riffaterre, M. 'Criteria for Style Analysis', *Word*, XV, 154-175,
    repr. in Chatman/Levin, *Essays on the language of Literature*,
    1959.
--- 'Stylistic Content', *Word*, XVI, 207-218, repr. in
    Chatman/Levin, *Essays on the Language of Literature*, 1960.
Rimmon-Kenan, Shlomith. *Narrative Fiction: Contemporary Poetics*,
    1973, rpt. 1983.
Ron, Moshe. 'Free Indirect Discourse, Mimetic Language Games
    and the Subject of Fiction', *Poetics Today*, 2, 2, pp. 17-39,
    1981.
Scholes, Robert. *Structuralism in Literature*, 1974.
Scholes, R. & Kellogg, R. *The Nature of Narrative*, 1966.
Shaw, V. *The Short Story: A Critical Introduction*, 1983.
Spender, Stephen. *The Struggle of the Modern*, 1963.
Spitzer, Leo. 'Zur Entstehung der sogenannten 'Erlebten Rede'',
    GRM, XVI, pp. 327-332, 1928.
Spurgeon, Carolyn F.E. *Shakespeare's Imagery and what it tells us*,
    1935.
Stanzel, Franz K. *Die Typischen Erzählsituationen im Roman*,
    dargestellt an 'Tom Jones', 'Moby Dick', 'The Ambassadors',
    'Ulysses' u.a., *Wiener Beitrage zur Englischen Philologie*, 1963,
    pp. 145-156, 1955.
--- 'Episches Präterium, erlebte Rede, historisches Präsens', *DVLG
    XXXIII*, pp. 1-12, 1959.
--- *Die Typischen Erzählsituationen im Roman*, 1955. In English:
    Narrative Situations in the Novel, 1971.
--- *Typische Formen des Romans*, 1964.

--- 'Zwei Erzähltechnische Termini im Komparatischer Sicht: Erlebte Rede und Erzähler in Deutschen und Englishen, *Sprachkunst*, Vol. 10, pp. 192-200, 1979.

--- 'Teller-characters and reflector-characters in narrative theory', *Poetics Today*, 2, 2, pp. 5-16, 1981.

Stone, Harry. 'Dickens and Interior Monologue', *Philological Quarterly*, XXXVIII, pp. 52-65, 1959.

Swinnerton, Frank. *The Georgian Literary Scene*, 1910-1925, 1935.

Symons Arthur. *The Symbolist Movement in Literature*, 1967.

Temple, Ruth. *The Critic's Alchemy: A Study of the Introduction of French Symbolism to England*, 1953.

Thibaudet, Albert. *Gustave Flaubert*, pp. 246-254, 1935.

Todorov, Tzvetan. *Théorie de la Litterature. Textes des Formalistes Russes*, 1965.

--- Les catégories du récit littéraire', *Communications*, 8, 125-51, 1966.

--- *Littérature et Signification*, 1967.

--- *Grammaire du Decameron*, 1969.

--- *Introduction à la Littérature Fantastique*, 1970. In English, *The Fantastic: A Structural Approach*, 1975.

--- *The Poetics of Prose*, Orig. publ. in French, 1971.

Trilling, Lionel. 'On the Modern Element in Modern Literature', *Varieties of Literary Experience*, ed. Stanley Urnshaw, pp. 407-433, 1962.

Ullmann, Stephen. 'Reported Speech and Internal Monologue in Flaubert', *Style in the French Novel*, pp. 94-120, 1957.

Van Ghent, Dorothy. *The English Novel: Form and Function*, 1953.

Van O'Connor, William, ed. *Forms of Modern Fiction*, 1959.

Voloshinov, V.N. *Marxism and the Philosophy of Language*, Chapter 4, 'Quasi-Direct Discourse and French, German and Russian', pp. 141-160, transl. Ladislaw Matejka & I.R. Titunik, 1973.

Walzel, Oskar. 'Von 'erlebter' Rede', *Zeitschrift fur Bücherfreunde*, 16, 1924.

Weimann, Robert, 'Erzählerstandpunkt und Point-of-View'. Zu Geschichte und Aesthetik der Perspektive im englischen Roman', *Zeitschrift fur Anglistik und Amerikanistik*, X, 369-416, 1962.

Weinsheimer, Joel. 'Theory of Character: *Emma, Poetics Today*, 1, 1-2, pp. 185-211, 1979.

Weisstein, Ulrich. 'Expressionism: Style or Weltanschauung?' *Criticism*, IX, pp. 42-62, 1967. Rept. in *Expressionism as an International Phenomenon*, ed. Ulrich Weisstein, pp. 29-45, 1973.

--- 'Verbal Paintings, Fugal Poems, Literary Collages and the Metamorphic Comparatist', *Yearbook of Comparative Literature*, 27, pp. 7-19, 1978.

--- 'Comparing Literature and Art: Current Trends and Prospects in Critical Theory and Methodology', *Interrelations of Literature*, ed. J.P. Barricelli & J. Gibaldi, Modern Language Association, pp. 19-31, 1982.

Wellek, René. 'The Parallelism between Literature and the Arts', *English Institute Annual*, pp. 29-64, 1941. rept. 'The Parallel of the Arts: Some misgivings and a Faint Affirmation', in *JAAC*, 31, pp. 154-161 and 309-321, 1972/73.

Wellek, René and Austin Warren. *Theory of Literature*, Chapter 'Style and Stylistics', pp. 177-189, 1949.

Woolf, Leonard. *Beginning Again: An Autobiography of the Years 1911-1918*, 1964.

--- *Downhill all the Way: An Autobiography of the Years 1919 to 1939*, 1967.

INDEX

266